Selected Readings in Business, Millennium Edition

Selected Readings in Business, Millennium Edition

Myra Shulman

The University of Michigan Press
Ann Arbor

To K

Preface

. . . .

Selected Readings in Business, Millennium Edition, has been written for international students who are studying business as undergraduates or pursuing an MBA so they can become business professionals. Such a career in the new millennium will involve a global perspective. The business world is vastly different from the world that existed when the first edition of *Selected Readings in Business* was published in 1991. Today e-commerce, m-commerce, and dot-coms are common terms for forms of commerce that had not yet been implemented in 1991. Since then, globalization has been transformed from a theoretical concept to an actual paradigm of our world system, and this paradigm has transformed our ways of doing business. Moreover, the terrorist attacks of September 11, 2001, had a global impact. This textbook addresses these new developments. The articles have been chosen from current business journals and newspapers from around the world and present the latest thinking on subjects ranging from information technology (IT) to women's professional status to scientific applications in business. The focus is global, and the context is the whole universe of commerce—electronic, mobile, and traditional.

The book, which is learner centered, focuses on reading as an interactive process involving reader, writer, and text. It incorporates the integrated skills approach to ESL learning, as the four skills of reading, writing, listening, and speaking are integrated in the various activities. Reading and writing tasks are balanced with vocabulary acquisition, analysis, discussion, teamwork, and Internet research. Each chapter contains at least two unaltered readings for intensive study, as well as suggested outside readings from the *Harvard Business Review, Harvard International Review,* and *The Economist.* Most of the articles are moderate in length, with the exception of the long articles in chapters 12, 13, and 14 and "Globalization's Last Hurrah?" in Appendix C. In general, the articles tend to move in the direction of greater length and difficulty. Students and teachers will find both the academic and the journalistic styles—the idiomatic mixed with the technical. Altogether, the text emphasizes the practical skills and major concepts needed to function successfully in the global environment of the 21st century.

Selected Readings in Business, Millennium Edition, has the following goals:

- To improve reading comprehension and speed;

- To increase general vocabulary and business vocabulary;

- To encourage critical analysis of ideas;

- To sharpen expertise in Internet research;

- To strengthen logical thinking in written and oral expression;

- To provide examples of well-written standard English; and

- To present current theories and techniques of global business.

The book contains three appendixes. Appendix A has definitions of writing terms and examples of writing styles. Appendix B: Strategies for Communication presents guidelines and models for the major academic writing genres: summary, essay, synthesis, and critical review. It also addresses the needs of the business professional by giving models of a memorandum, a business letter, a résumé, and an oral presentation. While the examples of the business letter and memorandum stress business style and tone, students are encouraged in the other writing tasks to adopt the academic style and tone that are characteristic of the writing done in U.S. colleges and universities. Throughout, the emphasis is on a strategic approach to communication that will enable students to master the assignment. Appendix C has the full text of the article "Globalization's Last Hurrah?" from *Foreign Policy* (January–February 2002), which supplements the readings in chapter 2.

Users of the first edition of *Selected Readings in Business* will notice four major changes in the millennium edition. First is the global context. There is no doubt that the future will be shaped in part by the forces of globalization, which have produced an interconnected and multifaceted world, and this new world is reflected in the readings. Second is the inclusion of relevant Internet activities. Third, the analytical tasks have been somewhat compressed, with an expansion of comprehension and discussion. Fourth, the case studies are not found in the text but will be added to the book's Web site.

Because of the complexities that characterize the global market, the new millennium is an unusually challenging time to enter the field of international business. *Selected Readings in Business, Millennium Edition,* provides a foundation that will prepare students to study the various areas of business—whether economics, information technology, marketing, finance, or management—from a global point of view. Through reading, thinking, and writing about the high-interest articles in this book, students can become familiar with current topics and trends, master essential academic writing genres, expand their Internet skills, and gain an understanding of the innovative and competitive business world of the 21st century.

Acknowledgments

. . . .

This book reflects the thoughtful suggestions of colleagues, friends, and family. First of all, my deepest gratitude to my editor Kelly Sippell, who always provides support and encouragement. It is a true pleasure to work with her. Also special thanks go to Christina Milton and the editorial team at the University of Michigan Press.

I am indebted to my colleague at American University Claire Dygert, the Electronic Resources librarian, who shared her state-of-the-art knowledge of online databases and Internet research. Judith Snoke, director of the English Language Institute at Virginia Polytechnic Institute, offered expert advice on integrating Web resources into this book.

I welcomed the chance to field-test the book in my classes at American University, and I want to express my appreciation to my American University students, who were full of enthusiasm, questions, and ideas. Their writing assignments serve as models in Appendix B and the instructor's manual. I also thank my Georgetown University students, with whom I used the manuscript in summer 2002 in the English for Professional Purposes course. Their insightful comments resulted in many practical improvements.

My family members were of great help in this endeavor: Margot and Ken Sarch, Vera and Marc Ovadia, Elsa and David Smithgall, Eve Mezvinsky, and David Shulman. Deana Shulman was a sensitive critic and reader. My husband K as usual offered his global experience and business expertise.

Grateful acknowledgment is made to the following authors, publishers, and journals for permission to reprint previously published materials.

Business Week for "Cracks in Mexico's Glass Ceiling" by Elisabeth Malkin, reprinted from July 10, 2000, issue of *Business Week* by special permission, copyright © 2000; "A Net Not Made in America" by Stephen Baker, reprinted from March 26, 2001, issue of *Business Week* by special permission, copyright © 2001; "For Developing Countries, Health Is Wealth" by Laura D'Andrea Tyson, reprinted from January 14, 2002, issue of *Business Week* by special permission, copyright © 2002 by The McGraw-Hill Companies, Inc.

Carlisle & Company for "Bit Player" by James Gleick, from the *New York Times Magazine,* December 30, 2001, copyright © 2001.

Steven Cohen for "Good Negotiation Equals Good Contracts," from *Contract Management,* August 2001, copyright © 2001. The Negotiations Skills Company online at <www.negotiationskills.com>.

Computerworld for "A Truly Global Web" by Peter G. W. Keen, December 2000, copyright 2000; "A Key Shift for IT" by Peter G. W. Keen, May 2001, copyright © 2001; "Go Mobile—Now!" by Peter G. W. Keen, June 2001, copyright © 2001.

Copyright Clearance Center, Inc., for "Globalization's Last Hurrah?" from *Foreign Policy Magazine Globalization Index,* January–February 2002, copyright © 2002.

Andrew Downie for "Rio Co-op Raises Worker Standards, Fashionably." This article first appeared in *The Christian Science Monitor,* November 7, 2001, copyright © 2001. Online at <www.csmonitor.com>.

The Economist for "The Next Society," November 3, 2001, copyright © 2001; "A World Empire by Other Means: The Triumph of English," December 22, 2001, copyright © 2001, The Economist

Newspaper Group, Inc.; and "Japanese Mergers: Marriage in Name Only," March 2, 2002, copyright © 2002 The Economist Newspaper Ltd. All rights reserved. Reprinted with permission. Further reproduction prohibited. <www.economist.com>.

Forbes Magazine for "You Say Tomato," May 21, 2001, Forbes Best of the Web, copyright © 2001; "Smart and Smarter," March 18, 2002, Forbes, copyright © 2002. Reprinted by permission of *Forbes Magazine* © 2002 Forbes, Inc.

Fortune Magazine for "Nationality Matters More Than Ever: That's No Joke" by Michael Schrage, November 13, 2000; "Beyond Babel" by Michael Schrage, March 19, 2001. Copyright © 2000 Time Inc. All rights reserved.

Reprinted by permission of *Harvard Business Review.* From "The New Atlantic Century" by Hermann Simon and Max Otte, January–February 2000, copyright © 1999; "Dream Deferred: The Story of a High-Tech Entrepreneur in a Low-Tech World" by Monique Maddy, May–June 2000, copyright © 2000; "How We Went Digital without a Strategy" by Ricardo Semler, September–October 2000, copyright © 2000; "The Biology Century Dawns," April 2001, copyright © 2001; "DNA: Handle with Care" by Bronwyn Fryer, April 2001, copyright © 2001; "Buying into Japan Inc." by Ryoji Itoh and Till Vestring, November 2001, © 2001. Copyright © 1999, 2000, 2001 by the Harvard Business School Publishing Corporation; all rights reserved.

Haymarket Business Publications for "Developing a Name to Work Worldwide" by Sam Solley, from *Marketing,* December 21, 2000, copyright © 2000. Reproduced from *Marketing* magazine with the permission of the copyright owner, Haymarket Business Publications.

IC Publications for "Turkey Logs On" by Jon Gorvett, from *The Middle East,* September 2000, © 2000; "Luxury Goods Firms Target the Middle East" by Pamela Ann Smith, from *The Middle East,* November 2000, © 2000; "All It Takes Is a Dream" by Shilpa Mathai, from *The Middle East,* January 2001.

Moises Naim for "Sizing up Global Integration." This article first appeared in *The Christian Science Monitor* on February 28, 2001, copyright © 2001. Online at <www.csmonitor.com>.

New York Times for "Separating Sheep from Goats as Start-ups Fall to Earth" by Jennifer L. Rich, March 11, 2001, copyright © 2001.

T+D for "Women Working Overseas" by Tracy Wilen, copyright © May 2001; "Expat Training" by Gary Wederspahn, copyright © February 2002; "An American Expat's View" by David Beadles, copyright © February 2002, American Society for Training & Development. Reprinted with permission. All rights reserved.

Time Inc. for "Can We Learn to Beat the Reaper?" by Jeffrey Kluger, January 21, 2002, copyright © 2002, Time Inc. reprinted by permission.

Contents

. . . .

To the Student

How to Read Efficiently

Reading, like any skill, can be improved by strong motivation and steady practice. Being a good reader means reading actively, efficiently, fairly quickly, and with maximum comprehension. It also means reading for the author's general ideas, not for specific words. If you come to an unfamiliar vocabulary word, try to guess the meaning from the context of the sentence and paragraph, rather than stopping to look up the word in the dictionary.

When reading the articles in this textbook, or any other reading material, follow these three steps to be an efficient reader:

Preview

Read

Review

A. Preview

1. Skim the article for the author's name, the title, and all headings.

2. Ask yourself what the title could mean.

3. Read the first and second paragraphs, looking for the author's purpose or main idea.

4. Read the last paragraph, looking for a summary or conclusion.

5. Look over the visual aids (pictures, graphs, or charts).

B. Read

1. Read actively, with a pen or pencil in your hand.

2. Underline or highlight the main idea, major points, and important examples and supporting data.

3. Make brief comments in the margin when you agree with the author ("yes") or disagree ("no") or have a question ("?").

4. Keep in mind what you want to learn from the article.

C. Review

1. Reread the article, concentrating on the words, phrases, and sentences you have underlined or highlighted.

2. Make brief notes in the margin when you react to specific ideas.

3. Write one or two sentences that express the main idea(s) of the article.

4. Write one or two sentences that express your reaction to the article.

How to Do Internet Research

This text integrates Internet research with writing and teamwork assignments. Thus, it is important for you to be able to use the Internet in the most efficient manner. The following information will help you to search for and access Web sites. Since every library has its own system of organization, you should become familiar with your library system and its e-resource collection.

The World Wide Web

Search Engines

Many different search engines can be used to locate a book, to locate a journal or newspaper article, or just to find information on a topic. Before using these search engines, take time to read their help screens. The most comprehensive one currently is Google.com (<www.google.com>). The following search engines are also available.

Alta Vista: <www.altavista.digital.com>

Excite: <my.excite.com>

HotBot: <hotbot.lycos.com>

Infoseek: <infoseek.go.com>

Lycos: <www.lycos.com>

WebCrawler: <web.webcrawler.com>

Yahoo!: <www.yahoo.com>

Resources Available on the World Wide Web

- **Almanacs**

  Learning Network: <www.infoplease.com>

  The Political Reference Almanac: <www.polisci.com>

- **Country studies**

  The Central Intelligence Agency, *The World Factbook:* <www.cia.gov>

  The Library of Congress: <www.loc.gov>

The United Nations: <www.un.org>

The World Bank Group: <www.worldbank.org>

- **Encyclopedias**

  Encarta Encyclopedia: <www.encarta.msn.com>

  Encyclopaedia Britannica Online: <www.britannica.com>

  Encyclopedia Smithsonian (SI Encyclopedia): <www.si.edu>

- **Online news sites**

  Alternet.org: <www.alternet.org>

  British Broadcasting Company: <www.bbc.co.uk>

  Business Week: <www.businessweek.com>

  Cable News Network: <www.CNN.com>

  The Christian Science Monitor: <www.scmonitor.com>

  Financial Times: <www.ft.com>

  Fortune: <www.fortune.com>

  MSNBC: <www.MSNBC.com>

  New York Times: <www.NYTimes.com>

  Time: <www.Time.com>

  Salon: <www.salon.com>

  Slate: <www.Slate.msn.com>

  USA Today: <www.USAToday.com>

  The Wall Street Journal: <online.wsj.com>

  Washington Post: <www.Washingtonpost.com>

  Wired News: <www.wired.com>

  World Press Review: <www.worldpressreview.com>

  Yahoo! News: <www.news.yahoo.com>

Academic Resources

Library Electronic Access to Resource Material (E-Resource Collection)

Libraries offer online databases and other resources that allow students and professors to do research over the Internet from their homes, offices, or dorm rooms. These databases provide an array of information, from library holdings of books and journals to statistics and company data and the full text of journal and newspaper articles. Some academic journals, such as the *Harvard Business Review* and the *Sloan Management Review*, only provide article abstracts to most databases. To read the full text of an article, you must go to the library and find the issue of the print journal in which it was originally published.

- **Specialized databases for business and economics that provide the full text of many articles**

  ABI/Inform

  LexisNexis Academic

  Business Source

  Business and Company Resource Center

- **Databases for journal articles**

  Proquest General Reference

  Infotrac

  EBSCO Academic

- **Selected journals that provide the full text of articles online through databases**

  Business Week

  Computerworld

  The Economist

  Forbes

  Foreign Policy

  Fortune

  Harvard International Review

  The Middle East

  Newsweek

  Time

Note: Changes often occur in Internet addresses (URLs) and online resources. Please visit <www.press.umich.edu/esl> to monitor changes to the URLs or online resources printed in this book. To notify monitors of changes, e-mail <esladmin@umich.edu>.

Chapter 1

The Future

. . . .

"The New Atlantic Century" Hermann Simon and Max Otte *Harvard Business Review* January–February 2000	**"The Next Society"** Peter Drucker *The Economist* November 3, 2001

This chapter is intended to serve as an introduction to the structure and methodology of this book. Therefore, each activity in this chapter begins with a brief explanation, and answers to certain exercises are provided and explained at the end of the chapter.

Preview "The New Atlantic Century"

Previewing, which gives you an overview of the text, is mental preparation for reading. It increases both reading comprehension and speed. Efficient readers generally preview a document before reading it thoroughly. Previewing can take from 30 seconds to 10 minutes, depending on the length and difficulty of the reading material. In this text, previewing includes skimming, questioning, scanning, and guessing the vocabulary from the context.

Skimming

Skimming involves quickly looking over the reading to gain a general impression of the content. Glance at the author's name, the title, headings, and the first and last paragraphs. If there are illustrations, cartoons, or graphic aids, briefly glance at them also.

Skim the article quickly to find the following general information.

1. Read the title and all headings and look at any illustrations.

2. Read the first and second paragraphs, looking for the authors' purpose and main idea.

3. Read the last paragraph, looking for a summary or conclusion.

4. Write a sentence containing your preliminary understanding of the main idea of the article.

Questioning

Questioning encourages you to think about the subject before reading the article in order to assess what, if any, knowledge you may already have about the subject. It increases comprehension by making you anticipate or predict what the author will discuss.

Answer the following questions and discuss your answers in class.

1. What countries do you predict will be the center of the world economy in the 21st century?

2. Which Asian countries will become economically powerful in the 21st century?

Scanning

Scanning involves quickly looking over the reading to find specific information. Glance over each page, trying to find the key word or words from the question. When you locate the information, write the answer and the number of the paragraph in which the answer is found.

Scan the article quickly to find the following specific information.

1. Who are the core members of "Transatlantica"?

2. What is the trade in Japan heavily weighted toward?

3. Which country dominates high-tech industries, such as computer software, biotechnology, and Internet applications?

4. How many Americans, Europeans, and Asians are now online?

Vocabulary in Context

Guessing the meaning of new or unfamiliar words by using context clues is an important reading skill. It is not necessary to guess the precise meaning; a general idea will enable you to proceed with your reading. Context includes the meaning of the individual words in the sentences as well as the overall meaning of the sentence or paragraph.

Read the following sentences from the article and try to guess the meaning of the italicized words by using the context. Then replace the italicized words with synonyms (words or phrases that have nearly the same or similar meanings).

1. "Although the recent financial crisis *dimmed* some of Asia's luster, many observers continue to believe that the strongest *engine* of growth will be found in the fast-developing Pacific Basin." (Paragraph 1)

2. "Even though Japan is slowly moving away from *mercantilism,* its trade is still heavily *weighted* toward imports of raw materials and exports of ready-made products." (Paragraph 5)

3. "It [the United States] has abundant *venture capital* and thriving *entrepreneurship*." (Paragraph 7)

4. "English is quickly becoming the *lingua franca* of the region, *facilitating* all sorts of dealings." (Paragraph 10)

5. "It does not appear, however, that any of those *potential* conflicts is liable to *flare up* soon and fundamentally damage the world's most productive economic relationship." (Paragraph 13)

Paraphrasing

Paraphrasing means restating an author's ideas in your own words by changing the sentence structure, word order, and vocabulary. A good paraphrase is accurate—that is, true to the author's meaning—and complete. Paraphrasing tests both your knowledge of English grammar and vocabulary and your comprehension of the ideas in the article.

After reading the article, reread the sentences under Vocabulary in Context. Now rewrite them using your own words. To do a complete paraphrase, change the vocabulary and sentence structure, but do not change the authors' intended meaning or paraphrase any technical terms. There are several ways of paraphrasing each sentence. Here is an example of a complete paraphrase.

Original: "But in Asia, only the elites, for the most part, can speak English."

Paraphrase: However, the ability to speak English is generally limited to the privileged members of Asian society.

1. _____

2. _____

3. _____

4. _____

5. _____

opinion

The New Atlantic Century

The economic relationship between the United States and Europe is about to enter its strongest period yet.

by Hermann Simon and Max Otte

1 Looking into the next century, where will the center of the world economy be? Although the recent financial crisis dimmed some of Asia's luster, many observers continue to believe that the strongest engine of growth will be found in the fast-developing Pacific Basin. They foresee Asia supplanting Europe as the primary economic partner of the United States, leading to a so-called Pacific century. But we believe the new century, like the one just ended, will be very much an Atlantic century, with North America and Europe strengthening their business ties and extending their economic leadership.

2 Just look at the data on cross-border mergers and acquisitions. The level of direct investment between the United States and Europe – the core members of what we call "Transatlantica" – is three times that between the United States and Asia. And although 1998 was admittedly a year of Asian weakness, it is still striking that not a single Asian acquirer was among the group of foreign companies making the 25 largest acquisitions of U.S. businesses that year. Europe alone accounted for 20 of those purchases.

3 It is true that U.S. trade with Asia's Pacific Rim exceeds U.S. trade with Europe. But those numbers don't include services, arguably the most dynamic sector of the economy. Trade in services such as banking and consulting also goes further than trade in products to bring the two continents together. It creates the commercial ties crucial to building the trust that makes global business work.

4 Indeed, despite their export successes, countries like Japan and China are still relatively isolated from other countries. If you combine imports and exports, Japan's foreign trade equals only 22% of its gross domestic product, while in most European countries that figure is over 50%. Even the United States, with its big internal market, reaches 24%.

5 What's more, the character of trade in Transatlantica countries is much more advanced than it is in either Japan or China. Even though Japan is slowly moving away from mercantilism, its trade is still heavily weighted toward imports of raw materials and exports of ready-made products. China follows an explicitly mercantilist policy. Transatlantica's countries are much further along in restructuring their trade portfolios around specialized industrial goods.

6 Mercantilism was well suited to capturing world markets when business conditions were stable and governments could try to promote entire industries within their own borders. But today the most advanced products – the ones that will fuel future economic growth – are coming from companies with international reach. Competition now means a struggle for the best global talent, access both to the world's business centers and to other dispersed regions of competence, and the international relocation of whole value chains and processes. In this transformation, national identities are minimized, and the power in corporations is increasingly distributed among many countries.

7 At present, the United States is certainly best positioned to capture the op-

portunities of this increasingly complex world market. More than any other big country, it has moved to a service economy based on the flow of ideas rather than the flow of materials. It has abundant venture capital and thriving entrepreneurship. As a result, the United States dominates high-tech industries such as computer software, biotechnology, and Internet applications.

8   By comparison, European companies are slower and more risk averse. Yet the continent is not as far behind as epithets like "Eurosclerosis" suggest. We are struck by the wave of optimism and entrepreneurial spirit that has been sweeping Europe in the past two years. Wherever we go, we see aggressive and innovative plans for the future. Funds for corporate restructuring, mostly coming from America, are acting as catalysts in the liberalization of the European economy. Venture capital is increasingly available, and, in tandem, a progressive shareholder culture is emerging. Companies are going public ever sooner to finance their growth, and those shares are going to informed private investors who are monitoring "their" companies closely.

9   In Asia, many would-be entrepreneurs still trust in the state, in large corporations, or in close family ties. That may have been appropriate when a few major industries dominated the economy and capturing market share within those industries was the main goal. In the age of innovative turbocapitalism, however,

speed is of the essence, even at the cost of occasional failure. Large corporations and the state are disadvantaged in this game. And family ties, for all their flexibility, inevitably hinder the free flow of talent that advanced companies need to draw on.

10   New ideas move fastest when there's a common language and communication medium. On both these counts, Transatlantica has clear advantages. English is quickly becoming the lingua franca of the region, facilitating all sorts of dealings. Although

But today the most advanced products – the ones that will fuel future economic growth – are coming from companies with international reach.

Daimler-Benz is undoubtedly the dominant partner in its merger with Chrysler, it chose English as its corporate language. And it doesn't even seem odd that the largest publisher of English-language books in the world – Bertelsmann – has its headquarters in a small town in Germany. But in Asia, only the elites, for the most part, can speak English.

11   The Internet, too, is drawing the United States and Europe closer together. About 90 million Americans and 80 million Europeans are now on-line, compared with only about 40 million Asians. The vast majority of Internet content is produced

in Transatlantica, most of it in English. When Amazon.com looked overseas to expand, it chose Great Britain and Germany as the sites of its first foreign subsidiaries.

12   Of course, the last golden age of Euro-American integration ended in two devastating world wars. Even though the national rivalries underlying those wars now belong to history, three possible areas of contention could undermine the prosperity of Transatlantica. Europe could decide to go it alone militarily, terminating the NATO alliance and with it one of the foundations of intercontinental cooperation. The euro could threaten the dollar as the global reserve currency, prompting greater economic rivalry. And trade disputes between Europe and North America could intensify.

New ideas move fastest when there's a common language and communication medium.

13   It does not appear, however, that any of those potential conflicts is liable to flare up soon and fundamentally damage the world's most productive economic relationship. Driven by a variety of market and cultural forces, the two continents are growing even closer, forging a partnership that is likely to guide the world in the new century.

Hermann Simon is chairman of Simon Kucher Consultants, a strategy-consulting firm in Cambridge, Massachusetts.
Max Otte is an assistant professor of international relations at Boston University.

Reprint F00104

Glossary

catalysts	agents that provoke or speed significant change or action
devastating	reduced to chaos and disorder; brought to ruin by violent action
dimmed	reduced
elites	the socially superior or privileged members of a society; the best
engine	agent or instrument
entrepreneurship	the act of organizing, managing, and assuming the risks of a business or enterprise
epithets	disparaging or abusive words or phrases
explicitly	formulated without ambiguity or fully developed
facilitating	making easier; helping to bring about
flare up	intensify suddenly
forging	forming or bringing into being, especially by an expenditure of effort
hinder	to hold back, delay, or block
in tandem	occurring in conjunction or partnership
lingua franca	common language among peoples of diverse speech
luster	superficial attractiveness or appearance of excellence
mercantilism	trade and commerce; an economic system to increase the power and wealth of a nation by strict government regulation of trade and commerce
NATO	North Atlantic Treaty Organization
potential	existing in possibility
risk averse	avoiding or disliking a situation of risk
rivalries	competitions
shareholder	stockholder; one that owns a share of property
subsidiaries	companies wholly controlled by another
thriving	flourishing, growing vigorously; characterized by success
Transatlantica	the United States and Europe
undermine	to weaken or ruin
venture capital	capital invested in the ownership of a new enterprise (also called *risk capital*)
weighted	inclined in a particular direction

Comprehension

This task strengthens your understanding of the main idea, major points, and supporting details in the article. The answers can be found in the text, with the exception of the last two questions, which ask for your opinion.

Answer the following questions by finding the relevant information in the article.

1. In the 21st century, what will guide the world market?

2. What is revealed by the data on cross-border mergers and acquisitions?

3. Why is trade less advanced in China and Japan than in the Transatlantica countries?

4. How do the authors describe competition today?

5. Why is the United States best positioned to capture the opportunities of the world market?

6. What two major factors are advantageous to Transatlantica countries and why?

7. What three possible areas of contention could undermine the prosperity of Transatlantica?

8. What other areas of the world besides the United States and Europe could become economically powerful in the 21st century?

9. What changes have taken place in the world market since this article was published in January–February 2000?

Analysis

These questions sharpen your critical thinking and analytical skills as you identify the main idea of the article; interpret the meaning of words; make a logical deduction (inference); and analyze an author's style, tone, and method of organization. (See Appendix A: Definitions of Writing Terms and Examples of Writing Styles.)

Circle the letter next to the best answer(s). Justify your choices with quotations from the text.

1. The main idea is the central subject or unifying theme of the article and is often composed of several sentences stated in more than one paragraph. What is the main idea of the article, and in which paragraph(s) is it stated?

   a. The Internet has changed the way countries engage in trade and conduct business.

   b. Competition in trade will increase between Asian and European countries.

   c. The communication medium and the language are critical factors in determining economic relationships.

   d. The major trade relationship in the future will be between the United States and Europe.

2. Interpreting the meaning of words depends on understanding the context, the overall meaning of the sentence or paragraph in which the word appears. Reread paragraph 1. Choose the best meaning of the italicized word in this sentence from the first paragraph. "They foresee Asia *supplanting* Europe as the primary economic partner of the United States, leading to a so-called Pacific century."

   a. imitating

   b. replacing

   c. supporting

   d. following

3. Drawing an inference means making a logical deduction based on information in the text. The answer is not stated explicitly (in so many words) but is strongly supported by the text. We can infer the following from this sentence in paragraph 9: "In the age of innovative turbocapitalism, however, speed is of the essence, even at the cost of occasional failure."

   a. Speed is more important today than in the past because the powerful capitalistic system is characterized by rapid innovation.

   b. Capitalism has overtaken other economic systems in the world because of its ability to innovate.

   c. Large corporations and the state have a disadvantage in terms of the speed at which they do business.

   d. It is essential for businesses to operate carefully in this creative capitalistic environment in order to avoid making costly mistakes.

4. Style refers to an author's manner of expression in language. Analysis of an author's style is helpful in understanding the ideas conveyed by the author. In business or technical writing, the author's choice of style is generally determined by three criteria: the purpose, audience, and type of information in the document. Styles may vary from formal to informal, technical to nontechnical, or personal to impersonal, and there are as many writing styles as there are writers. (See Appendix A: Definitions of Writing Terms and Examples of Writing Styles.) The authors' writing style in this article is _____

   and _____ .

   a. impersonal

   b. personal

   c. technical

   d. nontechnical

5. Tone, which is an inherent part of an author's style, reveals the author's attitude toward the subject and the audience. It results from the writer's word choice, sentence structure, and phrasing and can be described in a number of ways. For example, the author's tone may be objective, subjective, humorous, serious, emotional, balanced, positive, negative, authoritative, tentative, scholarly, or colloquial. The tone of this article is ＿＿＿＿＿＿ and ＿＿＿＿＿＿ .

   a. persuasive

   b. neutral

   c. straightforward

   d. ambiguous

6. Business writers usually present and develop their content logically so readers can understand their ideas. They structure their material according to a wide variety of organizational methods: analysis, argument, cause-effect, chronology, classification, comparison-contrast, definition, description, enumeration, exemplification (examples), problem-solution, process, and spatial order. What overall method of development is used in this article?

   a. comparing and contrasting two proposals

   b. supporting an argument with specific data and evidence

   c. defining a new system

   d. explaining the steps in a complex process

7. Effective writers employ specific writing techniques to capture the attention of the reader in the beginning of an article and to conclude an article in a meaningful and memorable way. These techniques range from quoting a well-known person to defining unfamiliar terms to using metaphoric language. What techniques do the authors use to get the reader's attention in the introduction to this article (paragraph 1)?

   a. making a humorous statement

   b. giving a definition

   c. asking a question

   d. adding a contrasting idea

The next society

Tomorrow is closer than you think. Peter Drucker explains how it will differ from today, and what needs to be done to prepare for it

By invitation

Peter Drucker is a writer, teacher and consultant who has published 32 books, mostly on various aspects of society, economics, politics and management. Born in 1909 in Vienna, Mr. Drucker was educated in Austria and England, and holds a doctorate from Frankfurt University. Since 1971 he has been Professor of Social Science and Management at Claremont Graduate University, California.

1 THE new economy may or may not materialise, but there is no doubt that the next society will be with us shortly. In the developed world, and probably in the emerging countries as well, this new society will be a good deal more important than the new economy (if any). It will be quite different from the society of the late 20th century, and also different from what most people expect. Much of it will be unprecedented. And most of it is already here, or is rapidly emerging.

2 In the developed countries, the dominant factor in the next society will be something to which most people are only just beginning to pay attention: the rapid growth in the older population and the rapid shrinking of the younger generation. Politicians everywhere still promise to save the existing pensions system, but they—and their constituents—know perfectly well that in another 25 years people will have to keep working until their mid-70s, health permitting.

3 What has not yet sunk in is that a growing number of older people—say those over 50—will not keep on working as traditional full-time nine-to-five employees, but will participate in the labour force in many new and different ways: as temporaries, as part-timers, as consultants, on special assignments and so on. What used to be personnel and are now known as human-resources departments still assume that those who work for an organisation are full-time employees. Employment laws and regulations are based on the same assumption. Within 20 or 25 years, however, perhaps as many as half the people who work for an organisation will not be employed by it, certainly not on a full-time basis. This will be especially true for older people. New ways of working with people at arm's length will increasingly become the central managerial issue of employing organisations, and not just of businesses.

4 The shrinking of the younger population will cause an even greater upheaval, if only because nothing like this has happened since the dying centuries of the Roman empire. In every single developed country, but also in China and Brazil, the birth rate is now well below the replacement rate of 2.2 live births per woman of reproductive age. Politically, this means that immigration will become an important—and highly divisive—issue in all rich countries. It will cut across all traditional political alignments. Economically, the decline in the young population will change

markets in fundamental ways. Growth in family formation has been the driving force of all domestic markets in the developed world, but the rate of family formation is certain to fall steadily unless bolstered by large-scale immigration of younger people. The homogeneous mass market that emerged in all rich countries after the second world war has been youth-determined from the start. It will now become middle-age-determined, or perhaps more likely it will split into two: a middle-age-determined mass market and a much smaller youth-determined one. And because the supply of young people will shrink, creating new employment patterns to attract and hold the growing number of older people (especially older educated people) will become increasingly important.

Knowledge is all

5 The next society will be a knowledge society. Knowledge will be its key resource, and knowledge workers will be the dominant group in its workforce. Its three main characteristics will be:
- Borderlessness, because knowledge travels even more effortlessly than money.
- Upward mobility, available to everyone through easily acquired formal education.
- The potential for failure as well as success. Anyone can acquire the "means of production", ie, the knowledge required for the job, but not everyone can win.

6 Together, those three characteristics will make the knowledge society a highly competitive one, for organisations and individuals alike. Information technology, although only one of many new features of the next society, is already having one hugely important effect: it is allowing knowledge to spread near-instantly, and making it accessible to everyone. Given the ease and speed at which information travels, every institution in the knowledge society—not only businesses, but also schools, universities, hospitals and increasingly government agencies too—has to be globally competitive, even though most organisations will continue to be local in their activities and in their markets. This is because the Internet will keep customers everywhere informed on what is available anywhere in the world, and at what price.

7 This new knowledge economy will rely heavily on knowledge workers. At present, this term is widely used to describe people with considerable theoretical knowledge and learning: doctors, lawyers, teachers,

accountants, chemical engineers. But the most striking growth will be in "knowledge technologists": computer technicians, software designers, analysts in clinical labs, manufacturing technologists, paralegals. These people are as much manual workers as they are knowledge workers; in fact, they usually spend far more time working with their hands than with their brains. But their manual work is based on a substantial amount of theoretical knowledge which can be acquired only through formal education, not through an apprenticeship. They are not, as a rule, much better paid than traditional skilled workers, but they see themselves as "professionals." Just as unskilled manual workers in manufacturing were the dominant social and political force in the 20th century, knowledge technologists are likely to become the dominant social—and perhaps also political—force over the next decades.

The new protectionism

8 Structurally, too, the next society is already diverging from the society almost all of us still live in. The 20th century saw the rapid decline of the sector that had dominated society for 10,000 years: agriculture. In volume terms, farm production now is at least four or five times what it was before the first world war. But in 1913 farm products accounted for 70% of world trade, whereas now their share is at most 17%. In the early years of the 20th century, agriculture in most developed countries was the largest single contributor to GDP; now in rich countries its contribution has dwindled to the point of becoming marginal. And the farm population is down to a tiny proportion of the total.

9 Manufacturing has travelled a long way down the same road. Since the second world war, manufacturing output in the developed world has probably tripled in volume, but inflation-adjusted manufacturing prices have fallen steadily, whereas the cost of prime knowledge products—health care and education—has tripled, again adjusted for inflation. The relative purchasing power of manufactured goods against knowledge products is now only one-fifth or one-sixth of what it was 50 years ago. Manufacturing employment in America has fallen from 35% of the workforce in the 1950s to less than half that now, without causing much social disruption. But it may be too much to hope for an equally easy transition in countries such as Japan or Germany, where blue-collar manufacturing workers still make up 25-30% of the labour force.

10 The decline of farming as a producer of wealth and of livelihoods has allowed farm protectionism to spread to a degree that would have been unthinkable before the second world war. In the same way, the decline of manufacturing will trigger an explosion of manufacturing protectionism—even as lip service continues to be paid to free trade. This protectionism may not necessarily take the form of traditional tariffs, but of subsidies, quotas and regulations of all kinds. Even more likely, regional blocks will emerge that trade freely internally but are highly protectionist externally. The European Union, NAFTA and Mercosur already point in that direction.

11 The future of the corporation

Statistically, multinational companies play much the same part in the world economy as they did in 1913. But they have become very different animals. Multinationals in 1913 were domestic firms with subsidiaries abroad, each of them self-contained, in charge of a politically defined territory, and highly autonomous. Multinationals now tend to be organised globally along product or service lines. But like the multinationals of 1913, they are held together and controlled by ownership. By contrast, the multinationals of 2025 are likely to be held together and controlled by strategy. There will still be ownership, of course. But alliances, joint ventures, minority stakes, know-how agreements and contracts will increasingly be the building blocks of a confederation. This kind of organisation will need a new kind of top management.

12 In most countries, and even in a good many large and complex companies, top management is still seen as an extension of operating management. Tomorrow's top management, however, is likely to be a distinct and separate organ: it will stand for the company. One of the most important jobs ahead for the top management of the big company of tomorrow, and especially of the multinational, will be to balance the conflicting demands on business being made by the need for both short-term and long-term results, and by the corporation's various constituencies: customers, shareholders (especially institutional investors and pension funds), knowledge employees and communities.

13 Against that background, this survey will seek to answer two questions: what can and should managements do now to be ready for the next society? And what other big changes may lie ahead of which we are as yet unaware? ■

Glossary

accessible	available, capable of being used or seen
alignments	arrangements, relationships
apprenticeship	learning by practical experience under skilled workers
arm's length	a distance discouraging personal contact
autonomous	existing independently without outside control
blue-collar	class of workers who wear work clothes; manual workers
bolstered	reinforced, supported, boosted
constituents	people involved in or served by an organization
dwindled	decreased, became steadily less
homogeneous	the same or similar, uniform
lip service	allegiance expressed in words but not in deeds
marginal	not of central importance
pension funds	funds that invest money paid to persons following retirement from service
pensions	money paid to persons following retirement from service
protectionism	government economic protection for domestic producers by restrictions on foreign competitors
shrinking	decreasing, becoming smaller
subsidiaries	companies wholly controlled by another
subsidies	money granted by government to persons or companies; public money given to private enterprise
tariffs	duties imposed by government on imported goods; price charge
trigger	to cause, initiate
upheaval	radical change

Discussion

These questions are intended to strengthen your understanding of the article, stimulate original thinking, and encourage you to express your point of view.

1. According to Drucker, what will be the dominant factor in the next society in the developed countries? What will cause this to happen?

2. What change will take place in the labor force in the new society?

3. What will result from the fact that in developed countries, as well as China and Brazil, the birthrate is below the replacement rate of 2.2 live births per woman?

4. How will the decline in the young population change the mass market?

5. What are the three main characteristics of the knowledge society?

6. Who will become the dominant social and political force in the new society?

7. Explain the meaning of the phrase "the new protectionism."

8. What will result from an explosion of manufacturing protectionism?

9. What will hold together and control multinational corporations in 2025?

10. How does Drucker differentiate tomorrow's top management from today's top management?

11. What can you predict about future social, political, and economic changes in your native country? Can you forecast any major improvements? Can you forecast any serious problems?

Teamwork

Working in teams to accomplish goals and objectives is a common approach used in the world of global business. Collaborative work means that all members of the group support each other, contribute equally, and cooperate in completing the project. After forming your group, choose a group leader, who will assign each person a section of the work and oversee the project's final form. This first team project introduces you to online research.

Peter F. Drucker, the author of "The Next Society," is a professor of social science and management at Claremont Graduate University in California. He has written 32 books on organization and management. Working in a group, make a list of Drucker's books. You can find this information by going online. Using the Internet offers you the following options.

1. Log on to your school's library catalog of books.

2. Log on to <http://www.Amazon.com>.

3. Use the Internet search engine Google at <http://www.google.com>. Do a search by typing the words *Peter Drucker*.

Writing Assignments

Each chapter contains four different writing assignments that meet the needs of a variety of students and course objectives. Some of the writing tasks involve library and Internet research. Writing strategies, guidelines, and models of writing assignments are presented in Appendix B: Strategies for Communication.

1. The authors of "The New Atlantic Century," printed in this chapter, believe that "the economic relationship between the United States and Europe is about

to enter its strongest period yet." Make a list of the arguments used by the authors to support their belief. Then write a 300-word summary of "The New Atlantic Century." (See Appendix B, Summary.)

2. Make an outline of Peter Drucker's article "The Next Society," printed in this chapter. Then write a 300-word summary of the article. (See Appendix B, Summary.)

3. Imagine that you work for an international investment company. Write a memorandum to your boss explaining why your company should invest in European companies, rather than Asian companies, in the coming year. The writing style of the memorandum should be informal and personal, and the tone should be persuasive and positive. (See Appendix B, Memorandum.)

4. Write a research paper on the topic of changes in the workforce in the 21st century. You may use the articles printed or mentioned in this chapter, including the expansion readings, as sources for your paper. Also find several recent sources. These books should be helpful.

Cooper, Richard N., and Richard Layard, eds. *What the Future Holds: Insights From Social Science.* Cambridge, MA: MIT Press, 2002.

DiMaggio, Paul, ed. *The 21st-Century Firm: Changing Economic Organization in International Perspective.* Princeton: Princeton University Press, 2001.

Drucker, Peter F. *Managing in the Next Society.* New York: St. Martin's Press, 2002.

Expansion Readings

Each chapter suggests readings from the *Harvard Business Review,* the *Harvard International Review,* or *The Economist* for outside reading. The Internet business database ABI/Inform provides the full text of articles from the *Harvard International Review* and *The Economist.* It provides only the abstracts of articles from the *Harvard Business Review;* the full text can be found in the bound volumes in the library. For chapter 1, the suggested readings are the following.

Handy, Charles. "Toqueville Revisited: The Meaning of American Prosperity." *Harvard Business Review* 79, no. 1 (January 2001): 57–63.

"The Next Society: A Survey of the Future." *The Economist,* 3 November 2001, 3–20.

Nye, Joseph. "America's Power: The New Rome Meets the New Barbarians." *The Economist,* 23 March 2002, 23–25.

Peterson, Peter G. "A Graying World." *Harvard International Review* 23, no. 3 (Fall 2001): 66–75.

"Trade Disputes: Dangerous Activities." *The Economist,* 11 May 2002, 63–66.

Oral Presentation

Working with a partner, give a 20-minute oral presentation to the class on one of the articles listed under Expansion Readings or an article of your choice on business in the future. Summarize the article by including the author's thesis, major points, and supporting data and evaluate its strengths and weaknesses. Be prepared to answer questions on your topic. If you have the technical capability, use the presentation graphics program PowerPoint for your presentation. Otherwise, make at least one overhead to use on the overhead projector. (See Appendix B, Oral Presentation.)

Travels on the Web

The Internet offers numerous opportunities to read more about business and technology in the 21st century. The following Web sites are excellent sources of state-of-the-art information.

1. Log on to the Futurist Society Web site, founded by Glen Hiemstra. Choose Portal to Content and click on Content Archive. More than 50 articles are in the article archive, including the 3 listed here. Read several of the articles the archive contains. Print out one article and write a brief reaction to it. Bring the article to class to share with your classmates.

   • <http://www.futurist.com>

   • Portal to Content

   • Content Archive

     1. "Four Jobs of the Future." Richard Wilkinson (February 2001). "A creative look at four jobs that are needed in the future but do not yet exist today."

     2. "Top Ten Careers of the Future." Glen Hiemstra (February 2001). "The top ten careers of the future, and a comparison of various views on future careers."

     3. "Over the Horizon." Glen Hiemstra (December 2000). "List and links for the ten key technological developments of the first decade of the 21st century."

2. Log on to the George Washington University Forecast of Technology and Strategy to read the annual report on future developments in business and technology. On the Site Map, choose About GW Forecast. Then choose Knowledge Base and click on Summary of Results and Latest Results. Print out the Summary of Results and Latest Results and bring them to class for discussion with your classmates.

   • <http://www.gwforecast.gwu.edu> (The GW Forecast: A Virtual Think-Tank for Tracking the Technology Revolution)

- About GW Forecast

- Knowledge Base

- Summary of Results

- Latest Results (Energy, Environment, Materials, IT Hardware, IT Software, Medicine)

Answers to Exercises

Preview   "The New Atlantic Century"

Scanning

1. Who are the core members of "Transatlantica"? (the United States and Europe: paragraph 2)

2. What is the trade in Japan heavily weighted toward? (imports of raw materials and exports of ready-made products: paragraph 5)

3. Which country dominates high-tech industries, such as computer software, biotechnology, and Internet applications? (the United States: paragraph 7)

4. How many Americans, Europeans, and Asians are now online? (90 million Americans, 80 million Europeans, 40 million Asians: paragraph 11)

Vocabulary in Context

1. Although the recent financial crisis *dimmed* (reduced) some of Asia's luster, many observers continue to believe that the strongest *engine* (agent) of growth will be found in the fast-developing Pacific Basin.

2. Even though Japan is slowly moving away from *mercantilism* (commercialism), its trade is still heavily *weighted* (inclined in a particular direction) toward imports of raw materials and exports of ready-made products.

3. It [the United States] has abundant *venture capital* (capital invested in the ownership of a new enterprise) and thriving *entrepreneurship* (organization and assumption of the risks of a business).

4. English is quickly becoming the *lingua franca* (common language) of the region, *facilitating* (making easier) all sorts of dealings.

5. It does not appear, however, that any of those *potential* (possible) conflicts is liable to *flare up* (intensify suddenly) soon and fundamentally damage the world's most productive economic relationship.

Paraphrasing

Examples of Possible Paraphrases

1. Many analysts are convinced that the greatest growth will take place in the Pacific Basin despite the fact that the economic downturn has weakened Asia.

2. Japan's trade is dominated by importing raw materials and exporting manufactured goods at the same time it is turning away from commercial trade.

3. Large sums of money are available for investment, and many people are starting their own businesses in the United States.

4. Business deals are made easier by the use of the English language, which is being adopted throughout the area.

5. This extremely strong economic partnership is unlikely to be affected by any possible conflicts that might develop in the future.

Comprehension

Note: Answers to the comprehension questions are taken directly from the article in most cases, without paraphrasing.

1. In the 21st century, what will guide the world market? (The economic relationship between the United States and Europe—that is, within Transatlantica—will guide the world market. paragraphs 1 and 12)

2. What is revealed by the data on cross-border mergers and acquisitions? (The level of direct investment between the United States and Europe is three times that between the United States and Asia. European acquisitions accounted for 20 of the 25 largest acquisitions of U.S. businesses in 1998. paragraph 2)

3. Why is trade less advanced in China and Japan than in the Transatlantica countries? (Transatlantica countries are much further along in restructuring their trade around specialized industrial goods. paragraph 5)

4. How do the authors describe competition today? (Today, competition means a struggle for the best global talent and access to the world's business centers and other regions of competence. National identities are minimized, and corporate power is distributed among many countries. paragraph 6)

5. Why is the United States best positioned to capture the opportunities of the world market? (The United States has moved to a service economy based on the flow of ideas rather than the flow of materials, it has abundant venture capital and thriving entrepreneurship, and, thus, it dominates high-tech industries. paragraph 7)

6. What two major factors are advantageous to Transatlantica countries and why? (The two factors are a common language, English, and a common communication medium, the Internet. paragraphs 10 and 11)

7. What three possible areas of contention could undermine the prosperity of Transatlantica? (Europe could terminate the NATO alliance, the euro could threaten the dollar as the global reserve currency, and trade disputes between Europe and North America could intensify. paragraph 12)

8. What other areas of the world besides the United States and Europe could become economically powerful in the 21st century? (Answers will vary. One possible suggestion is Asia, as the reading states.)

9. What changes have taken place in the world market since this article was published in January–February 2000? (Answers will vary.)

Analysis

1. What is the main idea of the article, and in which paragraph(s) is it stated?

   a. The Internet has changed the way countries engage in trade and conduct business.

   b. Competition in trade will increase between Asian and European countries.

   c. The communication medium and the language are critical factors in determining economic relationships.

   d. The major trade relationship in the future will be between the United States and Europe.

   The correct answer is **d.** The authors state this main idea in the first paragraph, again in the last paragraph, and in the title. The article contains a variety of points that support the authors' belief in Transatlantica as the center of the world economy. Sentence **a** is not discussed directly in the text, but it could be inferred as a supporting point. Sentence **b** is not stated in the text, and sentence **c** is a supporting point for the main idea.

2. What is the meaning of the italicized word in this sentence from the first paragraph? "They foresee Asia *supplanting* Europe as the primary economic partner of the United States, leading to a so-called Pacific century."

   a. imitating (copying)

   b. replacing

   c. supporting (helping, promoting)

   d. following (coming after)

   The correct answer is **b,** according to the context of the paragraph. The authors believe Europe will be the primary economic partner of the United States, but "many observers" believe Asia will take this role instead of Europe. Thus, the reader can guess that "replacing" is the correct meaning of the word *supplanting*.

3. We can infer the following from this sentence in paragraph 9: "In the age of innovative turbocapitalism, however, speed is of the essence, even at the cost of occasional failure."

   a. Speed is more important today than in the past because the powerful capitalistic system is characterized by rapid innovation. (correct: The word *turbocapitalism* implies the supercharged and speedy capitalistic system in which innovations occur daily. *Turbo* refers to turbine, a powerful driving engine.)

   b. Capitalism has overtaken other economic systems in the world because of its ability to innovate. (incorrect: This sentence is not supported by the text.)

   c. Large corporations and the state have a disadvantage in terms of the speed at which they do business. (incorrect: This sentence is stated explicitly in the text, not implied.)

   d. It is essential for businesses to operate carefully in this creative capitalistic environment in order to avoid making costly mistakes. (incorrect: This is not the meaning of the sentence.)

4. The authors' writing style in this article is _____ and _____ .

   a. impersonal (incorrect: The authors would not use the first-person pronoun *we* if the style were impersonal.)

   b. personal (correct: The authors use the first-person pronoun *we* and present their opinion, stating, for example, "But we believe . . .")

   c. technical (incorrect: The authors use very few technical terms. *Mercantilism* is one of the few.)

   d. nontechnical (correct: The authors are writing for the average businessperson, not an international trade expert.)

5. The tone of this article is _____ and _____ .

   a. persuasive (correct: The authors provide strong supporting arguments to persuade readers to accept their main idea.)

   b. neutral (incorrect: The authors take a stand and are not neutral about where the center of the world economy will be in the next century.)

   c. straightforward (correct: The authors present their points clearly, concisely, and directly.)

   d. ambiguous (incorrect: The authors' meaning is not open to several interpretations. It is clear and definite.)

6. What overall method of development is used in this article?

   a. comparing and contrasting two proposals

   b. **supporting an argument with statistical data and evidence (correct: The authors support their thesis that the major trade relationship will be between the United States and Europe by giving facts, statistics, and examples.)**

   c. defining a new system

   d. explaining the steps in a complex process

7. What techniques do the authors use to get the reader's attention in the introduction to this article (paragraph 1)?

   a. making a humorous statement

   b. giving a definition

   c. **asking a question (correct: "Looking into the next century, where will the center of the world economy be?")**

   d. **adding a contrasting idea (correct: "But we believe that the new century, like the one just ended, will be very much an Atlantic century . . .")**

Discussion

Note: Answers to the discussion questions are taken directly from the article in most cases, without paraphrasing.

1. According to Drucker, what will be the dominant factor in the next society in the developed countries? (The dominant factor will be the rapid growth in the older population and the rapid shrinking of the younger generation. paragraph 2) What will cause this to happen? (Leaders can infer that women are having fewer children—below the replacement rate of 2.2 live births per woman—and people are living longer because of better health care and diet.)

2. What change will take place in the labor force in the new society? (Within 25–30 years, as many as half the people who work for an organization will not be employed on a full-time basis. paragraph 3)

3. What will result from the fact that in developed countries, as well as China and Brazil, the birthrate is below the replacement rate of 2.2 live births per woman? (Politically, immigration will become an important and highly divisive issue. paragraph 4)

4. How will the decline in the young population change the mass market? (The homogeneous youth-determined mass market will change into a mass market determined by the middle-aged and a much smaller youth-determined market. paragraph 4)

5. What are the three main characteristics of the knowledge society? (It will be borderless, because knowledge travels effortlessly; it will have upward mobility, because knowledge will be available to everyone; it will offer the potential for failure as well as success, because not everyone can win. paragraph 5)

6. Who will become the dominant social and political force in the new society? (Knowledge technologists—computer technicians, software designers, and so on—will be the dominant force. paragraph 7)

7. Explain the meaning of the phrase "the new protectionism." (Subsidies, quotas, and regulations will protect farmers and manufacturers because farming and manufacturing have declined as producers of wealth and livelihoods. paragraphs 8–10)

8. What will result from an explosion of manufacturing protectionism? (Regional blocks that trade freely internally but are highly protectionist externally, like the European Union, NAFTA, and Mercosur, will emerge. paragraph 10)

9. What will hold together and control multinational corporations in 2025? (They will be held together and controlled by strategy. paragraph 11)

10. How does Drucker differentiate tomorrow's top management from today's top management? (Today's top management is an extension of operating management. Tomorrow's top management will be a distinct and separate organ that will have to balance the conflicting demands for both short-term and long-term results. paragraph 12)

11. What can you predict about future social, political, and economic changes in your native country? Can you forecast any major improvements? Can you forecast any serious problems?

Writing Assignments

1. The authors of "The New Atlantic Century," printed in this chapter, believe that "the economic relationship between the United States and Europe is about to enter its strongest period yet." Make a list of the arguments used by the authors to support their belief.

   • The level of direct investment between the United States and Europe is three times that between the United States and Asia.

   • European acquisitions accounted for 20 of the 25 largest acquisitions of U.S. businesses in 1998. Asian countries made no U.S. acquisitions.

   • Japan and China are still relatively isolated from other countries in regard to trade.

   • The character of trade in Transatlantica, which has been restructured around specialized industrial goods, is much more advanced than it is in Japan or China. China follows a mercantilist policy, and so does Japan to a lesser extent.

- The United States is best positioned to capture opportunities of the world market. It has moved to a service economy and dominates high-tech industries.

- A wave of optimism and entrepreneurial spirit has been sweeping Europe.

- New ideas move fastest when people share a common language and a common communication medium. Transatlantica has a common language (English) and a common communication medium (the Internet).

- No potential conflicts with Europe are likely to damage the world's most productive economic relationship.

2. Make an outline of Peter Drucker's article "The Next Society," printed in this chapter.

  I. Introduction: The next society will be very different from the society of the late 20th century.

    A. The dominant factor will be the rapid growth of the older population and the rapid shrinking of the younger generation.

    B. Half of all workers will be part-time, so the central managerial issue will be new ways of working with part-time employees.

    C. In developed countries, as well as Brazil and China, the birthrate is well below the replacement rate of 2.2 live births per woman.

    D. Immigration will become a highly divisive and political issue in rich countries.

    E. The mass market will split into a large middle-aged market and a small youth market.

  II. Knowledge Is All: The next society will be a knowledge society.

    A. Knowledge will be the key resource, and the knowledge society will have three characteristics:

      1. It will be borderless, because knowledge travels effortlessly.

      2. It will have upward mobility, because knowledge will be available to everyone through education.

      3. It will offer the potential for failure as well as success.

    B. The knowledge economy will rely on knowledge workers.

      1. Knowledge technologists do manual work based on knowledge acquired through formal education.

      2. They will become the dominant social and political force.

III. The New Protectionism: Structurally, the next society is diverging from the society we still live in.

    A. Agriculture has become marginal, so farm protectionism has spread.

    B. Manufacturing employment in the United States has declined from 35 percent to less than half that.

        1. Manufacturing protectionism will spread.

        2. Regional blocks, like the European Union, NAFTA, and Mercosur, which are highly protectionist externally, will emerge.

IV. The Future of the Corporation: Multinational corporations have changed since 1913.

    A. Multinationals are now organized globally along product or service lines.

    B. Multinationals of 2025 will be held together and controlled by strategy, not ownership.

    C. Alliances, joint ventures, and minority stakes will increase, creating a need for a new kind of top management.

    D. Top management will need to balance demands for both short-term and long-term results.

    E. Subsequent parts of this survey will seek to determine what management can and should do to be ready for the next society. (Note: "The Next Society" is part of a section in *The Economist* titled "A Survey of the Near Future.")

Chapter 2
Globalization

Preview   "Sizing Up Global Integration"

Skimming

Skim the article quickly to find the following general information.

1. Read the title and all headings and look at any illustrations.

2. Read the first and second paragraphs, looking for the authors' purpose and main idea.

3. Read the last paragraph, looking for a summary or conclusion.

4. Write a sentence containing your preliminary understanding of the main idea of the article.

Questioning

Answer the following questions and discuss your answers in class.

1. What factors determine the level of global integration of a country?

2. To what extent is your native country globally integrated?

3. How has globalization affected your native country and culture?

Scanning

Scan the article quickly to find the following specific information.

1. What four factors were used in the survey to determine global integration?

2. Which countries outpaced other countries in the diffusion of new information technologies?

3. What was the world's most global nation in the 2001 report?

4. What was the rank of the United States in the globalization index in 2001?

Vocabulary in Context

Read the following sentences from the article and try to guess the meaning of the italicized words by using the context. Then replace the italicized words with synonyms (words or phrases that have nearly the same or similar meanings).

1. "This finding offers a *counterpoint* to those who argue that developing countries are poor and unequal because of globalization. . . ." (Paragraph 9)

2. "It comes as little surprise that the world's industrialized economies *surpass* the rest of the globe in the development of information technologies." (Paragraph 11)

3. "These findings suggest that much of the common knowledge surrounding globalization remains *misguided*." (Paragraph 16)

4. "We believe that all sides are best served when these debates rely less on anecdotal evidence and more on *empirical* facts." (Paragraph 17)

Paraphrasing

After reading the article, reread the sentences under Vocabulary in Context. Now rewrite them using your own words. Change the vocabulary and sentence structure, but do not change the author's intended meaning or paraphrase any technical terms. There are several ways of paraphrasing each sentence.

OPINION

Sizing up global integration

The more globalized nations boast greater income equality, not less

By Moisés Naím
and Paul A. Laudicina

WASHINGTON

1 GLOBALIZATION has become the new century's most abused buzzword. Advocates and detractors alike bend its meaning to fit their arguments.

2 In truth, globalization entails a dense web of cross-border relationships that range from the very evident – one example is the exotic fruits found in supermarkets – to the very subtle, such as the opinions that become conventional wisdom as a result of the unprecedented boom in human interaction.

3 One aspect frequently missed in the debates about globalization is its measurement: How extensive is globalization? Which countries are the most globalized? The least? And why?

4 Those rare instances in which anyone attempts to measure globalization typically rely on data concerning international trade and investment flows, to the exclusion of other aspects of global integration.

5 To fill this gap, Foreign Policy magazine teamed up with A.T. Kearney to create the Globalization Index, which employs indicators spanning information technology, finance, trade, travel, and personal communication to gauge levels of global integration in 50 key developed countries and emerging markets.

6 The results of this exercise offer a fascinating three-dimensional glimpse of the nature, speed, and scope of globalization. Looking closely at the details, we find strong evidence that some of the most widely held notions surrounding global integration require reexamination. Consider just a few of our observations:

7 Globalization and income disparity need not go together. The world's most global countries boast greater income equality than their less-global counterparts.

8 Even among developing countries, those that are more integrated with their neighbors (such as Hungary, Poland, and the Czech Republic), tend to have more equitable patterns of income distribution than those that are not as well integrated (including Argentina, China, and Russia).

9 This finding offers a counterpoint to those who argue that developing countries are poor and unequal because of globalization, suggesting instead that history, economic policies, welfare programs, and education policies may play an important role in shaping income distribution.

10 More-globalized nations are freer and less corrupt. With few exceptions, countries that score well on the Globalization Index enjoy greater political freedom, as measured by the annual Freedom House survey of civil liberties and political rights. Similarly, a comparison of the index's rankings with Transparency International's survey of perceived corruption worldwide suggests that public officials in more-global countries are less corrupt than their counterparts in closed economies.

More than one digital divide

11 It comes as little surprise that the world's industrialized economies surpass the rest of the globe in the development of

Globalization and income disparity need not go together.

More-globalized nations are freer and less corrupt.

information technologies. However, various indicators of Internet use and access indicate that other gaps exist within the global digital divide.

12 The United States, Canada, and Scandinavian economies such as Finland and Sweden far outpace other advanced countries in the diffusion of new information technologies.

13 Meanwhile, globalization in many of the countries that are part of the euro currency bloc has been weighed down by their slow start in Internet development.

Bigger is not always better

14 The most-global economies tend to be small nations for which openness allows access to goods, services, and capital not readily available at home. Tiny Singapore ranks as the world's most-global nation, with the Netherlands, Sweden, and Switzerland not far behind.

15 Singapore boasts high levels of trade, heavy capital flows, and an annual stream

of international travelers nearly three times higher than the country's population of a little more than 4 million. And with international telephone traffic that totals 390 minutes per person each year, the country far outdistances its nearest rivals in cross-border contact between people. By contrast, the United States hosts only one-sixth that proportion of international travelers and claims less than one-fourth the international telephone traffic per capita.

16 These findings suggest that much of the common knowledge surrounding globalization remains misguided.

17 To be fair, the forces drawing nations together include many that are beyond the ability of governments to control, including global warming, the spread of disease, and the rise of transnational crime. But ongoing debates over the relative merits of global integration have very real implications, both for countries and for the people who live in them. We believe that all sides are best served when these debates rely less on anecdotal evidence and more on empirical facts.

■ *Moisés Naím is editor and publisher of Foreign Policy magazine. Paul A. Laudicina is the managing director of A.T. Kearney's Global Business Policy Council. The A.T. Kearney/Foreign Policy magazine Globalization Index™ is featured in the January/February issue of Foreign Policy magazine.*

The global top 20

The Globalization Index™ measures the level of global integration in 50 developed countries and key emerging markets worldwide. Singapore ranks No. 1, while the United States comes in 12th, because of its relatively low level of economic integration compared with the other countries in the survey.

Malaysia
Israel
Spain
Hungary
France
Portugal
Germany
Italy
United States
Denmark
Canada
Norway
United Kingdom
Austria
Ireland
Finland
Switzerland
Sweden
Netherlands
Singapore

TECHNOLOGY: population online, Internet hosts, and secure servers.

PERSONAL CONTACT: cross-border money remittances, international phone calls and travel.

FINANCE: foreign direct investments and capital flows.

GOODS/SERVICES: international trade, convergence of domestic and global prices.

Source: A.T. Kearney Inc. and Foreign Policy magazine

KAREN N. SCHNEIDER - STAFF

Glossary

advocates	supporters, defenders
anecdotal	based on reports of unscientific observers
buzzword	a popular word or phrase
capital	national or individual wealth as produced by industry and available for reinvestment; funds, assets, money
civil liberties	freedom from arbitrary governmental interference, as with the right of free speech, by denial of governmental power
conventional	ordinary, commonplace
corruption	impairment of integrity, virtue, or moral principle
counterpoint	a complementing or contrasting item; an opposite opinion
detractors	critics
diffusion	spreading out, distributing
digital divide	the gap between those who can use computer technology and those who cannot
disparity	differences
empirical	based on observation or experience; able to be verified by observation or experience
equitable	fair; dealing fairly and equally with all concerned
gauge	to measure precisely
globalization	integration of markets, nation-states, and technologies, characterized by free-market capitalism, computerization, the Internet, and innovation; the dominant international system (Thomas L. Friedman, *The Lexus and the Olive Tree: Understanding Globalization* [New York: Anchor Books, 2000])
implications	suggestions, possible significances
indicators	any of a group of statistical values that, taken together, give an indication of global integration
integration	forming or blending into a united whole; to unite with something else
misguided	led by wrong or inappropriate motives or ideals
sizing up	forming a judgment of
spanning	extending across
subtle	delicate; difficult to understand or perceive
surpass	to exceed, go beyond
transparency	state of being open; easily detected, readily understood
unprecedented	having no precedent; never seen

Comprehension

1. What do the authors believe about the connection between globalization and income disparity? How do they justify their opinion?

2. What four factors may play a role in shaping income distribution? Can you suggest any other factors?

3. Explain the meaning of the term *digital divide*. How is this factor slowing globalization?

4. Why is "openness" such a critical factor in global integration?

5. Why do the authors state that "much of the common knowledge surrounding globalization remains misguided"?

6. Do you believe that globalization is a force for integration and harmony, or does globalization make poor countries weaker? What are the negative effects of globalization, and what are the positive effects?

Analysis

Circle the letter of the best answer(s). Justify your choices with specific examples from the text.

1. What is the main idea of the article, and in which paragraph(s) is it stated?

    a. Empirical research should be conducted to determine the global integration of a country.

    b. Large countries are the most globally integrated because of their economic strength.

    c. Four major factors determine the extent to which a country is globally integrated.

    d. The United States is more globally integrated than other large countries.

2. What is the meaning of the italicized word in this sentence in paragraph 17? "But ongoing debates over the relative *merits* of global integration have very real implications, both for countries and for the people who live in them."

    a. criteria

    b. challenges

    c. demands

    d. value

3. We can infer the following from this statement in paragraph 7: "Globalization and income disparity need not go together."

   a. Income disparity has no relationship with globalization.

   b. Globalization is not the major cause of income disparity.

   c. Globalization and income disparity are often wrongly seen as interrelated.

   d. Income disparity has increased because of globalization.

4. The authors' writing style in this article is _____ and _____ .

   a. scholarly

   b. journalistic

   c. concise

   d. wordy

5. The tone of the article is _____ and _____ .

   a. emotional

   b. factual

   c. balanced

   d. argumentative

6. What overall method of development is used in this article?

   a. describing an empirical study and its results

   b. defining a problem and proposing a solution

   c. analyzing a scientific process

   d. attacking an argument by comparing data

7. In the concluding sentence, the authors state: "We believe that all sides are best served when these debates rely less on anecdotal evidence and more on empirical facts." (paragraph 17) What are the authors contrasting in this statement?

   a. written reports and oral debates

   b. the most globalized and the least globalized countries

   c. measurable, objective information and unscientific information

   d. the advantages and disadvantages of globalization

brave new work ● by michael schrage

Nationality Matters More Than Ever. That's No Joke

1 Stop me if you've heard this one before: In Heaven, the cooks are French, the police are English, the mechanics are German, the lovers are Italian, and the bankers are Swiss. But in Hell, the cooks are English, the police are German, the mechanics are French, the lovers are Swiss, and the bankers are Italian.

2 So did you smirk, or were you offended? (Please don't tell me.) Less than a generation ago, middlebrow publications such as *Reader's Digest* would print jokes like that one, gently mocking nationalist stereotypes and pretensions. Where you were from said something about who you were.

3 In today's era of political correctness, of course, humor that plays and preys upon ethnic imagery is *verboten*. The economic imperatives of global markets ostensibly trump the prejudices of cross-cultural caricature. As national economies become more intertwined, it is people's fundamental similarities—*not* their myriad differences—that drive globalization.

4 There's some truth to that. But another truth is that national, cultural, and ethnic differences will increasingly determine success in tomorrow's global markets. Why? For all the punditry proclaiming that globalization promotes homogeneity, simple economic reality dictates that firms competing in global markets are relentlessly driven to differentiate. A casual survey of the global business landscape reveals that it's become far harder for firms to differentiate themselves simply by being faster, better, and/or cheaper than their competition. "Faster, better, cheaper" is being commoditized. So where should companies turn for assets and insights that make them special? Those intangible ele-

ments that define a regional taste, an ethnic sensibility, a national culture. The intangible assets that go into "German engineering" or "Italian design" or "French fashion." They represent resources that can't so easily be emulated or reverse-engineered by business competitors.

5 This concept of cultural capital has been

As national economies become more intertwined, it is people's fundamental similarities—*not* their myriad differences—that drive globalization.

enthusiastically embraced by governments and trade ministries worldwide. Culture has become postindustrial policy. Prime Minister Tony Blair talks of "branding Britain" and aggressively promotes England as a world capital of pop culture and design. Malaysia's Mahathir Mohammed and Singapore's emeritus Prime Minister Lee Kwan Yew stridently emphasize "Asian values"—as opposed to Western values—as the reason for the resilience of Asian economies. Hungary, Bangalore, and Ireland celebrate the software development savvy of their people. Israel and Taiwan argue that their indigenous business cultures represent a future of high-tech entrepreneurship. Is there any country in the world more xenophobically arrogant about

its sensibilities than France? As the CEO of France's largest film company once observed, "American movies succeed because they are supposed to appeal to everybody. French movies succeed because they are French."

6 In fact, the past decade of globalization has seen a tremendous surge in the active marketing by governments of positive ethnic and nationalist stereotypes. Enlightened globalists may feel that nationalism and ethnicity in economics should matter less, but they should hardly be shocked when the Indians, Chinese, Hungarians, Brazilians, Indonesians, Koreans, and French insist they should matter more. And they are not the only ones. World Bank economists have become increasingly sensitive to cultural considerations in their efforts to promote development. Economic historians like Harvard's David Landes and strategic management gurus like Michael Porter argue that cultural and regional tastes have profound influences on a nation's ability to innovate.

7 But this resurgent strain of nationalistic and ethnic economics will prove extraordinarily volatile and dangerous. For every positive stereotype of a national economic character, there are ugly and destructive negatives. What's more, stereotypes can become chains of self-fulfilling prophecies: A country or region may define itself along its cultural competence to the exclusion of other opportunities.

8 Companies may become arbitrageurs of stereotypes and reorganize themselves accordingly: *We'll hire Hungarian and Indian software developers; Koreans and Mexicans to do the manufacturing based on our German subsidiary's engineering; the French can handle the high-end marketing, and we'll have the Americans do the mass marketing; and the Israelis can do the venture stuff.*

9 It's easy to see how that kind of cultural apartheid can breed resentment and backlash. Nevertheless, this is the direction in which global markets will go. So global managers with multinational, multi-ethnic work forces had better pay close attention to the kinds of jokes they hear: There may be a differentiation opportunity there. **F**

MICHAEL SCHRAGE *is co-director of the MIT Media Lab's e-markets initiative and author of* Serious Play. *Reach him at michael_schrage@fortunemail.com.*

ILLUSTRATION BY BORIS KULIKOV

Glossary

apartheid	separation, segregation
arbitrageurs	those who simultaneously buy and sell securities or foreign exchange
backlash	a strong adverse reaction or hostile response
caricature	cartoon; misrepresentation
commoditized	being made into an article of commerce, an economic good, a commodity
emulated	imitated; tried to equal
ethnicity	ethnic quality based on racial, national, tribal, religious, linguistic, or cultural origin
homogeneity	the quality of being the same or similar in nature
indigenous	native, local, original
intangible	indefinable, not able to be concretely specified
mocking	scornful, disrespectful
myriad	numerous, many, countless
ostensibly	apparently, supposedly
punditry	opinions given in an authoritative manner
resilience	an ability to recover from or adjust easily to misfortune or change; flexibility
resurgent	coming to life again
stereotypes	standardized mental pictures held by members of a group that represent a prejudiced attitude or oversimplified opinion
trump	to outdo, get the better of
verboten	forbidden (German)
volatile	unstable, unpredictable; explosive
xenophobically	fearful of what is foreign or strange and especially of people of foreign origin

Discussion

1. Michael Schrage writes that because of "political correctness," humor that focuses on ethnic differences is no longer acceptable. Explain what he means, and give your opinion on the principle of "political correctness."

2. Why will national, cultural, and ethnic differences increasingly determine success in tomorrow's global markets?

3. What is the meaning of the term *cultural capital?* What examples of cultural capital does Schrage give?

4. Why may "enlightened globalists" feel that nationalism and ethnicity in economics should matter less?

5. What do experts such as David Landes and Michael Porter argue about cultural considerations?

6. Why will nationalistic and ethnic economics prove extraordinarily dangerous?

7. What positive ethnic and national stereotypes of your native country could be an asset (advantage) in business? What negative ethnic and national stereotypes of your native country could be a liability (disadvantage) in business?

8. Do you agree with Michael Schrage that "national, cultural, and ethnic differences will increasingly determine success in tomorrow's global markets"? Explain your answer.

Teamwork

Working with a group, discuss the factors of global integration that are presented in "Globalization's Last Hurrah?" from the January–February 2002 issue of *Foreign Policy.* This article, located in Appendix C, presents the second annual A. T. Kearney/ *Foreign Policy* magazine Globalization Index. Then compare the 2002 Globalization Index with the Globalization Index in the 2001 article "Sizing Up Global Integration," printed in the present chapter. Make a list of the key indicators used in the reports, and explain how they were measured. Summarize the major findings.

Writing Assignments

1. Log on to the Web site for *Fortune* magazine: <http://www.fortune.com>. Click on Company Profiles and then click on Global 500 and Global Most Admired. Make a list of those companies you would be interested in working for, and read about them. Choose one company where you want to apply for a position. Write a cover letter and a résumé to send to its Department of Human Resources. (See Appendix B, Memorandum, Business Letter, and Résumé.)

2. The article "Measuring Globalization" in the January–February 2001 issue of *Foreign Policy* (pp. 56–65) discusses the first annual A. T. Kearney/*Foreign Policy* magazine Globalization Index. Appendix C in the present book contains "Globalization's Last Hurrah?" from the January–February 2002 issue of *Foreign Policy* (pp. 38–50), which discusses the second annual Globalization Index. Use the Internet business database ABI/Inform or the search engine Google to locate "Measuring Globalization" on the Internet. (Do a search by

typing the phrases *globalization index* and *foreign policy.*) After reading the articles, note the differences between the 2000 and 2001 Globalization Indexes, and compare the top 20 countries. Write a summary presenting the major findings of these annual studies.

3. Write an essay in which you discuss the level of global integration in a country in which you are interested. (See Appendix B, Essay.) Consider the four factors of technology, personal contact, finance, and goods/services. Use the Internet to do research on the globalization of this country. For example, to get current information, you can use the business database LexisNexis Academic. Select Site Map and under Reference, choose the options Country Profiles and World Almanac. You can also choose from the following country reports.

   - The Central Intelligence Agency (CIA) reports at <http://www.cia.gov>. Under Library & Reference, select *The World Factbook.*

   - The Library of Congress reports at <http://www.loc.gov>. Click on Search Our Web Site, click on the letter C, and select Country Studies/Area Handbooks.

   - The World Bank Group reports at <http://www.worldbank.org>. Click on Countries & Regions and also on Development Topics.

   - The United Nations reports at <http://www.un.org>. Click on Economic and Social Development and select Statistics or Site Index Statistics.

4. Write a research paper on the topic of the advantages and disadvantages of globalization. You may use the articles printed or mentioned in this chapter, including the expansion readings, as sources for your paper. Also find several recent sources. These books should be helpful.

   Friedman, Thomas L. *The Lexus and the Olive Tree: Understanding Globalization.* New York: Anchor Books, 2000.

   Fukuyama, Francis. *The End of History and the Last Man.* New York: Penguin Books, 1992.

   Hutton, Will, and Anthony Giddens, eds. *On the Edge: Living with Global Capitalism.* London: Jonathan Cape, 2000.

   Neipert, David. *Law of Global Commerce: A Tour.* Upper Saddle River, NJ: Prentice-Hall, 2002.

   Steger, Manfred B. *Globalism: The New Market Ideology.* Lanham, MD: Rowman and Littlefield Publishers, 2002.

   Stiglitz, Joseph. *Globalization and Its Discontents.* New York: Norton, 2002.

   Sullivan, Jeremiah J. *The Future of Corporate Globalization: From the Extended Order to the Global Village.* Westport, CT: Quorum Books, 2002.

Expansion Readings

Annan, Kofi. "Development without Borders: Globalization in the 21st Century." *Harvard International Review* 23, no. 3 (Summer 2001): 84.

Bartlett, Christopher A., and Sumantra Ghoshal. "Going Global: Lessons from Late Movers." *Harvard Business Review* 78, no. 2 (March–April 2000): 132–42.

Ghemawat, Pankaj. "Distance Still Matters: The Hard Reality of Global Expansion." *Harvard Business Review* 79, no. 8 (September 2001): 137–47.

Morse, Gardiner, and L. Paul Bremer. "Doing Business in a Dangerous World." *Harvard Business Review* 80, no. 3 (April 2002): 22–24.

"Special Report: Globalisation: Is It at Risk?" *The Economist,* 2 February 2002, 65–68.

"A Survey of Television: Think Local." *The Economist,* 13 April 2002, 12–14.

Oral Presentation

Working with a partner, give a 20-minute oral presentation to the class on one of the articles listed under Expansion Readings or the article "Measuring Globalization" from the January–February 2001 issue of *Foreign Policy* magazine. (See the second exercise under Writing Assignments). Summarize the article by including the author's thesis, major points, and supporting data and evaluate its strengths and weaknesses. Be prepared to answer questions on your topic. If you have the technical capability, use the presentation graphics program PowerPoint for your presentation. Otherwise, make at least one overhead to use on the overhead projector. (See Appendix B, Oral Presentation.)

Travels on the Web

The Internet offers numerous opportunities to read more about the nature of globalization. Log on to the following Web sites to search for an article about globalization. You can consider any relevant areas, including business, economics, politics, technology, and social policy. Print out an interesting article and write a summary of it. Bring the article and summary to class to share with your classmates.

- The British Broadcasting Company (BBC): <http://www.bbc.co.uk>

- *The Economist* magazine: <http://www.economist.com>

- *Foreign Policy* magazine: <http://www.foreignpolicy.com>

- The Institute for Policy Studies: <http://www.ips-dc.org>

- *World Press Review* magazine: <http://www.worldpressreview.com>

3
Mergers and Acquisitions

"Buying into Japan Inc." Ryoji Itoh and Till Vestring *Harvard Business Review* November 2001	"Japanese Mergers: Marriage in Name Only" *The Economist* March 2, 2002

....
Preview "Buying into Japan Inc."
....

Skimming

Skim the article quickly to find the following general information.

1. Read the title and all headings and look at any illustrations.

2. Read the first and second paragraphs, looking for the authors' purpose and main idea.

3. Read the last paragraph, looking for a summary or conclusion.

4. Write a sentence containing your preliminary understanding of the main idea of the article.

Questioning

Answer the following questions and discuss your answers in class.

1. What well known mergers have taken place recently?

2. What advantages do mergers offer to companies?

3. What are the disadvantages of mergers?

Scanning

Scan the article quickly to find the following specific information.

1. In 2001, what percent of all M&A activity in Japan did foreign purchases account for?

2. In what year did three Japanese banks form the Mizuho Group?

3. Which company acquired the Japanese telecommunications company International Digital Corporation (IDC)?

4. Under Carlos Ghosn, what net profits did Nissan achieve in 2000?

Vocabulary in Context

Read the following sentences and try to guess the meaning of the italicized words by using the context. Then replace the italicized words with synonyms (words or phrases that have nearly the same or similar meanings).

1. "Japan has long been an *inhospitable* place for foreign companies." (Paragraph 1)

2. "We've found that foreign acquirers now have considerable advantages over *domestic* acquirers." (Paragraph 3)

3. "They [Japanese mergers] rely heavily on *consensus* building, which slows down decision making and prevents decisive action." (Paragraph 4)

4. "The *specter* of a Western owner has long made Japanese workers nervous." (Paragraph 6)

5. "Ghosn had already *piloted* drastic restructuring programs at Michelin as well as at Renault." (Paragraph 8)

Paraphrasing

After reading the article, reread the sentences under Vocabulary in Context. Now rewrite them using your own words. Change the vocabulary and sentence structure, but do not change the author's intended meaning or paraphrase any technical terms. There are several ways of paraphrasing each sentence.

idea

Buying into Japan Inc.

Now may be the ideal time to acquire a Japanese company – if you do it right.

by Ryoji Itoh and Till Vestring

1 Japan has long been an inhospitable place for foreign companies. Yes, a few outsiders have built successful businesses in the country – McDonald's, IBM, and Microsoft spring to mind – but they're the exceptions. Most multinational corporations have had to settle for relatively small, low-profit businesses in the market.

2 But the climate is changing. After a decade of economic weakness, which has led to record levels of bankruptcies, the doors of Japan Inc. are opening for outsiders. Japanese managers and workers, traditionally fearful of incursions by foreign companies, are now beginning to recognize that their economy needs an influx of new ideas and ways of working if it is to rebound. In response, some aggressive U.S. and European companies are moving in to acquire struggling Japanese businesses. From 1998 through the first half of 2001, foreign acquisitions in Japan totaled $58 billion, up sharply from $7 billion in the eight years prior to 1998. Foreign purchases now account for 19% of all M&A activity in the country, up from 7%.

3 Our analysis of recent acquisitions provides some important guidelines for companies looking to buy in Japan. We've found that foreign acquirers now have considerable advantages over domestic acquirers. Seizing these advantages, though, requires thoughtful yet bold action.

Forget "Merger of Equals"

4 Japanese mergers are traditionally approached as mergers of equals. They rely heavily on consensus building, which slows down decision making and prevents decisive action. Take the 1999 merger of three of Japan's leading banks – Industrial Bank of Japan, Dai-Ichi Kangyo Bank, and Fuji Bank – into the Mizuho Group. Two years later, the banks continue to operate separately, with three co-CEOs overseeing the holding company. Integration efforts have slowed to a crawl.

5 In the meantime, foreign competitors have begun to grab hold of top spots in high-margin financial services businesses. Citigroup, for example, drove a hard bargain with Nikko Securities, a leading Japanese brokerage. Knowing that Nikko desperately needed capital, Citigroup agreed in 1998 to buy a relatively modest 20% of Nikko in return for control over its investment banking business. Citigroup left no doubt about who had the upper hand in the transaction. Although once considered culturally offensive, taking control in this way actually provides much-needed clarity to the management teams, employees, and customers of acquired companies.

Divulge Your Strategy

6 The specter of a Western owner has long made Japanese workers nervous. They fear that an American or European company will quickly move to cut employment rolls. In actuality, though, most foreign acquirers look to Japan, the world's second-largest market, as a source of growth, not cost savings. When this objective is made explicit – to senior executives and division managers alike – Japanese employees eventually begin to realize that their jobs may be more secure with a foreign company determined to prosper in Japan than with the merger of two ailing domestic companies.

7 Cable & Wireless prevailed in its long struggle to acquire the Japanese telecommunications company International Digital Corporation (IDC) because it articulated a clear growth strategy. C&W planned to make IDC the Asian hub for its global business, and it was committed to investing heavily in the company. IDC's other suitor, the dominant Japanese telecom company NTT, was much less open about its plans for IDC. C&W's clear vision for preserving IDC and expanding its business was far more attractive to IDC's people.

Let Outsiders Lead

8 Foreign acquirers have been timid about putting outsiders in charge of Japanese operations. That's a mistake. Western executives have far more experience integrating and restructuring companies than do their Japanese counterparts. Think of the spectacular success of Carlos Ghosn, the Brazilian executive whom Renault brought in to turn around Nissan. Ghosn had already piloted drastic restructuring programs at Michelin as well as at Renault. He and his team of seasoned turnaround artists identified and worked directly with Nissan's most talented and action-oriented middle managers, avoiding laborious, hierarchical consensus building. Under Ghosn, Nissan achieved net profits of $2.7 billion in 2000, after posting a loss of $6.8 billion the year before.

9 Ghosn's success underscores our central message: Foreign companies can play a major role in helping Japan revive its economy – but only if they act decisively.

Ryoji Itoh is the managing director of Bain & Company's Tokyo office, and Till Vestring is a vice president in the office.

Reprint FO110C

Glossary

acquisitions	companies bought by another company
ailing	unhealthy
articulated	put into words clearly and effectively
capital	amount of money that a company uses in carrying on a business; funds, assets, money; stock or value of accumulated goods
consensus	general agreement; the judgment arrived at by most of those concerned
counterparts	persons having the same function as others
domestic	relating to one's own country
drastic	extreme in effect or action
exceptions	cases to which a rule does not apply
explicit	unambiguous in expression; expressed without vagueness
hierarchical	arranged into ranks by ability or professional standing
high-margin	yielding a large profit
holding company	a company whose primary business is holding a controlling interest in the securities of other companies
hub	a center of activity
incursions	hostile entrances into a territory
influx	a coming in
inhospitable	not friendly or receptive
laborious	involving hard effort
M&A	merger and acquisition
merger	absorption by a corporation of one or more other corporations
offensive	causing displeasure or resentment
piloted	guided, led
rebound	to recover from a setback
specter	something that perturbs the mind
timid	lacking in boldness, courage, or determination
underscores	emphasizes, stresses

Comprehension

1. Why have only a few outsiders built successful companies in Japan?

2. What have most multinational corporations had to settle for?

3. Why is the climate in Japan changing?

4. How have Japanese companies traditionally approached mergers?

5. What are the negative effects of relying heavily on consensus building?

6. Explain the Citigroup and Nikko Securities transaction.

7. Why are Japanese workers nervous about Western ownership?

8. In actuality, why may the jobs of Japanese workers be more secure with foreign companies than with Japanese companies?

9. How did Cable and Wireless prevail over NTT in acquiring IDC?

10. Why should foreign acquirers be put in charge of Japanese operations?

11. How did Carlos Ghosn achieve success at Nissan?

Analysis

Circle the letter next to the best answer(s). Justify your choices with quotations from the text.

1. What is the main idea of the article, and in which paragraph(s) is it stated?

   a. Foreign companies should increase their acquisition and leadership of Japanese companies, which could help revive the Japanese economy.

   b. European companies, by investing heavily in Japanese companies, are becoming global.

   c. The economy in Japan is in a downturn, which has led to many domestic mergers.

   d. American companies have been buying Japanese companies recently, but serious cultural conflicts have emerged.

2. What is the meaning of the italicized words in this sentence in paragraph 5? "Citigroup left no doubt about who had the *upper hand* in the transaction."

   a. investment

   b. seniority

   c. power

   d. money

3. What can be inferred from the phrase *Japan Inc.*, which is often used to describe the country of Japan, as in the title of the article "Buying into Japan Inc."?

    a. Japan is an incorporated country whose government runs on business management principles.

    b. The country of Japan is similar to a large corporation because it is characterized by hierarchy and rigid rules.

    c. Japan has always focused on building up its international trade and direct investment.

    d. Japan offers opportunities to foreign acquirers because of its economic weakness.

4. The authors' writing style is _____ and _____ .

    a. conversational

    b. academic

    c. technical

    d. nontechnical

5. The tone of the article is _____ and _____ .

    a. subjective

    b. objective

    c. authoritative

    d. tentative

6. What overall method of development is used in this article?

    a. defining a complex method

    b. narrating a personal history

    c. comparing and contrasting two systems

    d. justifying a thesis with examples

7. What techniques do the authors use to get the reader's attention in the introduction (paragraphs 1–3)?

    a. contrasting ideas

    b. parallelism

    c. indirect quotations

    d. statistics

Japanese mergers

Marriage in name only

TOKYO
Salarymen find it hard to shift their allegiance

1 HERE is another reason why structural reform is hard for Japanese industry: employees are not good at transferring loyalty to a new company. Resentments between merger partners can fester for years. At Bank of Tokyo-Mitsubishi, formed in 1996 when Tokyo Bank merged with Mitsubishi Bank, a bigger but less prestigious institution, employees from Tokyo Bank were outnumbered three to one. Frustrated by Mitsubishi Bank's stodgy practices, many left; those that stayed were often sidelined. Insiders say there are still unofficial Tokyo Bank "societies" in which they air grievances to each other.

2 Nissan Motor, before its latest tie-up with Renault, a French car maker, was also legendary for bitter internal rivalries. In 1966, Nissan, then the second-biggest car company in Japan, merged with Prince Motor, the fourth-biggest. Hostilities between workers from Nissan and Prince lasted for years; even in the 1980s, older employees were still stamped with "Prince" or "Nissan" labels.

3 Nippon Steel, Japan's largest steel maker, had similar problems after it was formed in 1970 by a merger between Yawata Iron and Steel and Fuji Iron and Steel, even though the two had originally been part of the same company, Japan Iron and Steel, before it was broken up after the second world war. Nippon Steel is said to have kept separate personnel departments for the two sides for years. To this day, it scrupulously alternates its presidents between people of Yawata and Fuji origin.

4 Dai-Ichi Kangyo Bank (DKB), created in 1971, also kept two personnel departments for 20 years: one for former Dai-Ichi employees, another for ex-Nihon Kangyo folk. These days DKB is in a power struggle with its new partners, Fuji Bank and Industrial Bank of Japan, with which it has merged to create Mizuho Holdings, the world's largest bank. Employees at Mizuho complain that they get scolded for not fighting turf battles.

5 One reason why Japanese companies are prone to post-merger discord is their need to save face. Even when one is clearly stronger than the other, companies insist that theirs is a merger of equals. Preserving this balance creates false expectations. The latest example is the merger (due to take effect this autumn) between Japan Airlines, the top airline, with big domestic and international operations, and Japan Air System, which runs mostly domestic flights. Despite clear disparities in strength and size, both say the merger will happen in a "spirit of equality".

6 The time it takes companies to iron out details of their mergers provides plenty of time for rancour. Unlike America or Europe, where mergers can be concluded within two or three months of announcement, Japanese ones may take two to three years. The final stage of Mizuho's merger will take place this April, two-and-a-half years after it was originally announced. The merger of Sumitomo Chemical and Mitsui Chemical, announced in late 2000, is due to take place in October 2003. The government, which is hoping that more face-saving mergers will help mask the lack of reform in sagging industries, might want to bear these lessons in mind. ∎

Discussion

1. Explain the humor in the title of the article "Japanese Mergers: Marriage in Name Only."

2. What are the first two examples given by the author to show that "Japanese employees are not good at transferring loyalty to a new company"?

3. Why does Nippon Steel still alternate its presidents between people of Yawata and Fuji origin?

4. What do employees complain about at Mizuho Holdings, the world's largest bank?

5. Explain the meaning of the term *to save face*. How does the Japanese need to save face lead to postmerger discord?

6. Why do Japanese mergers take so much longer to implement than mergers in the United States and Europe?

7. In both "Buying into Japan Inc." and "Japanese Mergers: Marriage in Name Only," the authors describe the Japanese approach to mergers as "a merger of equals." How does this differ from mergers in other countries?

8. Name some recent mergers that have been successful.

Teamwork

Working with a group, analyze the merger between AOL and Time Warner or Compaq and Hewlett-Packard or another merger you are interested in. Use the Internet business database ABI/Inform to look up recent journal articles on these mergers. After reading the articles, check the stock prices of these companies in a newspaper or on the Internet. Then write a brief report on the status of one of these companies, including whether its stock price is rising or falling. At the end of the report, recommend whether or not to purchase stock in this company.

Writing Assignments

1. You can use the Internet business database ABI/Inform to locate articles about mergers and acquisitions. ABI/Inform is an international resource for business information. It indexes over 1,000 titles; the full text is available for articles from *Business Week, The Economist, Forbes, Foreign Policy, Fortune, Newsweek,* and *Time,* among others. Locate one of the following articles and read it. Then make an outline of the article and write a 400-word summary of it.

   • "Business: The Big Pitcher." *The Economist,* 20 January 2001, 63–64. This article discusses mergers in the beer industry. To access this article, do a search by typing the words *economist* and *business* and *the big pitcher.*

- "Computer Mergers: Over the Hill at 20." *The Economist,* 8 September 2001, 14. This article discusses mergers in the computer industry. To access this article, do a search by typing the words *economist* and *mergers* and *over the hill.*

- Dawson, Chester. "Ghosn's Way: Why Japan Inc. Is Following a Gaijin." *Business Week,* 20 May 2002, 58. This article discusses the success of Carlos Ghosn, the CEO of Nissan Motor Co. To access this article, do a search by typing the words *business week* and *Carlos Ghosn.*

2. Write an essay on the benefits and the drawbacks of mergers and acquisitions. Use the following thesis: Although mergers and acquisitions may limit innovation and competition, they can be advantageous in the global business world.

    Do research on the Internet or in the library to find current articles from business journals on this topic. Cite your sources in the in-text citation format (Itoh and Vestring 26). List your sources as Works Cited at the end of the paper and alphabetize them according to the authors' last names. When no author is listed for a source, alphabetize according to the first word of the title, excluding *a, an,* and *the.* (See Appendix B, Essay.)

3. Write a synthesis that discusses the two articles printed in this chapter, "Buying into Japan Inc." and "Japanese Mergers: Marriage in Name Only," and "Mizuho Bank: Undispensable" (*The Economist,* 27 April 2002, 72–73). Use the Internet business database ABI/Inform to access the article from *The Economist.* Do a search by typing the words *economist* and *Mizuho Bank.* You can also locate the article in the periodicals section of your library.

    Base your synthesis on the following thesis: Japanese mergers often have problems as a result of the Japanese belief in "a merger of equals." Cite your sources in the in-text citation format (Itoh and Vestring 26). List your sources as Works Cited at the end of the paper and alphabetize them according to the authors' last names. When no author is listed for a source, alphabetize according to the first word of the title, excluding *a, an,* and *the.* (See Appendix B, Synthesis.)

4. Write a research paper on the topic of global megamergers. You may use the articles printed in this chapter, including the expansion readings, as sources for your paper. Also use several recent sources. These books should be helpful.

    Gup, Benton E., ed. *Megamergers in a Global Economy: Causes and Consequences.* Westport, CT: Quorum Books, 2002.

    Harvard Business Review on Mergers and Acquisitions. Cambridge: Harvard Business School Press, 2001.

Expansion Readings

Aiello, Robert J., and Michael D. Watkins. "The Fine Art of Friendly Acquisition." *Harvard Business Review* 78, no. 6 (November–December 2000): 100–107.

Bower, Joseph L. "Not All M & As Are Alike—And That Matters." *Harvard Business Review* 79, no. 3 (March 2001): 92–101.

"European Merger Rules: Monti Braves the Catcalls." *The Economist,* 15 December 2001, 51–52.

Ghemawat, Pankaj, and Fariborz Ghadar. "The Dubious Logic of Global Megamergers." *Harvard Business Review* 78, no. 4 (July–August 2000): 64–72.

Ghosn, Carlos. "Saving the Business without Losing the Company. *Harvard Business Review* 80, no. 1 (January 2002): 37–45.

"Mizuho Bank: Undispensable." *The Economist,* 27 April 2002, 72–73.

Sulzer, Alessandra. "The Business of Cooperation: Peace and Profit through Joint Ventures." *Harvard International Review* 23, no. 2 (Summer 2001): 34–36.

Oral Presentation

Working with a partner, give a twenty-minute oral presentation to the class on one of the articles listed under Expansion Readings or an article of your choice on mergers. Summarize the article by including the author's thesis, major points, and supporting data and evaluate its strengths and weaknesses. Be prepared to answer questions on your topic. If you have the technical capability, use the presentation graphics program PowerPoint for your presentation. Otherwise, make at least one overhead to use on the overhead projector. (See Appendix B, Oral Presentation.)

Travels on the Web

The Internet offers numerous opportunities to read more about mergers and acquisitions. Log on to the following Web sites and look for information that relates to recent mergers. Find an interesting article, print it out, and bring it to class to share with your classmates.

- Business Wire: <http://www.businesswire.com>
  Click on Mergers and Acquisitions.

- RCW MIRUS: <http://www.merger.com>
  Under Recent Transactions, select M&A News by Industry.

- Thomson Mergers & Acquisitions Report:
  <http://www.mareport.com>
  Under News Updates, you can read articles about recent mergers.

Chapter 4
Language

Preview "Beyond Babel: Why the Babble Below
Will Matter Less"

Skimming

Skim the article quickly to find the following general information.

1. Read the title and all headings and look at any illustrations.

2. Read the first and second paragraphs, looking for the author's purpose and main idea.

3. Read the last paragraph, looking for a summary or conclusion.

4. Write a sentence containing your preliminary understanding of the main idea of the article.

Questioning

Answer the following questions and discuss your answers in class.

1. What is your native language? How many languages do you speak?

2. Do you know how to do multimedia presentations and use spreadsheets?

3. How important is it for businesspeople to be able to communicate in English in your native country?

Scanning

Scan the article quickly to find the following specific information.

1. What has happened to linguistic fluency in the global economy?

2. What will smart global firms look for?

3. What do global manufacturers rely on to manage their innovation efforts?

4. What do words so often create?

Vocabulary in Context

Read the following sentences from the article and try to guess the meaning of the italicized words by using the context. Then replace the italicized words with synonyms (words or phrases that have nearly the same or similar meanings).

1. "But linguistic fluency decays into a cost-ineffective *anachronism* in the global economy—nice but not necessary." (Paragraph 2)

2. "The *inherent* linguistic inefficiencies create more uncertainty than they resolve." (Paragraph 3)

3. "Firms that care deeply about design consistently *subordinate* language to image." (Paragraph 6)

4. "Words must be *demoted* as technology is promoted." (Paragraph 7)

5. "Language shifts from the center (of the page and of the discourse) to the *periphery*." (Paragraph 7)

Paraphrasing

After reading the article, reread the sentences under Vocabulary in Context. Now rewrite them using your own words. Change the vocabulary and sentence structure, but do not change the author's intended meaning or paraphrase any technical terms. There are several ways of paraphrasing each sentence.

brave new work ● by michael schrage

Beyond Babel:
Why the Babble
Below Will Matter Less

1　A flair for languages is a wonderful gift, *n'est-ce pas*? An ability to shift seamlessly between Mandarin and English or French and Arabic is undeniably impressive. In theory, the right word is worth a thousand pictures. As Tom Lehrer, the brilliant '60s parodist once observed, "I believe that if a person can't communicate, the very least he can do is to shut up!"

2　But linguistic fluency decays into a cost-ineffective anachronism in the global economy—nice but not necessary. Ignore the irritating American triumphalists who crow that, since English is now the lingua franca of business, the rest of the world's languages have become passé. No, the new reality is much starker. Language itself, both as a medium and a tool for value creation, is devolving into a trivial ingredient for postindustrial economic success.

3　Anybody who has had to sit though a five-hour global management meeting of a multinational firm whose participants are not-quite-fluent-in-English-but-trying-really-hard immediately grasps the point. *Faux* fluency is a major obstacle to understanding, not its enabler. The inherent linguistic inefficiencies create more uncertainty than they resolve. English *über Alles* doesn't mean managers necessarily understand what's going on.

4　Diversity creates its own imperatives. As organizations globalize, the need for simpler, less ambiguous communication intensifies. Smart global firms will not foolishly pursue the chimera of an internal Esperanto like, say, English, for business conversations; they will instead look for ways to reduce their dependence on language altogether.

5　Odds are more business-oriented Asians speak fluent Microsoft Excel than speak fluent English. Which fluency better helps their business? We'll tolerate the executive who mutters malaprops and garbles his gerunds; but we'll fire the ones who screw up the numbers. Who do you think is more successful at Jack Welch's General Electric or Sir John Browne's British Petroleum: the clever manager with a gift for explaining his Big Ideas? Or the bright manager with rigorous spreadsheets that speak more eloquently than she does?

6　Global manufacturers increasingly rely upon computer-aided design and computer-aided engineering software to manage their innovation efforts. These digital visualizations—not the written specifications or detailed product descriptions—drive the development process. Firms that care deeply about design consistently subordinate language to image.

7　Words must be demoted as technology is promoted. As bandwidth creeps higher, text gets squeezed out; it's literally marginalized. Language shifts from the center (of the page and of the discourse) to the periphery. Words *annotate* spreadsheets and simulations. The Executive Summary becomes the Executive Annotation; the words reinforce an image instead of conjuring up images of their own. Language's role shifts from the narrative to the declarative: *Look at this! This is important!* The managerial goal here is not a mute, inchoate, or inarticulate interaction but a business world where language is dedicated to making other forms of representation clearer.

8　Icons, animation, and cartoonlike communication will assume ever greater proportions of network bandwidth and managerial mind share as the dominant media for organizational communication. Multicultural constituencies—as much as multimedia opportunities—are forcing global organizations to recognize that most people would rather watch than read. There's no question that people are communicating more than ever—they're just not depending on language to do it.

9　Sophisticated multinationals should aggressively invest in "language-free" projects and management techniques to reduce the ambiguities and misunderstandings that words so often create. Managers should be rewarded less for their multilinguistic fluency and more for their ability to communicate and motivate through multimedia representations.

10　There's no denying the beauty and power of the right words in the right combinations. There's a poetry to artful expression. Then again, look at the global marketplace for the poetry of Pablo Neruda, compared with, say, sales of books like *Who Moved My Cheese?* Tomorrow's unhappy reality is that columns like this one will rapidly descend into irrelevance. I'm learning how to draw.

MICHAEL SCHRAGE *is co-director of the MIT Media Lab's e-markets initiative and author of* Serious Play. *Reach him at michael_schrage@fortunemail.com.*

Glossary

ambiguous	doubtful or uncertain; capable of being understood in two or more ways
anachronism	a thing from a former age that is incongruous in the present
annotate	to make critical or explanatory notes or comments
babble	meaningless, unintelligible words
Babel	a city in Shinar (Babylonia) where the building of a tower was halted by the confusion of languages, according to the Bible (Genesis 11); a scene of noise or confusion
chimera	an unrealizable dream; an illusion of the mind
demoted	reduced to a lower rank or a less important position
devolving	degenerating through a gradual change
Esperanto	an artificial language based on words common to the chief European languages
faux	false; imitation (French)
imperatives	rules, guides, duties
inchoate	formless; imperfectly formed
inherent	belonging by nature, intrinsic
irrelevance	the quality of not having meaning or applicability to the matter at hand
lingua franca	common language among people of diverse speech
malaprops	words sounding somewhat like the ones intended but wrong in the context
marginalized	relegated to an unimportant position; put in the margin of a page
mutters	utters words or sounds indistinctly or with a low voice
n'est-ce pas	isn't it (French)
Pablo Neruda	Chilean poet and diplomat (1904–73) who won the Nobel Prize in literature
passé	outdated (French)
periphery	the outward bounds of something as distinguished from its center
subordinate	to treat as of less value or importance
triumphalists	people who believe that English is superior to other languages
trivial	of little worth or importance
über Alles	above all else (German)
Who Moved My Cheese?	popular nonfiction book for businesspeople by Spencer Johnson, M.D.

Comprehension

1. Michael Schrage refers to the Tower of Babel in his title. Have you heard of the Tower of Babel, which is mentioned in the Bible? Can you explain the meaning of the Tower of Babel in terms of Schrage's argument in this article?

2. According to Schrage, what is the new reality about language?

3. Explain the meaning of the following statement: "Diversity creates its own imperatives."

4. What happens as organizations globalize?

5. What drives the development process in global manufacturing firms?

6. What has happened to the role of language as technology has been promoted?

7. What should managers be rewarded for?

8. Explain the meaning of Schrage's closing statement: "I'm learning how to draw."

9. Do you agree with Michael Schrage's argument that "language . . . is devolving into a trivial ingredient for postindustrial economic success"? Explain your answer.

10. How likely is it that "icons, animation, and cartoonlike communication," rather than language, will become the dominant media for organizational communication? Justify your answer.

Analysis

Circle the letter next to the best answer(s). Justify your choices with quotations from the text.

1. What is the main idea of the article, and in which paragraph(s) is it stated?

   a. It is easier to learn to use digital visualizations, such as computer-aided design, than to learn to speak English.

   b. The globalization of organizations has led to a greater dependence on the English language.

   c. Global organizations should emphasize the use of technology rather than language to communicate clearly.

   d. Economic success in the 21st century will depend equally on knowledge of the English language and mastery of technology.

2. What is the meaning of the italicized word in this sentence in paragraph 5? "We'll tolerate the executive who mutters malaprops and *garbles* his gerunds; but we'll fire the ones who screw up the numbers."

   a. misunderstands

   b. rejects

   c. forgets

   d. distorts

3. We can infer the following from this statement in paragraph 1: "In theory, the right word is worth a thousand pictures."

   a. Theories about the acquisition of language are unproven.

   b. Words and pictures are so different that they cannot be compared.

   c. In theory, pictures are more valuable than words.

   d. In reality, the right picture is worth a thousand words.

4. What can be inferred from the title of the article "Beyond Babel: Why the Babble Below Will Matter Less"?

   a. Communication with words has become less important since the Tower of Babel was built in ancient times.

   b. Communication with words has become more important since the Tower of Babel was built in ancient times.

   c. Because of the Tower of Babel, words have become meaningless and unimportant.

   d. It doesn't matter that people can no longer understand each other by communicating with words.

5. The author's writing style in this article is _____ and _____ .

   a. colorful

   b. academic

   c. formal

   d. informal

6. The tone of the article is _____ and _____ .

    a. ironic

    b. serious

    c. bureaucratic

    d. colloquial

7. What overall method of development is used in this article?

    a. supporting an unusual argument

    b. describing a chronological process

    c. explaining a quantitative method

    d. defining a technological problem

8. What techniques does the author use to get the reader's attention in the introduction (paragraphs 1 and 2)?

    a. negative statements

    b. vivid adjectives, adverbs, and verbs

    c. a direct quotation

    d. personal revelations

A world empire by other means

The new world language seems to be good for everyone—except the speakers of minority tongues, and native English-speakers too perhaps

1 IT IS everywhere. Some 380m people speak it as their first language and perhaps two-thirds as many again as their second. A billion are learning it, about a third of the world's population are in some sense exposed to it and by 2050, it is predicted, half the world will be more or less proficient in it. It is the language of globalisation—of international business, politics and diplomacy. It is the language of computers and the Internet. You'll see it on posters in Côte d'Ivoire, you'll hear it in pop songs in Tokyo, you'll read it in official documents in Phnom Penh. Deutsche Welle broadcasts in it. Bjork, an Icelander, sings in it. French business schools teach in it. It is the medium of expression in cabinet meetings in Bolivia. Truly, the tongue spoken back in the 1300s only by the "low people" of England, as Robert of Gloucester put it at the time, has come a long way. It is now the global language.

2 How come? Not because English is easy. True, genders are simple, since English relies on "it" as the pronoun for all inanimate nouns, reserving masculine for *bona fide* males and feminine for females (and countries and ships). But the verbs tend to be irregular, the grammar bizarre and the match between spelling and pronunciation a nightmare. English is now so widely spoken in so many places that umpteen versions have evolved, some so peculiar that even "native" speakers may have trouble understanding each other. But if only one version existed, that would present difficulties enough. Even everyday English is a language of subtlety, nuance and complexity. John Simmons, a language consultant for Interbrand, likes to cite the word "set", an apparently simple word that takes on different meanings in a sporting, cooking, social or mathematical context—and that is before any little words are combined with it. Then, as a verb, it becomes "set aside", "set up", "set down", "set in", "set on", "set about", "set against" and so on, terms that "leave even native speakers bewildered about [its] core meaning."

3 As a language with many origins—Romance, Germanic, Norse, Celtic and so on—English was bound to be a mess. But its elasticity makes it messier, as well as stronger. When it comes to new words, English puts up few barriers to entry. Every year publishers bring out new dictionaries listing neologisms galore. The past decade, for instance, has produced not just a host of Internettery, computerese and phonebabble ("browsers", "downloading", "texting" and so on) but quantities of teenspeak ("fave", "fit", "pants", "phat", "sad"). All are readily received by English, however much some fogies may resist them. Those who stand guard over the French language, by contrast, agonise for years over whether to allow *CD-Rom* (no, it must be *cédérom*), *frotte-manche*, a Belgian word for a sycophant (sanctioned), or *euroland* (no, the term is *la zone euro*). Oddly, *shampooing* (unknown as a noun in English) seemed to pass the French Academy *nem con*, perhaps because the British had originally taken "shampoo" from Hindi.

Albion's tongue unsullied

4 English-speakers have not always been so *Angst*-free about this *laisser-faire* attitude to their language, so ready to present a *façade* of *insouciance* at the *de facto* acceptance of foreign words among their *clichés*, *bons mots* and other *dicta*. In the 18th century three writers—Joseph Addison (who founded the *Spectator*), Daniel Defoe (who wrote "Robinson Crusoe") and Jonathan Swift ("Gulliver's Travels")—wanted to see a committee set up to regulate the language. Like a good protectionist, Addison wrote:

> I have often wished that…certain Men might be set apart, as Superintendents of our Language, to hinder any Words of Foreign Coin from passing among us; and in particular to prohibit any French Phrases from becoming current in this Kingdom, when those of our own stamp are altogether as valuable.

5 Fortunately, the principles of free trade triumphed, as Samuel Johnson, the compiler of the first great English dictionary, rather reluctantly came to admit. "May the lexicographer be derided," he declared, "who shall imagine that his dictionary can embalm his language…With this hope, however, academies have been instituted to guard the avenues of their languages…but their vigilance and activity have hitherto been vain…to en-

chain syllables, and to lash the wind, are equally the undertakings of pride."

Pride, however, is seldom absent when language is under discussion, and no wonder, for the success or failure of a language has little to do with its inherent qualities "and everything to do with the power of the people who speak it." And that, as Professor Jean Aitchison of Oxford University points out, is particularly true of English.

6 It was not always so. In the eastern half of the Roman empire, Greek remained the language of commerce, and of Christians such as St Paul and the Jews of the diaspora, long after Greek political supremacy had come to an end. Latin continued to be the language of the church, and therefore of any West European of learning, long after Rome had declined and fallen. But Greek and Latin (despite being twisted in the Middle Ages to describe many non-Roman concepts and things) were fixed languages with rigid rules that failed to adapt naturally. As Edmund Waller wrote in the 17th century,

> Poets that lasting marble seek,
> Must carve in Latin or in Greek.
> We write in sand, our language grows,
> And like the tide, our work o'erflows.

7 English, in other words, moved with the times, and by the 19th century the times were such that it had spread across an empire on which the sun never set (that word again). It thus began its rise as a global language.

8 That could be seen not just by the use of English in Britain's colonies, but also by its usefulness much farther afield. When, for instance, Germany and Japan were negotiating their alliance against America and Britain in 1940, their two foreign ministers, Joachim von Ribbentrop and Yosuke Matsuoka, held their discussions in English. But however accommodating English might be, and however

> **The real reason for the triumph of English is the triumph of the United States. Therein lies a huge source of friction**

much of the map was once painted red, the real reason for the latterday triumph of English is the triumph of the English-speaking United States as a world power. Therein lies a huge source of friction.

Damn Yanks, defensive Frogs

9 The merit of English as a global language is that it enables people of different coun-

tries to converse and do business with each other. But languages are not only a medium of communication, which enable nation to speak unto nation. They are also repositories of culture and identity. And in many countries the all-engulfing advance of English threatens to damage or destroy much local culture. This is sometimes lamented even in England itself, for though the language that now sweeps the world is called English, the culture carried with it is American.

On the whole the Brits do not complain. Some may regret the passing of the "bullet-proof waistcoat" (in favour of the "bullet-proof vest"), the arrival of "hopefully" at the start of every sentence, the wholesale disappearance of the perfect tense, and the mutation of the meaning of "presently" from "soon" to "now". But few mind or even notice that their old "railway station" has become a "train station", the "car park" is turning into a "parking lot" and people now live "on", not "in", a street.

Others, however, are not so relaxed. Perhaps it is hardest for the French. Ever since the revolution in 1789, they have aspired to see their language achieve a sort of universal status, and by the end of the 19th century, with France established as a colonial power second only to Britain and its language accepted as the *lingua franca* of diplomacy, they seemed to be on their way to reaching their goal. As the 20th century drew on, however, and English continued to encroach, French was driven on to the defensive.

One response was to rally French-speakers outside France. Habib Bourguiba, the first president of independent Tunisia, obligingly said in 1966 that "the French-language community" was not "colonialism in a new guise" and that to join its ranks was simply to use the colonial past for the benefit of the new, formerly French states. His counterpart in Senegal, Léopold Senghor, who wrote elegantly in the language of Molière, Racine and Baudelaire, was happy to join La Francophonie, an outfit modelled on the (ex-British) Commonwealth and designed to promote French language and culture. But though such improbable countries as Bulgaria and Moldova have since been drawn in—France spends about $1 billion a year on various aid and other programmes designed to promote its civilisation abroad—French now ranks only ninth among the world's languages.

The decline is everywhere to be seen. Before Britain joined the European common market (now the European Union) in 1973, French was the club's sole official language. Now that its members also include Denmark, Finland and Sweden, whose people often speak better English

than the British, English is the EU's dominant tongue. Indeed, over 85% of all international organisations use English as one of their official languages.

In France itself, the march of English is remorseless. Alcatel, the formerly state-owned telecoms giant, uses English as its internal language. Scientists know that they must either "publish in English or perish in French". And though one minister of "culture and the French language", Jacques Toubon, did his utmost to banish foreign expressions from French in the mid-1990s, a subsequent minister of education, Claude Allègre, declared in 1998 that "English should no longer be considered a foreign language… In future it will be as basic [in France] as reading, writing and arithmetic."

That does not mean that France has abandoned its efforts to stop the corruption of its beautiful tongue. Rearguard actions are fought by Air France pilots in protest at air-traffic instructions given in English. Laws try to hold back the tide of insidious Albion on the airwaves. And the members of the French Academy, the guardians of *le bon usage*, still meet in their silver-and-gold-embroidered uniforms to lay down the linguistic law.

Those who feel pity for the French, however, should feel much sorrier for the Quebeckers, a minority of about 6m among the 300m English-speakers of North America. It is easy to mock their efforts to defend their beleaguered version of French: all those absurd language police, fighting *franglais*, ensuring that all contracts are written in French and patrolling shops and offices to make sure that any English signs are of regulation size. But it is also easy to understand their concern. After all, the publishing onslaught from the United States is enough to make English-speaking Canadians try to put up barriers to protect their magazines in apparent defiance of the World Trade Organisation: Canada's cultural industries are at stake, they say. No wonder the French-speakers of Quebec feel even more threatened by the ubiquity of English.

Germans, Poles and Chinese unite

French-speakers are far from alone. A law went into effect in Poland last year obliging all companies selling or advertising foreign products to use Polish in their advertisements, labelling and instructions. Latvia has tried to keep Russian (and, to be more precise, Russians) at bay by insisting on the use of the Latvian language in business. Even Germany, now the pre-eminent economic and political power in Europe, feels it necessary to resist the spread of *Denglisch*. Three years ago the Institute for the German Language wrote to Deutsche Telekom to protest at its

adoption of "grotesque" terms like City-Call, HolidayPlusTarif and GermanCall. A year earlier, an article in the *Frankfurter Allgemeine Zeitung* in which a designer had been quoted using expressions like "giving story", "co-ordinated concepts" and "effortless magic" so infuriated Professor Wolfgang Kramer that he founded the Society for the Protection of the German Language, which now awards a prize for the *Sprachpanscher* (language debaser) of the year.

For some countries, the problem with English is not that it is spoken, but that it is not spoken well enough. The widespread use of Singlish, a local version of Shakespeare's tongue, is a perpetual worry to the authorities in Singapore, who fear lest their people lose their command of the "proper" kind and with it a big commercial advantage over their rivals.

In Hong Kong, by contrast, the new, Chinese masters are promoting Cantonese, to the concern of local business. And in India some people see English as an oppressive legacy of colonialism that should be exterminated. As long ago as 1908 Mohandas Gandhi was arguing that "to give millions a knowledge of English is to enslave them." Ninety years later the struggle was still being fought, with India's defence minister of the day, Mulayam Singh Yadav, vowing that he would not rest "until English is driven out of the country". Others, however, believe that it binds a nation of 800 tongues and dialects together, and connects it to the outside world to boot.

Some countries try, like France, to fix their language by fiat. A set of reforms were produced in Germany a few years ago by a group of philologists and officials with the aim of simplifying some spellings—*Spagetti* instead of *Spaghetti*, for example, *Saxifon* instead of *Saxophon*—reducing the number of rules governing the use of commas (from 52 to nine), and so on. Dutifully, the country's state culture ministers endorsed them, and they started to go into effect in schoolrooms and newspaper offices across the country. But old habits die hard, unless they are making way for English: in Schleswig-Holstein the voters revolted, and in due course even such newspapers as the *Frankfurter Allgemeine Zeitung* abandoned the new practice.

Spain strives for conformity too, through a Spanish Royal Academy similar to the French Academy. The job of the 46 Spanish academicians is to "cleanse, fix and give splendour" to a language that is very much alive, although nine out of ten of its speakers live outside Spain. The academy professes a readiness to absorb new words and expressions, but its director admits that "changes have become very rare now." No wonder Spanish-speaking countries in Latin America—as well as the Philippines and the United States—have set up their own academies.

Keeping tiny tongues alive

22 Rules alone may be unable to withstand the tide of English, but that does not mean it is impossible to keep endangered languages in being. Mohawk, for instance, spoken by some indigenous people in Quebec, was in retreat until the 1970s, when efforts were made first to codify it and then to teach it to children at school. Welsh and Maori have both made a comeback with the help of television and government interference, and Navajo, Hawaiian and several languages spoken in Botswana have been reinvigorated artificially.

23 Iceland has been extraordinarily successful at keeping the language of the sagas alive, even though it is the tongue of barely 275,000 people. Moreover, it has done so more by invention than by absorption. Whereas the Germans never took to the term *Fernsprechapparat* when *Telefon* was already available, and the French have long preferred *le shopping* and *le weekend* to their native equivalents, the Icelanders have readily adopted *alnaemi* for "AIDS", *skjar* for "video monitor" and *toelva* for "computer". Why? Partly because the new words are in fact mostly old ones: *alnaemi* means "vulnerable", *skjar* is the translucent membrane of amniotic sac that used to be stretched to "glaze" windows, and *toelva* is formed from the words for "digit" and "prophetess". Familiarity means these words are readily intelligible. But it also helps that Icelanders are intensely proud of both their language and their literature, and the urge to keep them going is strong.

24 Perhaps the most effective way of keeping a language alive, however, is to give it a political purpose. The association of Irish with Irish nationalism has helped bring this language back from its increasing desuetude in the 19th century, just as Israeli nation-building has converted Hebrew from being a merely written language into a national tongue.

25 For some nations, such as the Indians, the pain felt at the encroachments of English may be tempered by the pleasure of seeing their own words enriching the invading tongue: Sir Henry Yule's 1886 dictionary, "Hobson-Jobson", lists thousands of Anglo-Indian words and phrases. But for many peoples the triumph of English is the defeat, if not outright destruction, of their own language. Of the world's 6,000 or 7,000 languages, a couple go out of business each week. Some recent victims from the rich world have included Catawba (Massachusetts), Eyak (Alaska) and Livonian (Latvia). But most are in the jungles of Papua New Guinea, which still has more languages than any other country, or Indonesia, or Nigeria (India, Mexico, Cameroon, Australia and Brazil follow).

26 Pundits disagree about the rate at

> Of the world's 6,000 or 7,000 languages, a couple go out of business each week. Most are in the jungles of Papua New Guinea or in Indonesia

which languages are disappearing: some say that by the end of the century half will have gone, some say 90%. But whenever a language dies, a bit of the world's culture, history and diversity dies with it. This is slowly coming to be appreciated. The EU declared 2001 to be "European year of languages", and it is striking that even France—whose hostility to linguistic competition is betrayed by the constitution's bald statement that "the language of the Republic is French"—now smiles more benignly on its seven regional tongues (Alsatian, Basque, Breton, Catalan, Corsican, Flemish and Provençal).

27 Yet the extinction of most languages is probably unstoppable. Television and radio, both blamed for homogenisation, may, paradoxically, prolong the life of some by narrow-casting in minority tongues. And though many languages may die, more people may also be able to speak several languages: multilingualism, a commonplace among the least educated peoples of Africa, is now the norm among Dutch, Scandinavians and, increasingly, almost everyone else. Native English-speakers, however, are becoming less competent at other languages: only nine students graduated in Arabic from universities in the United States last year, and the British are the most monoglot of all the peoples of the EU. Thus the triumph of English not only destroys the tongues of others; it also isolates native English-speakers from the literature, history and ideas of other peoples. It is, in short, a thoroughly dubious triumph. But then who's for Esperanto? Not the staff of *The Economist*, that's for sure. ∎

Discussion

1. What reasons does the author give for the fact that English has become "the global language"?

2. What is the real reason for the "latterday triumph of English," and why is this reason a "source of friction"?

3. Which countries are complaining that the dominance of English is damaging or destroying their local culture? Have you experienced this problem in your native country?

4. In 1908, Mohandas Gandhi of India said that "to give millions a knowledge of English is to enslave them." What did Ghandi mean by this statement? Do you agree with him?

5. The author states that native English speakers are becoming less competent at other languages, although more people in the world are becoming multilingual. How many languages do you speak?

6. The author uses many foreign words that are common in English. Guess the meaning of these loanwords: *bona fide, angst, laisser-faire, façade, insouciance, de facto, clichés, bon mots,* and *dicta.*

7. Although the articles "Beyond Babel: Why the Babble Below Will Matter Less" and "The Triumph of English: A World Empire by Other Means" both focus on language, the authors take different approaches to the topic. What are the major differences in content, style, and purpose?

Teamwork

Working in a group, design, develop, and give a presentation using the presentation graphics program PowerPoint on the article "Beyond Babel: Why the Babble Below Will Matter Less." The purpose of the presentation is to summarize the article. However, to examine Schrage's theory that "people would rather watch than read," emphasize visual images (e.g., cartoons, icons) to get your message across, and use as few words as possible.

Writing Assignments

1. Write an essay on the differences between English and your native language or another language you know. Discuss three major differences, such as the alphabet, pronunciation, grammar, punctuation, or style of writing. You may develop your own thesis, or you may use the following thesis: Although my native

   language _____ and English are different in _____ ,

   _____ , and _____ , English is an easier language to learn

   than _____ .

2. Use the Internet business database ABI/Inform to locate recent articles on the English language. Choose one article to read and write a 400-word summary of it. For example, you could read "A Long Trip to School" by Moon Ilhwan (*Business Week,* August 27, 2001, p. 62) or "The Great English Divide" by Stephen Baker and Inka Resch (*Business Week,* August 13, 2001, p. 36). Attach a copy of the article to the summary.

3. Make a topic outline of Michael Schrage's article "Beyond Babel: Why the Babble Below Will Matter Less," printed in this chapter. Then write a critical review of this article. In your thesis, state whether you agree or disagree with his idea that "words must be demoted as technology is promoted."

   A possible thesis for this critical review is the following: I disagree with Schrage that "words must be demoted as technology is promoted," because language is a more precise and effective method of communication than visual images in the international business world. (See Appendix B, Critical Review.)
   Use this format for the critical review.

   I. Introduction (background and thesis)

   II. Summary

   III. Critique

   IV. Conclusion (restatement of thesis)

4. Write a research paper on the topic of the development of English as the world language. You may use the articles printed or mentioned in this chapter, including the expansion readings, as sources for this paper. Also find several recent sources. These books should be helpful.

   Baron, Naomi S. *Alphabet to E-mail: How Written English Evolved and Where It's Heading.* London and New York: Routledge, 2000.

   Burns, Anne, and Caroline Coffin, eds. *Analysing English in a Global Context: A Reader.* London and New York: Routledge, 2001.

Expansion Readings

"A Conversation with Literary Critic Harold Bloom." *Harvard Business Review* 79, no. 5 (May 2001): 63–68.

"Gender in France: The Mystery of Language and Ideology." *The Economist*, 25 May 2002, 49.

Kirby, Julia, and Diane L. Coutu. "The Beauty of Buzzwords." *Harvard Business Review* 79, no. 5 (May 2001): 30–32.

"Language across Frontiers: The English Invasion." *The Economist*, 21 December 2002, 120–21.

Roche, Eileen. "Words for the Wise." *Harvard Business Review* 79, no. 1 (January 2001): 26–27.

Oral Presentation

Working with a partner, give a 20-minute oral presentation to the class on one of the articles listed under Expansion Readings or an article of your choice on the use of English in business. Summarize the article by including the author's thesis, major points, and supporting data and evaluate its strengths and weaknesses. Be prepared to answer questions on your topic. If you have the technical capability, use the presentation graphics program PowerPoint for your presentation. Otherwise, make at least one overhead to use on the overhead projector. (See Appendix B, Oral Presentation.)

Travels on the Web

The Internet has hundreds of Web sites that contain information on the English language.

1. Read one of the articles listed below or a more recent one that discusses the use of English in the business world and on the Internet. Use the Internet business database ABI/Inform to find articles on this topic. You can do a search for the articles from *Computerworld* by typing the words *Computerworld* and *web site globalization*. Print out the article you read and bring it to class to share with your classmates.

   • *Fortune* magazine: <http://www.fortune.com>

      • Fox, Justin. "The Triumph of English." *Fortune*, 18 September 2000, 209–12.

   • *Computerworld:* <http://www.computerworld.com>

      • Betts, Mitch, Carol Sliwa, and Jennifer DiSabatino. "Global Web Sites Prove Challenging." *Computerworld*, 21 August 2000, 17.

      • DiSabatino, Jennifer. "Web Site Globalization." *Computerworld* 10 July 2000, 56.

      • Weiss, Todd R. "Multilingual Domain Name Registrations Hit 700,000." *Computerworld*, 1 January 2001, 16.

2. Many Web sites are devoted to helping nonnative speakers study English, both online and in schools. If you want to know about English language schools in the United States and other English-speaking countries, log on to the following Web sites.

   • Apply ESL.com <http://www.applyesl.com>. This site offers "direct online applications to the best ESL schools."

   • Study English in the USA: <http://www.studyusa.com>. By selecting English as a Second Language (ESL), you can gather information on graduate, under-graduate, and summer programs throughout the United States.

   • American English Language Foundation: <http://www.aelf.com>. This site identifies itself as "the best way to improve and learn new English skills online."

3. One of the most useful online handbooks on writing is found at the following Web site.

   • The University of Illinois at Urbana-Champaign: <http://www.english.uiuc.edu>. Choose Programs and then select Programs and Affiliations. Under Department Facilities, click on Writers' Workshop. The workshop menu includes such valuable topics as Tips & Techniques, ESL Resources, Bibliography Styles, Grammar Handbook, and Writing Websites. Print out a section of the Writers' Workshop that you find helpful and bring it to class to share with your classmates.

Chapter 5
Brand Names

Preview   "Developing a Name to Work Worldwide"

Skimming

Skim the article quickly to find the following general information.

1. Read the title and all headings and look at any illustrations.

2. Read the first and second paragraphs, looking for the author's purpose and main idea.

3. Read the last paragraph, looking for a summary or conclusion.

4. Write a sentence containing your preliminary understanding of the main idea of the article.

Questioning

Answer the following questions and discuss your answers in class.

1. Do you usually purchase products because of their brand name?

2. What are your favorite brands for food, drinks, and clothing?

3. What kind of ethical responsibility do brands have?

Scanning

Scan the article quickly to find the following specific information.

1. What percent of the English dictionary has already been registered as Web sites?

2. What type of tool helps the client feel there are real processes to name creation?

3. Why are short-listed brand names "disaster checked"?

4. What brand name did Dragon develop for the new global range of bodycare products?

Vocabulary in Context

Read the following sentences and try to guess the meaning of the italicized words by using the context. Then replace the italicized words with synonyms (words or phrases that have nearly the same or similar meanings).

1. "A marketer's life does not get any more challenging than a *brief* to create a new global brand." (Paragraph 1)

2. "Without using a failsafe research process, it is unlikely that any marketer could propose a name with no *adverse* global connotations or interpretations." (Paragraph 1)

3. "He points out that consumers travel everywhere, so brands need to be *consistent* in whichever country they are seen." (Paragraph 7)

4. "Like Marathon (now Snickers) and Opal Fruits (now Starburst), it has *altered* its U.K. name to fit with the rest of the world." (Paragraph 8)

Paraphrasing

After reading the article, reread the sentences under Vocabulary in Context. Now rewrite them using your own words. Change the vocabulary and sentence structure, but do not change the author's intended meaning or paraphrase any technical terms. There are several ways of paraphrasing each sentence.

Developing a name to work worldwide

Discovering an original name in a global economy is a difficult task. By Sam Solley

1 A marketer's life does not get any more challenging than a brief to create a new global brand. Without using a failsafe research process, it is unlikely that any marketer could propose a name with no adverse global connotations or interpretations.

2 Yet it is not totally unheard of for major companies to make mistakes when naming products for a global market. Famous faux-pas include Vauxhall's Nova meaning 'don't go' in Spanish, while Colgate introduced a toothpaste in France called Cue, the name of a notorious French adult magazine.

3 The likes of Coke, Pepsi and Levi's picked names that were apparently effortlessly successful all over the world. Certainly there wasn't quite the competition for names that there is now. "Ninety-eight per cent of the English dictionary has already been registered as web sites, so it's a real creative process to develop a product name that is as yet undiscovered," says Keith Wells, director of creative consultancy Dragon.

The name game

4 As a result there has been an explosion of naming consultancies – set up as offshoots of advertising or NPD agencies – to cash in on the naming crisis. Carat, St Luke's and Leo Burnett have all launched consultancy arms in recent years dedicated to naming. FutureBrand, a relative newcomer to the naming scene, was launched last April following the merger of US brand consultancy Diefenbach Elkins and UK design agency Davies Baron.

5 Jane Wyckham, head of naming at FutureBrand, says: "The client doesn't want creatives sat around coming up with various names. They like to know there is a science behind the process."

6 Tools such as etymology – tracing of words to their origins – helps the client feel there are real processes to name creation.

7 According to Mark Gandy, managing partner at Brandhouse WTS, creating a global brand is simply a matter of extending the existing national brand. He points out that consumers travel everywhere, so brands need to be consistent in whichever country they are seen.

8 This is the problem that brands such as Lever Brothers' Jif have chosen to leave behind. Jif, which will shortly be known to UK consumers as Cif, will be relaunched with a TV and press campaign by Lowe Lintas early next year. Like Marathon (now Snickers), and Opal Fruits (now Starburst), it has altered its UK name to fit with the rest of the world. Jif is now called Cif in 39 of the 60 countries where it is available.

Creative process

9 Simon Anholt, partner at ad agency Cave Anholt Jonason, says the process of naming a global brand starts with a creative team generating a long list of raw names, which is whittled down to a shortlist that meets the brief.

10 The short-listed names are then disaster checked by the agency to ensure they don't have an unfortunate meaning in any other languages. The chances of the chosen names not resembling any other word in any other language are slim to nil.

11 Finally, the names on the shortlist go forward for legal checks, to see if other companies have already registered the proposed names. If they have, back to square one, if not, you've struck lucky. "By the time a name is chosen and registered, it has usually come so far down the original shortlist, it's a minor miracle if anybody likes it at all," says Anholt.

12 Ultimately a name is just a word, and it's important to appreciate how much it can do, but also how much it can't do.

13 "It must be a good, strong, unique vessel with no holes in it," says Anholt. "So you can start pouring in that brand value, secure in the knowledge that it's not running out at the bottom as fast as you pour it in." ■

LEVI'S ENGINEERED JEANS™
TWISTED TO FIT

Levi's: national brand extended globally

AQEO: CREATING A GLOBAL BRAND

Boots Healthcare International's new global range of bodycare products for psoriasis sufferers called for a global brand, so BHI decided it was important to call in naming specialists to create the name.

Silvia Enzig-Strohm, the senior product manager at BHI, says: "We wanted to go abroad for the name generation process, as we didn't want to use a German company and possibly limit the global appeal. By using an international company we hoped to create a brand that would appeal on a global scale."

The chosen agency was Dragon, which developed the name Aqeo for the bodycare brand. Deborah Carter, creative consultant at Dragon, says: "It is very much a mainstream brand and we wanted the name to be as short as possible, but also to be friendly and easily pronounced. The client also wanted a link with water to relate to the cleansing side of the product. The name we generated, Aqeo, provides a short and international feel to the product. We were asked to create the whole package, so the graphics and packaging were also created by us and continued the strong visual message the new name gives consumers."

Glossary

adverse	harmful, unfavorable
altered	changed, made different
brand	a class of goods identified by name as the product of a single firm or manufacturer
brand value	intrinsic worth, utility, importance of brand
brief	an assignment
connotations	suggested meanings of a word apart from the thing it explicitly names
consistent	free from variation; marked by steady continuity
consultancies	agencies that provide consulting services
context	the interrelated conditions in which a word exists; environment
etymology	the history of a word, tracing its development since its earliest occurrence
eureka factor	expression of triumph on a discovery; *eureka*, a Greek word shouted out by Archimedes upon discovering the principle of buoyancy, means "I have found it."
failsafe	having no chance of failure
faux-pas	mistake, blunder; this French term literally means "false step."
flack	criticism
generating	originating, producing
launched	introduced, released
mainstream	prevailing direction of influence or activity
notorious	widely and unfavorably known
packaging	presentation of a product in such a way as to heighten its appeal to the public
raw	in a natural, unrefined, or crude state
slim to nil	slight to nothing
square one	starting point or beginning stage
vessel	container
whittled down	reduced gradually

Comprehension

1. Why is it so challenging to create a new global brand name today?

2. Why was it easier to choose the names of Coke, Pepsi, and Levi's than it is to choose a name now?

3. What has resulted from the naming crisis?

4. What do clients like to know when they hire a naming consultancy?

5. Why is creating a global brand "simply a matter of extending the existing national brand"?

6. Explain the process of naming a global brand.

7. How important is a brand name, according to Simon Anholt?

8. Which famous brands have been a failure in your native country? Why have they failed?

Analysis

Circle the letter next to the best answer(s). Justify your choices with quotations from the text.

1. What is the main idea of the article, and in which paragraph(s) is it stated?

    a. It is essential to think creatively when choosing a global brand name.

    b. A good brand name can usually ensure that a product or service will be a success.

    c. Globalization has increased the difficulty of choosing a brand name, so it is important to follow a research process.

    d. Many possible brand names have negative connotations and, therefore, must be carefully screened.

2. What is the meaning of the italicized word in this sentence in paragraph 12? "*Ultimately* a name is just a word, and it's important to appreciate how much it can do, but also how much it can't do."

    a. finally

    b. definitely

    c. unfortunately

    d. surprisingly

3. We can infer the following from this statement in paragraph 2: "Yet it is not totally unheard of for major companies to make mistakes when naming products for a global market."

    a. Major companies do not make mistakes when naming products for a global market.

    b. Major companies make many mistakes when naming products for a local market.

    c. No one has heard of mistakes made by major companies when naming global products.

    d. Mistakes are sometimes made by major companies when naming products for a global market.

4. The author's writing style in this article is _____ and _____ .

    a. formal

    b. informal

    c. literary

    d. businesslike

5. The tone of the article is _____ and _____ .

    a. analytical

    b. emotional

    c. factual

    d. dramatic

6. What overall method of development is used in this article?

    a. enumerating the advantages and disadvantages of a plan

    b. supporting a controversial thesis with examples

    c. testing the evidence supporting a theory

    d. explaining a series of steps in a process

7. A metaphor is a literary device used by writers to make their writing more vivid, and it involves the comparison of two dissimilar objects or ideas. In the concluding paragraphs, the author uses metaphoric language: "It [a brand name] must be a good, strong, unique vessel with no holes in it . . . so you can start pouring in that brand value, secure in the knowledge that it's not running out at the bottom as fast as you pour it in."
What is being compared in this metaphor?

    a. A good brand name is compared to a strong, unique container.

    b. A strong brand name is compared to a weak brand name.

    c. A brand name is compared to brand value.

    d. A unique brand name is compared to a common brand name.

LUXURY GOODS FIRMS TARGET THE MIDDLE EAST

By Pamela Ann Smith

The Middle East has been targeted by international brand leaders whose outlets in regional shopping malls are increasing rapidly

1 luxury took on a new meaning in the Middle East with the opening in May of the $320 million Al Faisaliah centre in Riyadh. But its anchor outlet, Britain's prestigious department store, Harvey Nichols, is just one of a host of international retailers and luxury brand manufacturers looking to expand in the region. The question is, will they thrive, or is the competition too great?

2 The desire to possess the world's finest merchandise is growing around the globe, not least because of the increase in the numbers of those wealthy enough to afford the best. The number of people worldwide with more than $1 million in financial assets reached seven million last year, up from six million in 1998 according to Merrill Lynch & Company's annual World Wealth Report. Of these, 4.5 million reside outside North America, the report notes, including a substantial number in Saudi Arabia and the Gulf states. The return of high oil prices, in the view of directors sitting in boardrooms in New York, London and Paris, is likely to increase the Middle East's share of the world's nouveau riche.

The Middle East is open to all levels of demand in the luxury goods sector

3 This rapidly growing market, especially the sector aged under 30, is one of the reasons that brands such as Hermès, Louis Vuitton, Chopard, Calvin Klein and Christian Dior are investing in new outlets outside their traditional markets in Europe, the US and Japan. Analysts and consultants advising them or their franchisees say that getting in first can make a huge difference, provided it is done well.

4 Another factor is that while buyers in America and Europe may provide a staple base of demand, their tastes are becoming more conservative. 'Superluxe', which London's *Financial Times* defines as "the yearning for pieces that will endure for more than one season and that you can hand down to your grandchildren", is the latest trend, making those brands which sport conspicuous logos or which have spread their licensing and franchising arrangements too widely less desirable. The Middle East, the analysts say, is open to all levels of demand in the luxury goods sector, with the result that some of the largest profits, and fastest growth curves, are to be found in countries like Kuwait, the UAE and Lebanon as well as Saudi Arabia.

5 Another factor is that Middle Eastern

investors, as well as some of the region's largest trading houses, are beginning to get in on the act themselves. This was spectacularly evident when Saudi Prince Al Waleed bin Talal and Mohamed Al Fayed, the head of Britain's premier emporium, Harrods, announced a partnership aimed at creating 'signature shops' in the Gulf. "Mohamed Al Fayed and I want to bring the exclusivity of Harrods goods to clients in the Middle East who otherwise could only obtain the items in London," the prince was quoted as saying. The shops are to be located in airports and tourist centres as well as "outstanding locations", the prince added, signalling the two partners' intentions to become a dominant, independent force in the high-end retail market.

Harrods of Knightsbridge, London, the inspiration for 'signature shops' in the region

Riyadh appears to have become the major focus of attention for luxury goods manufacturers

6   Prince Al Waleed has already enticed the distinguished New York City retailer, Saks Fifth Avenue, to take up the anchor position in his vast new skyscraper taking shape on the Riyadh horizon, not far from Al Faisaliah. Costing some $453 million, the Kingdom Centre is due to open at the end of this year and will include a Four Seasons hotel, bank head quarters and prestigious offices as well as vast shopping areas, spread over 30 floors in a building 70 storeys high.

7   While Saks may have been persuaded by the fact that the prince is an important shareholder in the company, international consultants have noted that Riyadh appears

to have become the major focus of attention for luxury goods manufacturers and retailers in the past year. Larger in geographical area than Paris and only slightly smaller than London, the Saudi capital boasts a homogeneous consumer market, large households and an inclination to spend, as well as a sizeable middle class eager to purchase the latest in western fashions while preserving their own culture at home.

8   "The market is fairly high net worth," Shavak Srivastava, general manager of Al Ghurair Retail in Dubai told the Dubai-based monthly, *Gulf Business*. "People have high disposable incomes relative to other parts of the world, with a propensity to spend. The bulk of the population is below 30 years of age and they are 'with it' in terms of trends and fashion. The expatriates, as well as the local population travel a lot, so they are aware of international brands."

9   Abu Dhabi, which has lagged behind its

more commercial neighbour, Dubai, is catching up with the opening of a spate of new malls including Fetouh Al Khair, where the UK chain Marks & Spencer is the anchor, and the new women-only She Zone. Gianfranco Ferre and Christian Dior are just two of the names that have opened, or are due to open, single-brand stores.

10   Even Oman, which has attracted relatively fewer internationally known outlets given its lower per capita income, is being targeted. The German luxury leather goods brand, Aigner, has a boutique in Muscat's Sabco Centre, while other names are being drawn to newly built malls such as the Al Khamis Plaza in Qurum.

11   Elsewhere in the region, Lebanon is once again boasting fine shopping despite its disappointing economic performance. Interna-

International designers enjoy a high profile in the Gulf

tional retailers now have almost 150 shops in the country, including 38 US chains. Many of the luxury brands are to be found in the five-star hotels springing up, or newly refurbished, in Beirut and the mountain resorts.

Riyadh, Kuwait and Abu Dhabi attract their own single brand stores or mall boutiques

12   However, Dubai remains the undisputed capital of international shopping in the region in the eyes of many, not least because of its low duties, huge range of products and liberal life style. Yet most analysts agree that the days when it reigned supreme in the region are drawing to a close as Riyadh, Kuwait and Abu Dhabi attract their own single-brand stores or mall boutiques.

13   Throughout the region, competition will remain fierce. Only those retailers, distributors and franchisees willing to invest to maintain the quality of the brand image are likely to prosper. ■

Mohamed Al Fayed (above) has joined forces with Saudi Arabia's Prince Al Waleed bin Talal

Discussion

1. Which sector of the market for luxury goods in the Middle East is growing the most rapidly?

2. What factors explain the growth in the demand for luxury brands in the Middle East?

3. Why is Riyadh in Saudi Arabia the major focus of attention for luxury goods retailers?

4. In this fierce competition, which brand names are likely to succeed and prosper?

5. Which luxury brands have opened stores in your native country? Which are the most successful?

6. What is your definition of a luxury brand? Do you buy these brands?

Teamwork

Working in a group, create a new brand name for a range of bodycare products that will be marketed globally. Follow the process that advertising executive Simon Anholt describes in "Developing a Name to Work Worldwide." According to Anholt, "the process . . . starts with a creative team generating a long list of raw names, which is whittled down to a shortlist." Make certain that the new brand name you develop has no unfortunate meanings in other languages. Also create a slogan (a short promotional phrase like the McDonald's slogan "We love to see you smile") to go with the brand name. Translate the slogan from English into every language used by your teammates. When you have made your decisions, present the new brand name and the slogan to the class.

Writing Assignments

1. Do research on a famous brand name, such as Coca Cola, Sony, Mercedes-Benz, Absolut (vodka), or Levi's (jeans). Discover who created the name and when, what range of products the name includes, what the connotations of the name are, and what factors have led to its success. Then write a report on the brand name. Write an abstract (a short summary of the report) as the first section. Use this format.

    I. Abstract (50 words)

    II. Introduction (background and thesis)

    III. Major point

    IV. Major point

    V. Conclusion (restatement of thesis)

2. Use the Internet business database ABI/Inform to find two articles from *The Economist,* September 8, 2001: "Pro Logo: The Case for Brands" (p. 11) and "Brands: Who's Wearing the Trousers?" (pp. 26–28). Print out the articles, read them and write a synthesis based on them. (Search for the first article by typing the words *pro logo* and *brands* and *economist;* search for the second article by typing the words *brands* and *trousers* and *economist.*)

Cite your sources in the in-text citation format, giving the title and page number since there is no author ("Pro Logo" 11). List your sources at the end of the paper as Works Cited and alphabetize them according to the first word of the title. Develop your own thesis, or you may use the following thesis: Although antiglobalists criticize corporate brands for exploiting consumers, brand names actually protect consumers by providing reliability, quality, and value.

3. Use the Internet business database ABI/Inform to access the magazine *Advertising Age.* Click on Search Methods, select Publication, and type the words *advertising age.* Examine the table of contents of recent issues. After choosing an article on advertising or brand names, print out the article, read it, and make an outline of it. Hand in a copy of the article with your outline.

4. Write a research paper on the topic of the powerful effects of brands. You may use the articles printed or mentioned in this chapter, including the expansion readings, as sources for your paper. Also find several recent sources. These books should be helpful.

Aaker, David A., and Eric Joachims Thaler. *Brand Leadership.* New York: Free Press, 2000.

Dufour, François, and Jose Bové. *The World Is Not for Sale: Farmers against Junk Food.* London and New York: Verso, 2001.

Frank, Robert. *Luxury Fever: Why Money Fails to Satisfy in an Era of Excess.* New York: Free Press, 2001.

Klein, Naomi. *No Logo: Taking Aim at the Brand Bullies.* New York: Picador, 2000.

Schlosser, Eric. *Fast Food Nation: The Dark Side of the All-American Meal.* New York: Houghton, 2001.

Expansion Readings

Aaker, David A., and Erich Joachimsthaler. "The Lure of Global Branding." *Harvard Business Review* 77, no. 6 (December 1999): 137–44.

"Brands: Pro Logo." *The Economist,* 8 September 2001, 11.

"Brands: Who's Wearing the Trousers?" *The Economist,* 8 September 2001, 26–28.

Clancy, Kevin J., and Jack Trout. "Brand Confusion." *Harvard Business Review* 80, no. 3 (March 2002): 22.

Deighton, John. "How Snapple Got Its Juice Back." *Harvard Business Review* 80, no. 1 (January 2002): 47–53.

Ettenson, Richard, and Jill Klein. "Branded by the Past." *Harvard Business Review* 78, no. 6 (November–December 2000): 28.

"Face Value: The Branding of Saint Rudy." *The Economist,* 23 November 2002, 60.

"Face Value: Selling Energy." *The Economist,* 11 May 2002, 62.

Oral Presentation

Working with a partner, give a 20-minute oral presentation to the class on one of the articles listed under Expansion Readings or an article of your choice on brand names. Summarize the article by including the author's thesis, major points, and supporting data and evaluate its strengths and weaknesses. Be prepared to answer questions on your topic. If you have the technical capability, use the presentation graphics program PowerPoint for your presentation. Otherwise, make at least one overhead to use on the overhead projector. (See Appendix B, Oral Presentation.)

Travels on the Web

The Internet offers numerous opportunities to build and manage the brand identity of an individual, a family, or a company on a Web site. Log on to Network Solutions, which enables you to create a personal or professional domain name in over 350 languages. Select a name and check on whether the name you selected has already been registered.

Then log on to AllAboutYourOwnWebSite to get advice on designing and building a Web site. If you can create your own Web site, print out your home page and bring it to class to share with your classmates.

- Network Solutions: <http://www.netsol.com >

  - Domain Names

  - Web Sites

- AllAboutYourOwn Website: <http://www.allaboutyourownwebsite.com>

  - About Us

  - Languages

Chapter 6
The Internet

<table>
<tr><td>

"A Net Not Made in America"
Stephen Baker
Business Week
March 26, 2001

</td><td>

"Turkey Logs On"
Jon Gorvett
The Middle East
September 2000

</td></tr>
</table>

Preview   "A Net Not Made in America"

Skimming

Skim the article quickly to find the following general information.

1. Read the title and all headings and look at any illustrations.

2. Read the first and second paragraphs, looking for the author's purpose and main idea.

3. Read the last paragraph, looking for a summary or conclusion.

4. Write a sentence containing your preliminary understanding of the main idea of the article.

Questioning

Answer the following questions and discuss your answers in class.

1. How much time do you spend surfing the Internet? What is your favorite search engine?

2. Do you have your own computer? Do you own a cell phone that can access the Internet?

3. Have you done academic research on the Internet? What type?

Scanning

Scan the article quickly to find the following specific information.

1. What standard did analysts devise to measure a nation's progress in terms of Internet penetration?

2. What is the prediction for Internet penetration in 2005 in Europe and the United States?

3. In 2001, what percent of Americans surfed the Net?

4. What led Japan to produce the best small cars in the world in the 50's and 60's?

Vocabulary in Context

Read the following sentences and try to guess the meaning of the italicized words by using the context. Then replace the italicized words with synonyms (words or phrases that have nearly the same or similar meanings).

1. "Now foreign dot-coms seem to be following their American *prototypes* over the financial cliff." (Paragraph 2)

2. "That's because these days everyone is on *equal footing* in the search for money-making e-business models." (Paragraph 3)

3. "Oh, just typing these words I can hear *rebuttals* pouring in from America." (Paragraph 4)

4. "Mobile telephony will be essential for the Net to attain its potential." (Paragraph 7)

5. "The time has come for the rest of the world to put its *stamp* on the Net." (Paragraph 7)

Paraphrasing

After reading the article, reread the sentences under Vocabulary in Context. Now rewrite them using your own words. Change the vocabulary and sentence structure, but do not change the author's intended meaning or paraphrase any technical terms. There are several ways of paraphrasing each sentence.

COMMENTARY By Stephen Baker

A NET NOT MADE IN AMERICA

[1] They came in like an invading army. It was the American dot-com brigade, and over the past four years it swept through Europe, Asia, and Latin America. Cisco Systems Inc. laid down the railways and bridges. Dell Computer Corp. and Sun Microsystems supplied the materiel. Amazon.com Inc. and AOL Time Warner Inc., flanked by venture capitalists, attacked the mass online markets. Soon, these foreign frontiers for the Internet were operating on the U.S. model. The goal: a personal computer on every office desk and in every home, all surfing local variants of Amazon, Yahoo!, and eBay. Analysts even devised a standard to measure each nation's progress: how many months behind the U.S. in terms of Internet penetration. A year ago, France was 24 months back, Japan 18. Whatever the pace, everyone seemed to be marching in formation.

[2] Now foreign dot-coms seem to be following their American prototypes over the financial cliff. But while these companies and their investors suffer, the Internet proceeds. Like tens of thousands of others in Paris, I'm logged on now through a broadband hookup that was unavailable until a year ago. I order books from Amazon.fr and Spanish Rioja wine through a site in Madrid. Whether or not these providers go bust, the Net will remain a force in France.

[3] And the rest of the world will not wait for new leadership from America. In fact, non-U.S. users could well drive the Net to the next stage. That's because these days everyone is on equal footing in the search for money-making e-business models. What's more, growth in PC sales is slowing. Net consultant Jupiter Research 2000 even predicts PC penetration in Europe will plateau at 52% of households in 2005, compared with 73% in the U.S. Thus, the Net will likely migrate onto other machines, principally the mobile phone, where Asia and Europe dominate.

[4] Oh, just typing these words I can hear rebuttals pouring in from America. The European phone companies will go broke building these mobile systems, and they made a mess of the first generation of the wireless Web. The Japanese? They're just a bunch of kids sending cartoons on cell phones! But let's agree that there will be many failed business models for the mobile Net. That's also true of the PC-centric Net.

[5] **GOLD.** The advantage of handheld, Net-enabled machines, though, is that they can extend e-mail, ticket orders, inventory levels, and music downloads into the hands of buyers and sellers every waking hour. In an economy that runs on information, this power is gold. Why assume nobody will figure out how to profit? People already are putting these tools to use. And many are outside the U.S.

[6] Consider the Philippines on Jan. 16, where the Senate was deliberating on corruption charges against President Joseph Estrada. When word spread that the charges could be dropped, opposition leaders hurried to mobilize a demonstration that night. Not enough Filipinos were online to reach them by e-mail. But 6 million have cell phones and use them to send text messages. Using this medium, within hours the organizers convened a throng outside Malacanang Palace, sending the clear message Estrada was history.

[7] Mobile telephony will be essential for the Net to attain its potential. Since 43% of Americans surf the Net, compared with 3% of the rest of the world, most of the growth is sure to be abroad. And as in Manila, many in this next generation lack PCs—but do have cell phones. The Web also will have to become more multilingual: Billions of Chinese, Brazilians, and French struggle to navigate in English. U.S. giants such as Intel Corp. and Microsoft Corp. are establishing wireless research centers across the world to tap these markets. But America's PC titans will have less of a stranglehold on software and content, giving rise to more innovative products, such as the Web browser used in NTT DoCoMo's wildly successful i-mode phones. Other breakthroughs could originate in small cities in China or India as companies struggle to build businesses for customers on tight budgets. It was this type of market pressure in the '50s and '60s that led Japan to produce the best small cars in the world. The time has come for the rest of the world to put its stamp on the Net.

> . . . the rest of the world will not wait for new leadership from America. In fact, non-U.S. users could well drive the Net to the next stage. That's because these days everyone is on equal footing in the search for money-making e-business models.

Baker covers the European tech scene from Paris.

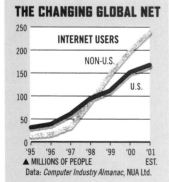

THE CHANGING GLOBAL NET

INTERNET USERS

NON-U.S.

U.S.

250
200
150
100
50
0

'95 '96 '97 '98 '99 '00 '01 EST.

▲ MILLIONS OF PEOPLE

Data: *Computer Industry Almanac, NUA Ltd.*

Glossary

breakthroughs	sudden advances in knowledge or technique
brigade	a large body of troops
broadband	high-speed Internet access utilizing a wide band of frequencies for transmission of data
corruption	impairment of integrity, virtue, or moral principle
devised	invented
equal footing	the same in status, position, or rank in relation to others
flanked	protected; supported
go bust	to become bankrupt
medium	channel or system of communication
migrate	to move from one place to another
mobilize	to put into movement
navigate	to get around; to manage
pace	rate of movement or progress
plateau	to reach a level of stability or attainment
potential	future capability, something that can develop, promise
prototypes	original models on which something is patterned
rebuttals	arguments
stamp	distinctive character
stranglehold	force or influence that suppresses freedom of expression
tap	to make an advantageous connection with
titans	companies that are gigantic in size or power
wireless	information technology equipment that transmits data through the air

Comprehension

1. What was the goal of the American dot-com business model?

2. Who will provide the new leadership for the next stage of the Net? Why?

3. If growth in the sales of personal computers slows, what machines will the Net likely migrate onto?

4. Why are handheld, Net-enabled machines as valuable as gold?

5. What does the economy of the 21st century run on?

6. Why will the Web have to become more multilingual?

7. Where will innovations and breakthroughs come from?

8. What major innovation would you like to see for the Internet?

9. Similes and metaphors, which are figures of speech, add vividness to writing. They involve comparisons of dissimilar objects or ideas. Stephen Baker uses similies and metaphors in the first six sentences of paragraph 1. Explain how these comparisons clarify Baker's meaning: "They came in like an invading army. It was the American dot-com brigade. . . . Soon, these foreign frontiers for the Internet were operating on the U.S. model."

Analysis

Circle the letter next to the best answer(s). Justify your choices with quotations from the text.

1. What is the main idea of the article, and in which paragraph(s) is it stated?

   a. In the next stage of Internet innovation and development, the leaders will be from countries other than the United States.

   b. The most valuable technology today is not personal computers but Net-enabled machines.

   c. Although other languages will become more common on the Internet, the Net will continue to use English primarily.

   d. The most significant breakthrough for the Internet will be in the area of music downloads.

2. What is the meaning of the italicized word in this sentence in paragraph 3? "In fact, non-U.S. users could well *drive* the Net to the next stage."

   a. expand

   b. help

   c. open

   d. lead

3. What can be inferred from the title of the article "A Net Not Made in America"?

   a. The Internet will gain more users in countries around the world.

   b. The Internet of the future will be dominated by non-U.S. countries.

   c. The United States will buy its Internet technology from other countries.

   d. The United States will stop making software for personal computers.

4. The author's writing style in this article is ＿＿＿＿＿ and ＿＿＿＿＿ .

   a. idiomatic

   b. formal

   c. personal

   d. impersonal

5. The tone of the article is ＿＿＿＿＿ and ＿＿＿＿＿ .

   a. subjective

   b. objective

   c. colloquial

   d. academic

6. What overall method of development is used in this article?

   a. comparing and contrasting two approaches

   b. choosing and describing one alternative out of several

   c. supporting an argument by giving specific examples

   d. defining a technical system

7. The graph titled "The Changing Global Net" shows that in 2001 there were almost 250 million non-U.S. Internet users compared to about 170 million U.S. users. Which of the following statements made by Baker are supported by these statistics?

   a. "Mobile telephony will be essential for the Net to attain its potential."

   b. "Now foreign dot-coms seem to be following their American prototypes over the financial cliff."

   c. "Non-U.S. users could well drive the Net to the next stage."

   d. "The Web also will have to become more multilingual."

TURKEY LOGS ON

Jon Gorvett reports from Istanbul

Customers can now buy cards with so many hours of net usage on them, rather like a phone card

1 Travelling through the bizarre, science fiction landscape of Cappadocia, one of the most impressive sites on the tourist itinerary is always the underground Byzantine city of Derinkoyu. A massive subterranean complex, the contrast between the below ground world and the above ground one is enormous, with the contemporary village a huddle of small houses. Yet look amongst those humble dwellings, and there, right on the village high street, you'll find not one, but two internet cafes.

2 It's a picture repeated throughout Turkey. No matter how small or remote the settlement, chances are that in this day and age, the local youth will spend a great proportion of its time online, surfing the net or engaging in chat line conversation with people around the globe at their local cafe.

3 Only a few months ago, a Turk, known as Mahir, hit world headlines with the most visited web site on the planet — over a million hits in just a few days. It's also not so long ago that the internet was scarcely known amongst the republic's 60 million inhabitants.

4 Estimates vary over the actual number of internet users in Turkey, but one thing every-

By the start of this year there were some 750,000 dial up account holders in Turkey

one agrees on is that the sector is booming.

5 Pre-1995, usage was limited to a number of academic institutions, but with the establishment of a national internet backbone in that year, things took off.

6 The INTURNET consortium set up in 1996 to put this in place pushed the first

ISPs into action, but by the following year, the system had become so overloaded it could barely function.

7 Companies such as Superonline and Turk.net then set up their own systems, and in 1998, PRI lines and Cisco Access entered the market, with start up costs falling dramatically, along with subscription rates. Others followed, particularly Vestel, which began offering a computer and internet package whereby customers would buy a computer in instalments which was complete with Vestel's own internet software. Others, such as Is Bank, Beko, Aidata, IhlasNet and Zetnet soon followed suit, also boosting the number of PC owners dramatically. Ixil has now also started offering a unit-based system, where customers can buy cards with so many hours of net usage on them, rather like a phone card.

Some conservatives have pushed for a ruling forbidding internet cafes near schools and other areas where young people congregate

8   By the start of this year there were some 750,000 dial-up account holders in Turkey, a figure probably swelling to around a million when academic institutions are added in. Recent projections suggest a 50 per cent annual growth rate over the next three years.

9   There has also been a recent growth in e-commerce. Turkey now ranks 39th in the top 60 countries. As one example, an internet cafe set up in the central Anatolian city of Kayseri by local businessmen has, according to local chamber of commerce director Erdal Cinar, helped local firms make a whole series of deals in mini refrigerators, acrylics and fibres with companies in Israel and as far away as China.

10   Elsewhere, the Obase Computer and Consultancy Company, established by four Turkish youths in 1994, has also netted 38 per cent of Turkey's chain stores and hypermarkets with its services. Haluk Alpay, Obase Executive Board Chairman, says they are now planning to enter the US and European markets in two years' time, and provide services to 835 national businesses in 1999, with a target of 1,200 for 2000.

11   And e-commerce is also having a powerful effect on tourism. Used mainly by younger travellers, the internet has provided a fast way to book hotels, reserve tickets or even lay on entire tour packages.

12   "Some of even the smallest hostels have amazing websites now. Before they travel, people want to book somewhere to stay. The number of people making tour bookings on the internet is booming," says Genjay Acar, of Pasifik Tours in Istanbul.

13   Another recent development has been the introduction of e-training, a market expected to be worth $11.4 billion world wide by 2003. Reha Ayata, the Turkish representative of Intuition, a company that offers web-based training to more than 150 banks and financial establishments through-

The growth in servers and users has not been completely matched by developments in the telephone network

out the world, says "although electronic training is not as widespread in Turkey as it is in many other countries, we are expecting a boom in the very near future." Yuksel Onden, of Onden Instruction Consultants Ltd, confirmed small businesses, known as "KOBIs", were likely to make up the main part of e-training as they would benefit most from its lower costs. KOBIs account for 98 per cent of work places in Turkey and represent 65 per cent of the country's workforce," he says. "One of their main problems is finding qualified employees... Consortiums of computer, printing, marketing and internet companies in the sector, which has been growing at an average of 35 per cent annually, are currently offering resolution packages with e-training packs, specifically directed at KOBIs."

14   However, there are a number of factors causing a glich in the system. First amongst these is the technological infrastructure. The growth in servers and users has not been completely matched by developments in the telephone network, with many areas still using analogue exchanges. Another problem is that many companies have underestimated the size of the market and have failed to install equipment sufficiently powerful to deal with such a quantity of e-traffic.

15   Then there's the government. While committed to a more free market approach than previously, there are still significant political groupings that are wary of the spread of internet usage. Conservatives and Islamists in particular have pushed for controls, with a ruling last year forbidding the locating of internet cafes near schools or other areas where young people congregate.

16   On top of these factors, there is also the overall economic performance of the country. Growth has slowed — indeed, last year saw shrinkage — which cuts the number of PCs sold and thus subscribers. It may also be behind the boom in internet cafes, as a cheaper short term alternative to home subscription.

17   However, there is no mistaking the overall trend. A number of companies have also recently started marketing WAP systems, taking advantage of the massive mobile phone market, due for expansion soon when GSM 1800 networks replace the existing lower frequency 900 ones.

18   Last year's earthquakes have also had an unexpected effect on the market. "In the areas worst affected by the quake," says Ayse Polat, a marketing consultant, "we've found the highest number of people using internet cafes. It seems that it's a way for people who suffered to make contact — to escape from towns still devastated by the disaster."

19   A cafe in the quake-hit town of Yalova is one example. "Since then," explains Ali Karaoglu, "the young people especially haven't had much chance to lead a normal life. But at the internet cafe, I can talk to people all over the world, or play games — it's possible to go into another world."

20   It seems that for a variety of reasons, many Turks are also flocking to this other, electronic realm. ■

Discussion

1. Who used the Internet in Turkey before 1995?

2. What factors have led to the growth of Internet users in Turkey?

3. How successful has e-commerce been in Turkey?

4. Explain the electronic training that is being offered to small businesses.

5. What problems does Turkey have to solve in its technological infrastructure?

6. What is the government's attitude toward the spread of Internet usage?

7. How did the earthquakes in 1999 affect the use of Internet cafés?

8. How strong is the technological infrastructure in your native country?

9. What is the attitude of your native country's government toward the spread of the Internet?

Teamwork

Working with a group, do research on the World Wide Web to discover Web sites that use languages other than English. (Do not include Hotmail.com or Yahoo.com in your research.) Access at least five of these Web sites and print out copies of their home pages. Then write a short description of each of the Web sites, translating their information into English. Bring the home pages to class to share with your classmates.

Writing Assignments

1. Do research to discover the statistics on telephone lines, Internet use, and cell phone use in a country in which you are interested. What is the current situation in this country in regard to use of the Internet and of cell phones? What percent of the population can access the Internet? What percent uses cell phones? One useful Internet source is the United Nations Global Statistics at <http://www.un.org>. Select Site Index and Statistics. Then choose Millennium Country Profiles. After completing your research, write an essay in which you discuss your findings and draw conclusions.

2. Write a synthesis using the following three articles from *The Middle East* magazine: "Turkey Logs On" by Jon Gorvett (September 2000: pp. 35–36), printed in this chapter; "Syrian Surfers Take to the Net" by Alan George (October 2000: pp. 31–32); and "How Dot.Com Is Cairo?" by Michael A. Gordon (December 2001: pp. 26–27). Find the latter two articles by using the Internet business database ABI/Inform. Search for the George article by typing the words *Middle East*

and *Syrian surfers* and *net*. Search for the Gordon article by typing the words *Middle East* and *dot.com* and *Cairo*. Cite your sources in the in-text citation format (Gorvett 35). List your sources at the end of the paper as Works Cited and alphabetize them according to the authors' last names.

3. Working with a partner, conduct an interview with an information technology expert on the future uses of handheld, Net-enabled machines (mobile telephony). (See "DNA: Handle with Care" in chapter 8 for an example of an interview.) Use a tape recorder during the interview and write up the information as a report in three sections: introduction, interview questions and answers, conclusion.
You may use the questions listed below in your interview.

   - What types of high-tech machines will be developed?

   - Which countries will develop the new technology?

   - How will this technology be marketed globally?

   - What type of Web browser will be developed?

   - What is your favorite handheld, Net-enabled machine?

   - What is your favorite cell phone brand?

4. Write a research paper on the topic of freedom versus regulation on the Internet. You may use the articles printed or mentioned in this chapter, including the expansion readings, as sources for your paper. Also find several recent sources. These books should be helpful.

   Cothran, Helen, ed. *The Internet: Opposing Viewpoints*. San Diego, CA: Greenhaven, 2002.

   Grossman, Wendy. *From Anarchy to Power: The Net Comes of Age*. New York: New York University Press, 2001.

   Hiller, Janine S., and Ronnie Cohen. *Internet Law and Policy*. Upper Saddle River, NJ: Prentice-Hall, 2002.

   Lessig, Lawrence. *Code and Other Laws of Cyberspace*. New York: Basic Books, 1999.

   ———. *The Future of Ideas*. New York: Random House, 2001.

Expansion Readings

"The Internet and the Law." *The Economist*, 13 January 2001, 21–25.

Porter Michael. "Strategy and the Internet." *Harvard Business Review* 79, no. 3 (March 2001): 62–78.

"Survey: The Internet Society." *The Economist*, 25 January 2003, 3–26.

Worf, Richard. "Speaking Out: The Internet in China." *Harvard International Review* 23, no. 4 (Winter 2002): 7–8.

Oral Presentation

Working with a partner, give a 20-minute oral presentation to the class on one of the articles listed under Expansion Readings or an article of your choice on the Internet. Summarize the article by including the author's thesis, major points, and supporting data and evaluate its strengths and weaknesses. Be prepared to answer questions on your topic. If you have the technical capability, use the presentation graphics program PowerPoint for your presentation. Otherwise, make at least one overhead to use on the overhead projector. (See Appendix B, Oral Presentation.)

Travels on the Web

1. The Internet offers numerous opportunities to read more about changes in the World Wide Web and the impact of the Internet. The three articles listed below are excellent. To find "The Surveillance Society" you can go directly to the Web site of *Wired* magazine's archives. Use the Internet business database ABI/Inform to locate the articles from *The Economist* and *Foreign Policy*. For example, to find the article from *The Economist* using ABI/Inform, do a search by typing the words *Internet* and *law* and *stop signs* and *economist*. Print out one of these articles and bring it to class to discuss with your classmates.

   - *The Economist* magazine: <http://www.economist.com>

     - "The Internet and the Law: Stop Signs on the Web." 13 January 2001, 21–25.

   - *Foreign Policy* magazine: <http://www.foreignpolicy.com>

     - Litan, Robert E. "The Internet Economy." *Foreign Policy* (March–April 2001): 16–24.

   - *Wired* magazine: <http://www.wired.com/wired/archive/9.12/surveillance>

     - Penenberg, Adam L. "The Surveillance Society." *Wired* (December 2001).

2. Today, as more and more computers are connected to the Internet, the number of computer crimes has increased, and cybercrime has become a growing problem throughout the world. These crimes include financial fraud, computer break-in and sabotage, and identity theft. Log on to the following Web sites that provide protection against global computer crime. Print out some of the most useful information and bring it to class to share with your classmates.

   - Council of Europe: <http://www.coe.int>

   - Critical Infrastructure Assurance Office: <http://www.ciao.gov>

   - Cyber Defenders: <http://www.cyberdefenders.com>

   - Federal Bureau of Investigation's (FBI) National Infrastructure Protection Center: <http://www.nipc.gov>

   - Interpol: <http://www.interpol.int>

Chapter 7
Information Technology

"Go Mobile—Now!"
Peter G. W. Keen
Computerworld
June 2001

"Key Shift for IT"
Peter G. W. Keen
Computerworld
May 2001

"A Truly Global Web"
Peter G. W. Keen
Computerworld
December 2000

"Bit Player"
James Gleick
The New York Times Magazine
December 30, 2001

Preview   "Go Mobile—Now!"
"Key Shift for IT"
"A Truly Global Web"

Skimming

Skim the articles quickly to find the following general information.

1. Read the titles and all headings of the articles and look at any illustrations.

2. Read the first and second paragraphs of each article, looking for the author's purpose and main idea.

3. Read the last paragraph of each article, looking for a summary or conclusion.

4. For each article, write a sentence containing your preliminary understanding of the main idea of the article.

Questioning

Answer the following questions and discuss your answers in class.

1. Do you have a Palm handheld or a wireless laptop computer?

2. Have you bought anything over the Internet?

3. What are your favorite Web sites?

Scanning

Scan the articles quickly to find the following specific information.

"Go Mobile—Now!"

1. What has e-commerce been paced by, especially in the business-to-business market?

2. According to *Consumer Reports,* what were the satisfaction levels with mobile phones?

3. Where is the largest mobile phone company in the world located?

4. What is the world's most profitable and fastest-growing mobile Web and messaging service?

"Key Shift for IT"

1. What are the main issues IT must increasingly address?

2. What is Moore's law?

3. What will result from the huge international imbalance in e-commerce purchases?

4. In many consumer protection cases, what are troubles caused by?

"A Truly Global Web"

1. In the United States, where have the main growth areas in business-to-consumer e-commerce been?

2. What fee do credit card companies charge merchants in Japan?

3. In China, how many television sets are there for every personal computer?

4. Where is half the world's manufacturing now done?

Vocabulary in Context

Read the following sentences and try to guess the meaning of the italicized words by using the context. Then replace the italicized words with synonyms (words or phrases that have nearly the same or similar meanings).

"Go Mobile—Now!"

1. "The next major *shift* in the use of IT will obviously be toward wireless and mobile commerce." (Paragraph 1)

2. "Their effectiveness and range of applications today is limited by a lack of bandwidth, but that bottleneck is being removed, albeit in a piecemeal and *fragmented* way." (Paragraph 1)

3. "But in wireless and m-commerce, the U.S. is a *laggard.*" (Paragraph 3)

4. "M-commerce is international, and the more that IT professionals look beyond the U.S., the more they'll be able to *accelerate* their companies' moves into the next innovation space of online business." (Paragraph 6)

"Key Shift for IT"

1. "Historically, their *sphere* of concern was managing technology: expenditures, development, operations and support." (Paragraph 1)

2. "So, expect the next *massive* and complex software investments to center on tax collection." (Paragraph 4)

3. "There are few *precedents*, established practices and laws to cover online business." (Paragraph 4)

4. "IT will *thrive* or fail during the next few years on the diversity of its roles and responsibilities—and of its people and their skills." (Paragraph 5)

"A Truly Global Web"

1. "Shopping isn't the main *priority;* communication is." (Paragraph 2)

2. "The success of e-commerce *rests* on credit cards." (Paragraph 3)

3. "Europe, *lagging* the U.S. in business-to-business e-commerce, is moving fast to catch up." (Paragraph 6)

4. "There's an old *precept,* 'Think globally, act locally.'" (Paragraph 7)

Paraphrasing

After reading the articles, reread the sentences under Vocabulary in Context. Now rewrite them using your own words. Change the vocabulary and sentence structure, but do not change the author's intended meaning or paraphrase any technical terms. There are several ways of paraphrasing each sentence.

PETER G. W. KEEN

Go Mobile - Now!

1 HE NEXT MAJOR SHIFT in the use of IT will obviously be toward wireless and mobile commerce. It will happen in fits and starts, with the usual hype, chaos and clutter, disappointments and brilliant innovations - just like with e-commerce. In many ways, m-commerce is the continuation of e-commerce with the Palm handheld, wireless laptops and a new generation of Web-enabled digital phones already on the market. Their effectiveness and range of applications

today is limited by a lack of bandwidth, but that bottleneck is being removed, albeit in a piecemeal and fragmented way.

2 In one key regard, though, m-commerce is very different from e-commerce. E-commerce has been paced by U.S. technology and business innovation, particularly in the business-to-business market; there are approximately 20 firms selling $1 billion to $20 billion worth of goods over the Internet - yet none are outside the U.S.

3 But in wireless and m-commerce, the U.S. is a laggard. This has substantial implications for IT organizations. They largely don't know what's going on elsewhere and risk getting left behind in exploiting m-commerce. The fragmentation, unreliability, cost and poor quality of U.S. cell phone services, as well as the equally fragmented rollout of broadband services like Digital Subscriber Line, have all resulted in close to zero interest among consumers in wireless Internet tools, according to surveys. Early this year, *Consumer Reports* said that satisfaction levels with mobile phones were among the lowest in any of its studies, below that for lawyers.

4 Meanwhile, the rest of the world is moving fast, and IT developers in this country must play the role of followers in the m-commerce arena. Here are a few questions (followed by the answers) that can help you calibrate your knowledge:

1. Which company is the largest provider of mobile phone services?
2. What is GPRS?
3. What is WAP?
4. Which country has close to 100% mobile phone coverage among its adults and is the world leader in m-commerce applications?
5. What is DoCoMo?
6. What is SMS?
7. Which company has the largest share - 35% - of the world mobile handset market?

5 These aren't trick questions; the answers appear in many articles in the daily press. They are as follows:

1. The U.K.'s Vodafone is the largest mobile company in the world, with a well-established strategy of massive acquisitions worldwide.
2. General Packet Radio Service (GPRS) is the 2.5G bit/sec. broadband wireless capability that fills the gap between first-generation digital phones and the massive, planned - and much-delayed - third generation wireless services.

3. **Wireless Application Protocol (WAP) is a specification being developed in a European-led effort to bring the wireless Web to mobile phones and personal digital assistants. WAP has been a major disappointment so far, but the lessons for designers have been substantial. Trying to shrink HTML pages onto a phone display with deadly slow wireless transmission speeds doesn't work.**
4. **Finland has set the pace for m-commerce with a flood of applications that are profitable and that show the extent to which there is real demand, given a solid wireless technology infrastructure. Many Finland households and small businesses no longer bother with wired phones.**
5. **NTT DoCoMo is the world's most profitable and fastest-growing mobile Web and messaging service and also shows the proven demand for wireless messaging everywhere.**
6. **Simple Messaging System (SMS) is the foundation of the first generation of consumer m-commerce applications. It's almost nonexistent in the U.S., but in Europe, it's everywhere.**
7. **Nokia has 35% of the handset market; Motorola has just 13%.**

6   **M-commerce is international, and the more that IT professionals look beyond the U.S., the more they'll be able to accelerate their companies' moves into the next innovation space of online business.**

PETER KEEN's new book, co-authored with Ron Mackintosh, *The Freedom Economy: Gaining the M-commerce Edge in the Era of the Wireless Internet,* is being published this month by McGraw-Hill. Contact him at <u>peter@peterkeen.com</u>.

Glossary

accelerate	to cause to move faster; to speed up
albeit	even though
bandwidth	the data transfer rate of an electronic communications system; the capacity of a country's cable, telephone lines, and fiber optics to carry digital communications
bottleneck	situation that halts free movement and progress
broadband	high-speed Internet access utilizing a wide band of frequencies for transmission of data
calibrate	to adjust precisely
chaos	state of confusion
exploiting	making productive use of
fragmented	broken up into small pieces
hype	extravagant promotion
infrastructure	underlying foundation or basic framework
IT	information technology
laggard	one that moves or functions with comparative slowness
massive	impressively large
paced	moved along; led
rollout	public introduction of a new product
shift	change in direction
shrink	to make smaller or more compact

PETER G. W. KEEN

Key Shift for IT

1 **THERE'S AN IMMENSE SHIFT UNDER WAY in the responsibilities of effective IT organizations. Historically, their sphere of concern was managing technology: expenditures, development, operations and support. Now, about five years into the e-commerce era, the main issues IT must increasingly address are the impacts of technology.**

2 The Internet, PCs, e-commerce and mobile commerce have accelerated the shift of technology from the periphery to the center of more areas of business, society and everyday life. Here are just four areas that will need new IT expertise, experience and education: energy and conservation, privacy, taxation, and consumer protection. This list may seem surprising, but in a way, it reflects how successful IT, e-commerce and the computer and telecommunications industries have been in helping turn the academic network infrastructure of the old Internet into a force that's at the center of the most far-reaching, progressive changes in our world today and into tomorrow.

3 IT's impacts go well beyond the management of technology now; my list adds up to an essential extension of its skill and responsibility base.

4 The following are reasons why:

- Energy and conservation. About 12% of all electrical energy consumption in the U.S. is for IT operations. In some ways, the corollary to Moore's Law (that hardware price-performance doubles every 18 months) is that demands for air conditioning, which helps cool data centers, and managing that energy, increases faster than energy supply, if not proportionately. Add the growing problems of disposal of batteries, obsolete equipment and print cartridges, and it's clear that IT will increasingly need to take energy and conservation into account in its planning and operations.

- Privacy. This is becoming a growing concern, and it's climbing political and legislative agendas across the world. There has always been a tension between convenience and privacy, between access and control, and between personal service and anonymity in any telecommunications-dependent service. E-commerce has increased that tension. Mobile commerce will increase it even more because of FCC regulations and business applications that track the locations of subscribers. Any IT professional must become knowledgeable about privacy in terms of technology issues, best practices and the law.

- Taxation. Within the next three years, taxation will be a key IT planning issue. In the U.S., the issues will center on legislation, state and local taxes vs. federal taxes, and collection. Internationally, a trade war is coming. The huge international imbalance in e-commerce purchases means more goods and services will be sold out of the U.S. Europe wants to collect a value-added tax of, typically, 18% at the buyer's end. The U.S. will favor collection of a 5% to 10% sales tax at the seller's end. So, expect the next massive and complex software investments to center on tax collection.

- Consumer protection. There are few precedents, established practices and laws to cover online business. There are growing reports of customers having problems resolving, for instance, the blocking of "opt-out" marketing procedures. In these situations, they're automatically billed for renewing a service unless they explicitly opt out in writing. But they can't get their letters to the people who can process the cancellations, and they can't get redress on incorrect charges of dispute transactions. In many cases, the troubles are caused by IT system design problems and poor handling of the business processes behind the system.

5 IT will thrive or fail during the next few years on the diversity of its roles and responsibilities - and of its people and their skills. Diversity and creativity go together. The IT organization that doesn't take on these four issues as responsibilities is implicitly deciding to confine itself to too narrow a role to be central in managing technology's impacts, rather than just managing technology.

PETER G. W. KEEN is chairman of Keen Innovations (formerly The International Center for Information Technologies) in Fairfax Station, Va.; a senior fellow of Differentis, a European business-to-business consultancy; and a distinguished visiting professor at the University of Delft in the Netherlands. Contact him at peter@peterkeen.com.

Glossary

agendas	lists of things to be considered or done
anonymity	quality of being unidentified, anonymous
corollary	something that naturally follows
dispute	controversy, argument
imbalance	lack of balance, proportion
immense	enormous; marked by greatness in size or degree
implicitly	involved in the nature of something, though not expressed
obsolete	no longer in use or no longer useful; old-fashioned
opt out	to decide against something
periphery	the outward bounds of something
precedents	earlier occurrences of something similar that may serve as examples
proportionately	corresponding in size, degree, or intensity
redress	compensation for wrong or loss; relief from distress
sphere	area within which something acts
thrive	to grow vigorously, flourish

PETER G. W. KEEN

A Truly Global Web

T HE WORLD WIDE WEB (W3) is anything but worldwide in its impact on business. It's highly local. Internet "users" are people and companies who are very different both regionally and nationally in their demand patterns and behaviors. This is unlike the market for

standard phone services, where the global differences are fairly narrow and mainly relate to price. With the Internet, one country's experiences may not in any way apply to another's. Here are examples of the differences around the world:

- In the U.S., the main growth areas in business-to-consumer e-commerce have been in books, plane tickets and consumer electronics. It certainly won't be the same for Latin American and Asian countries with lower average incomes and weak telephony services. It's hard to see people in those countries yearning to get on the Internet to order books from Amazon and to bid on eBay. They're most likely to use e-mail, access entertainment and use the Net to help their children with their education. Shopping isn't the main priority; communication is.

Next year should be the year when W3 becomes W5.

- The success of e-commerce rests on credit cards. Yet in much of Latin America, credit cards can only be used in the countries in which they're issued, and business credit is far more limited there than in the U.S. and Europe. And in Japan, business-to-consumer Internet commerce has been greatly constrained by the high fees that credit card companies charge merchants - around 10% of the amount of the sale, compared with 3% in the U.S. and Europe.

- In the U.S., goods move simply and quickly, credit is widely available and there are few regulatory blockages. A small business can import and export easily. Many Asian and Latin American nations need improvements in these basic areas before business-to-business e-commerce can take off. So ports, customs agencies and trade financing are the key factors in those countries.

- The primary access tools for Internet service vary widely. The U.S. has close to 40 personal computers per 100 inhabitants. Germany has just half that, and Latin American nations average around four. In China, there are 25 television sets for every personal computer. In India, telephone and Internet services are highly regulated, but cable TV service is a free-for-all. So in those two giant nations, it's the television and not the PC that's likely to drive the mass market. In Finland, however, it will certainly be wireless as the growth in new wireless subscribers has overtaken those of wired phones.

6   Next year should be the year when W3 becomes W5: the World Wide World Wide Web. Europe, lagging the U.S. in business-to-business e-commerce, is moving fast to catch up. It's way ahead of the U.S. in wireless technology and it's taking the lead in mobile commerce. Given that half the world's manufacturing is now in Asia, extending supply chains across the globe is obviously a priority for e-commerce logistics leaders everywhere. Many of the largest recent mergers and acquisitions are creating truly global firms targeting the consumer market, with German giants Mannesmann (Vodafone) and Bertelsmann (which holds a large stake in Barnesandnoble.com) taking the lead. Lycos is now owned by Telefonica, the Spanish phone company that dominates Latin America.

7   What does all this mean for IT and IT professionals? Whatever they decide it means. W5 is coming fast, and its growth will be more explosive than W3's growth to date. Almost all the discussion of e-commerce until today has been U.S.-centered. IT needs a new knowledge base in order to play a significant role in the W3-to-W5 expansion of e-commerce. It can't carry U.S. assumptions and experience about customers, supply-chain management, business-to-business, business-to-commerce, markets and technology into the global arena. There's an old precept, "Think globally, act locally." There's a danger for IT in thinking locally, then trying to act globally. So, think globally, and act globally.

Keen is chairman of Keen Innovations in Fairfax Station, Va., a senior fellow of Differentis, a European B2B consultancy and a distinguished visiting professor at the University of Delft in the Netherlands. Contact him at peter@peterkeen.com.

Glossary

access	to gain entry to
bid	to offer a price for payment
constrained	restricted, limited
drive	to direct the course of, to give shape to
explosive	large-scale, rapid expansion
lagging	moving with comparative slowness
logistics	the handling of the details of an operation; procurement, maintenance, and transportation of personnel, equipment, and materials
precept	command or principle intended as a general rule of action
priority	something given attention before competing alternatives
rests	is based on; depends on
stake	a share or interest in a commercial venture
take off	to spring into wide use or popularity
yearning	longing, desiring

Comprehension

"Go Mobile—Now!"

1. What will the next major shift in the use of IT be?

2. In what way is e-commerce very different from m-commerce?

3. What has caused the low interest among U.S. consumers in wireless Internet tools?

4. What lessons have designers learned from Wireless Application Protocol (WAP)?

5. Where is Simple Messaging System (SMS) used?

6. Where should IT professionals look for the next innovation space of online business?

"Key Shift for IT"

1. What shift has taken place in the responsibilities of IT organizations?

2. What four areas will need new IT expertise, experience, and education?

3. What tensions exist in any telecommunications-dependent service?

4. Why is an international trade war coming?

5. Why are there growing reports of problems for consumers involved in online business?

"A Truly Global Web"

1. What is the difference between the market for standard phone services and the market for Internet services?

2. In American and Asian countries with average incomes that are lower than those in the United States, what are people most likely to use the Internet for?

3. How are credit cards used in much of Latin America?

4. In which areas do many Asian and Latin American countries need improvements before business-to-business e-commerce can take off?

5. What is a priority for e-commerce logistics leaders everywhere?

6. Why does IT need a new knowledge base for the expansion of e-commerce?

Analysis

Circle the letter next to the best answer(s). Justify your choices with quotations from the text.

1. What is the main idea of the article "Go Mobile—Now!" and in which paragraph(s) is it stated?

    a. IT developers in the United States must catch up with international advances in m-commerce.

    b. The best IT product to market in the future is the mobile phone.

    c. Sales of mobile phones have outpaced sales of personal computers around the world.

    d. Japan's instant messaging service is extremely successful.

2. What is the main idea of the article "Key Shift for IT," and in which paragraph(s) is it stated?

    a. Consumer protection is the most serious problem facing IT.

    b. The field of IT must become aware of not only the management but also the impacts of technology.

    c. The difficulty of protecting the privacy of consumers engaged in e-commerce has been increasing.

    d. U.S. domination of e-commerce is causing complaints from other countries.

3. What is the main idea of the article "A Truly Global Web," and in which paragraph(s) is it stated?

    a. The use of the Internet varies from one country to another, but it is most often used for e-mail.

b. Credit cards have changed the way business is done in every country in the world.

c. Business-to-business e-commerce is growing rapidly in Asian countries.

d. IT must adopt a global perspective if e-commerce is to succeed and expand.

4. What is the meaning of the italicized word in this sentence from paragraph 1 of "Key Shift for IT"? "Now, about five years into the e-commerce era, the main issues IT must increasingly *address* are the impacts of technology."

a. look over

b. revise

c. deal with

d. clarify

5. We can infer the following from this statement in paragraph 3 of "Go Mobile— Now!" "Early this year, *Consumer Reports* said that satisfaction levels with mobile phones were among the lowest in any of its studies, below that for lawyers."

a. The United States has to improve and update the IT used in its m-commerce.

b. Cell phones are not popular in the United States because they are expensive.

c. *Consumer Reports* is a reliable source of information on the quality of products.

d. Satisfaction levels for lawyers are lower in the United States than in most other countries.

6. The author's writing style in these articles is _____ and _____ .

a. formal

b. informal

c. technical

d. nontechnical

7. The tone of these articles is _____ and _____ .

a. objective

b. subjective

c. authoritative

d. tentative

8. What overall method of development is used in these three articles?

   a. outlining problems and offering solutions

   b. classifying and analyzing methods

   c. refuting arguments through examples

   d. defining technological processes

9. In "Go Mobile—Now!" the author structures his article around seven questions and answers. What is the purpose of this test?

   a. to entertain readers with an easy quiz

   b. to explain the diverse forms of m-commerce

   c. to increase readers' awareness of their lack of global knowledge

   d. to prove the point that m-commerce is international

Bit Player

The mathematician invented the very essence of the Information Age.

By James Gleick

1 Halfway through the last century, information became a thing. It became a commodity, a force — a quantity to be measured and analyzed. It's what our world runs on. Information is the gold and the fuel. We measure it in bits. That's largely because of Claude Shannon.

2 Shannon is the father of information theory, an actual science devoted to messages and signals and communication and computing. The advent of information theory can be pretty well pinpointed: July 1948, the Bell System Technical Journal, his landmark paper titled simply "A Mathematical Theory of Communication." Before that, no such theory existed. Suddenly, there it was, almost full grown.

3 To treat information scientifically, engineers needed to answer the kinds of questions they were asking about matter and energy: how much? How fast? For fundamental particles, an irreducible unit of measure, Shannon proposed the word "bits" — as shorthand (suitably compressed) for "binary digits." A bit is a choice. On or off. Yes or no. One or zero. Shannon saw that these pairs are all the same. Information is fungible: smoke signals and semaphores, telegraph and television, all channels carrying bits.

4 Back then, the main technologies for sending and storing information were analog, not digital, so this was far from obvious. Phonograph records embodied sound waves in vinyl, and Shannon's telephone-company employers trafficked mostly in wavy signals, too. Yet some interesting communications channels were not continuous but discrete: the telegraph and teletype.

5 Mainly, though, Shannon was thinking of electrical circuits. The marriage of on-off to yes-no meant that circuits could carry out something akin to logic. They could not only transmit bits; they could manipulate them. Not coincidentally, in that same year Bell Labs was preparing to announce a new invention: the transistor. "It is almost certain," Scientific American declared bravely in 1952, "that 'bit' will become common parlance in the field of information, as 'horsepower' is in the motor field." Sure enough, bits led to bytes and, inexorably, to kilobytes, megabytes, gigabytes and terabytes.

6 All that still rests on the theoretical foundation laid by this playful mathematician and electrical engineer. Shannon was born in rural Michigan in 1916, the son of a language teacher and a probate judge. He was an early and enthusiastic tinkerer in the new American style. Thomas Edison was his hero. Once he built a crude telegraph using a half-mile of barbed wire between his house and a friend's.

7 Nor did he stop playing just because he grew up. At Bell Labs, and then as a professor at the Massachusetts Institute of Technology, he amused colleagues by building juggling machines, unicycles, chess-playing computers and robotic turtles. He left a body of work comprising more than a hundred technical papers along the lines of "Reliable Circuits Using Less Reliable Relays," as well as others, not quite so influential, like "Scientific Aspects of Juggling" and "The Fourth-Dimensional Twist, or a Modest Proposal in Aid of the American Driver in England." He was also the author of "A Rubric on Rubik Cubics," which can be sung to the tune of "Ta-ra-ra-boom-de-ay."

8 When modern theorists worry about compressing data, maximizing bandwidth and coping with noise, they use the tools Shannon provided. They also keep in mind a paradox he emphasized from the very beginning — one that is either lovely or perverse, depending on your point of view. Information, in its new scientific sense, is utterly divorced from meaning. Chaotic systems, and strings of random numbers, altogether meaningless, are dense with information.

9 The medium, it turns out, is not the message. Words, sounds, pictures or gibberish — it's still just bits. ∎

[Note: This article in *The New York Times Magazine* commemorated the life of Claude Shannon, who died in 2001.]

Glossary

advent	arrival, beginning
akin	similar, like
analog	relating to a mechanism in which data is represented by continuously variable physical quantities; a device that operates with numbers represented by directly measurable quantities
chaotic	disordered, disorganized
commodity	product, goods
digital	transmitting data in the form of numerical units; a device that operates with numbers expressed directly as digits
discrete	separate, distinct; consisting of unconnected elements
divorced	separated, broken up
fungible	interchangeable
gibberish	unintelligible or meaningless language; nonsense
irreducible	impossible to restore to a simpler condition
juggling	keeping several objects in the air at the same time by tossing and catching them
medium	channel of communication, mode, means
paradox	contradiction in terms, inconsistency
parlance	manner of speaking, idiom, jargon
perverse	contrary, stubborn, wicked
random	chance, accidental, haphazard
robotic	having the characteristics of a device that automatically performs complicated repetitive tasks
unicycle	a vehicle that has a single wheel and is usually propelled by pedals

Discussion

1. What great contribution did Claude Shannon make?

2. Where does the word *bits* come from?

3. What is the difference between analog technology and digital technology?

4. What did Shannon understand about electrical circuits?

5. Thomas Edison was Shannon's hero. Who was Thomas Edison, and why is he famous?

6. Gleick writes that "information, in its new scientific sense, is utterly divorced from meaning. . . . The medium, it turns out, is not the message." Explain what Gleick means.

Teamwork

Working with a group, conduct a survey of 20 people to determine the level of customer satisfaction with cell phones in your area. First decide on the methodology of your survey (telephone or face-to-face interview), then develop a questionnaire with at least 10 questions to ask your survey participants. For example, you should ask each cell phone user the following questions.

1. How would you rate your cell phone service: excellent, very good, good, fair, or poor?

2. What brand of cell phone do you use?

3. What problems have you experienced in using it?

After you have completed your survey, write a brief report, including the survey's purpose, methodology, results, and the conclusions you have reached based on the questionnaire answers. Present your survey results in a table if possible.

Writing Assignments

1. Using the three *Computerworld* articles in this chapter, write a synthesis that discusses the future developments of information technology and business. Cite your sources in the in-text citation format (Keen 2). List your sources at the end of the paper as Works Cited and organize them according to their dates of publication, with the most recent source first. (See Appendix B, Synthesis.)

2. After reading the following articles from *The Economist,* write a synthesis that discusses the future of computing. (You may also find more current articles.) Access these articles by using the Internet business database ABI/Inform. Cite your sources in the in-text citation format ("Computing's New Shape" 11). List your sources at the end of the paper as Works Cited and alphabetize them according to the first word of the title. (See Appendix B, Synthesis.)

   • "Computing's New Shape." *The Economist,* 23 November 2002, 11–12.

   • "Nokia v Microsoft: The Fight for Global Dominance." *The Economist,* 23 November 2002, 61–63.

3. Peter G. W. Keen says that information technology will have an impact on business, society, and everyday life in four major areas in the future: energy and conservation, privacy, taxation, and consumer protection. Write an essay

in which you focus on one of these areas, the problems involved, and future solutions to these problems. Find information on these areas by searching the Internet. You can access online magazines, such as *Computerworld* (<http://www.computerworld.com>) and *Wired* (<http://www.wired.com>), and also use Google or your favorite search engine.

4. Write a research paper on the topic of information technology and the right to privacy. You may use the articles printed or mentioned in this chapter, including the expansion readings, as sources for your paper. Also find several recent sources. These books should be helpful.

Bergeron, Bryan P. *Dark Ages II: When the Digital Data Die*. Upper Saddle River, NJ: Prentice-Hall, 2002.

Denning, Peter J. *The Invisible Future: The Seamless Integration of Technology into Everyday Life*. New York: McGraw-Hill, 2002.

Le Goc, Michel. *Development Techniques for International Technology Transfer*. Westport, CT: Quorum Books, 2002.

Lewis, Michael. *Next: The Future Just Happened*. New York: Norton, 2001.

Expansion Readings

"Computer Viruses: Throttled at Birth." *The Economist,* 23 November 2002, 74–75.

"Computers and Language: The Elements of Style." *The Economist,* 9 February 2002, 70–71.

"E-Commerce: Profits at Last." *The Economist,* December 2002, 91–92.

Kenny, David, and John F. Marshall. "Contextual Marketing: The Real Business of the Internet." *Harvard Business Review* 78, no. 6 (November–December 2000): 119–25.

Oral Presentation

Working with a partner, give a 20-minute oral presentation to the class on one of the articles listed under Expansion Readings or an article of your choice on information technology. Summarize the article by including the author's thesis, major points, and supporting data and evaluate its strengths and weaknesses. Be prepared to answer questions on your topic. If you have the technical capability, use the presentation graphics program PowerPoint for your presentation. Otherwise, make at least one overhead to use on the overhead projector. (See Appendix B, Oral Presentation.)

Travels on the Web

The Internet offers a wide variety of opportunities to become involved in e-commerce.

1. Log on to the following well-known Web sites and consider the products that you can purchase there. Make a list of 10 books or other items you want to buy, including their prices.

   - Advanced Book Exchange: <http://www.abebooks.com>

   - Amazon.com: <http://www.amazon.com>

   - Barnes and Noble: <http://www.bn.com>

   - eBay Auctions: <http://www.ebay.com>

2. Rakuten, which is one of the most popular Internet shopping destinations for Japanese Web users, is a cybermall with 8,000 retailers. If you can read Japanese, log on to the Rakuten Web site (<http://www.rakuten.co.jp>) and consider the products you can purchase there. Print out a copy of the site's home page and bring it to class.

3. The Fair Trade Federation (FTF) works to provide fair wages and employment to economically disadvantaged artisans and farmers worldwide. Members of the Fair Trade Federation have a common goal: to live up to the fair-trade credo, which is to create a just and sustainable economic system through free trade. Log on to the FTF Web site (<http://www.fairtradefederation.org>) and read about the organization and its members. Make a list of members that are located outside of the United States.

4. The following Web sites, which are all members of the Fair Trade Federation (FTF), deal with international products. Log on to several of these sites and consider the products that you can purchase there. Make a list of the products that you find most appealing.

   - Carvings International: <http://www.carvings-international.com>

   - DGImports: <http://www.dgimports.org>

   - Mountcastle International Trading: <http://www.mountcastle.com>

   - Peace Coffee: <http://www.peacecoffee.com>

   - Susan Hebert Imports: <http://www.ecobre.com>

   - Tribal Fiber: <http://www.tribalfiber.com>

Chapter 8
Science

"The Biology Century Dawns"	"DNA: Handle with Care"
Harvard Business Review	Bronwyn Fryer
April 2001	*Harvard Business Review*
	April 2001

Preview   "The Biology Century Dawns"

Skimming

Skim the article quickly to find the following general information.

1. Read the title and all headings and look at any illustrations.

2. Read the first and second paragraphs, looking for the author's purpose and main idea.

3. Read the last paragraph, looking for a summary or conclusion.

4. Write a sentence containing your preliminary understanding of the main idea of the article.

Questioning

Answer the following questions and discuss your answers in class.

1. What science courses have you taken? Did you enjoy studying science?

2. Would you like to study genetics?

3. What is the meaning of cloning?

Scanning

Scan the article quickly to find the following specific information.

1. What field of science was the source of business innovation in the 20th century?

2. What is DNA, in essence?

3. How much data can a single gram of DNA theoretically store?

4. Why have researchers been studying ants, bees, and termites?

Vocabulary in Context

Read the following sentences and try to guess the meaning of the italicized words by using the context. Then replace the italicized words with synonyms (words or phrases that have nearly the same or similar meanings).

1. "The mapping of the human genome, largely complete, is the most obvious sign of biology's *ascendance*." (Paragraph 2)

2. "One new field, dubbed biomimicry or biomimetics, is already producing commercial *breakthroughs*." (Paragraph 3)

3. "Biological experimentation has, of course, always *stirred* controversy, particularly when it's pursued for profit." (Paragraph 5)

4. "Undoubtedly, cloning will be *ground zero* in this brave new world." (Paragraph 5)

Paraphrasing

After reading the article, reread the sentences under Vocabulary in Context. Now rewrite them using your own words. Change the vocabulary and sentence structure, but do not change the author's intended meaning or paraphrase any technical terms. There are several ways of paraphrasing each sentence.

The
Biology
Century
Dawns

1 FROM THE INTERNAL COMBUSTION ENGINE to the atomic bomb to the microprocessor, advances in physics underpinned many of the product breakthroughs that shaped life – and business – in the twentieth century. But the dominance of physics as the source of business innovation may soon be broken. It's looking more and more like the twenty-first will be the century of biology.

2 The mapping of the human genome, largely complete, is the most obvious sign of biology's ascendance. As Juan Enriquez and Ray Goldberg show in "Transforming Life, Transforming Business: The Life-Science Revolution" (HBR, March–April 2000), our new understanding of the code of life is transforming many industries, from agriculture and chemicals to health care and pharmaceuticals. And that's just the beginning. Genetically modified organisms, the authors argue, will come to play central roles in mining, energy, defense, cosmetics, and many other industries. Since DNA is in essence only another form of software code, computer processing and the Internet will both influence and be influenced by scientists' progress in genetics.

3 But it would be wrong to think that genetics is the whole story. As companies realize the treasure trove hiding in the life sciences, a great deal of research and development money will flow into biology, creating all sorts of revolutionary products. One new field, dubbed biomimicry or biomimetics, is already producing commercial breakthroughs. At last year's Olympic Games in Sydney, for example, many swimmers wore bodysuits made from a material with exceptionally low drag that researchers had developed by mimicking sharkskin. Similarly, scientists have been studying leaves to build more efficient solar cells, and they believe that understanding and adapting the way butterfly wings dissipate heat could lead to a novel cooling system to prevent computer chips from overheating. Some biologists even believe that DNA molecules could one day be used for storing and processing data – a single gram of DNA can theoretically store as much data as one trillion CDs!

4 Beyond product innovation, biological research may help increase the efficiency of human organizations. In the new field of swarm intelligence, researchers have been studying social insects such as ants, bees, and termites to understand the principles and behaviors of self-organizing systems. Recent research in this field may have enormous implications for how companies can organize themselves and develop more effective business strategies.

5 Biological experimentation has, of course, always stirred controversy, particularly when it's pursued for profit. Just think of animal testing and genetically modified foods. The controversies are certain to multiply and intensify. Undoubtedly, cloning will be ground zero in this brave new world. The cloning of humans is already well within our grasp and, as Brian Alexander writes in "(You)^2" (*Wired*, February 2001), may be under way at this moment in some secret laboratory.

6 Get ready for the ultimate in luxury goods: a whole new version of you.

Reprint RO104H

HARVARD BUSINESS REVIEW

Glossary

ascendance	rise; domination
breakthroughs	sudden advances in knowledge or techniques
cloning	a scientific method in which an individual is grown from a cell of its parent and is genetically identical to the parent
dawns	begins
dissipate	to break up and scatter
DNA	deoxyribonucleic acid; any of various nucleic acids that are the molecular basis of heredity
dubbed	called
genetics	a branch of biology that deals with the heredity and variation of organisms
ground zero	the center or origin of rapid, intense activity or change
implications	suggestions; possible significance
mimicking	imitating closely
molecule	the smallest particle of a substance that retains all the properties of the substance and is composed of one or more atoms
stirred	brought into debate; raised
swarm	a great number of insects massed together and in motion
underpinned	served as a foundation for; supported

Comprehension

1. What field of science will break the dominance of physics as the source of business innovation in the 21st century?

2. What is the most obvious sign of biology's ascendance?

3. Why will computer processing and the Internet both influence and be influenced by scientists' progress in genetics?

4. What is an example of a commercial breakthrough produced by the new field of biomimicry?

5. Why do some biologists believe that DNA molecules could one day be used for storing and processing data?

6. What are the business implications from research in the field of swarm intelligence?

7. What does the author predict about biological experimentation when pursued for profit?

8. How do you feel about reproductive cloning, which is the cloning of a human being? Explain your answer.

Analysis

Circle the letter next to the best answer(s). Justify your choices with quotations from the text.

1. What is the main idea of the article, and in which paragraph(s) is it stated?

   a. The 21st century will be dominated by biology, primarily as a result of the developments in genetics.

   b. Business will be affected by the numerous innovations in the field of genetics.

   c. Major controversies over the ethics of cloning may result in legislation that outlaws cloning.

   d. When DNA is completely understood, scientists will be able to use it for storing computer data.

2. What is the meaning of the italicized word in this sentence in paragraph 6? "Get ready for the *ultimate* in luxury goods: a whole new version of you."

   a. most expensive

   b. most popular

   c. most extreme

   d. most common

3. What can be inferred from this statement in paragraph 5? "Undoubtedly, cloning will be ground zero in this brave new world."

   a. Advances in biology in the 21st century may include cloning.

   b. Cloning experiments will have to start from an advanced level of research.

   c. The new world of the future will be brave enough to reject cloning.

   d. The center of controversy in the future will be cloning.

4. The author's writing style in this article is _____ and _____ .

   a. simple

   b. complex

   c. businesslike

   d. poetic

5. The tone of the article is _____ and _____.

   a. positive

   b. negative

   c. judgmental

   d. nonjudgmental

6. What overall method of development is used in this article?

   a. chronologically describing a process

   b. supporting a thesis with examples

   c. justifying an argument by contrasting two approaches

   d. refuting the assumptions of an argument

7. The author concludes her article with one short sentence: "Get ready for the ultimate in luxury goods: a whole new version of you." What is your response to this statement?

   a. disbelief

   b. doubt

   c. concern

   d. excitement

DNA: Handle with Care

The genetics boom is upon us,
promising everything from cures for
inherited diseases to smarter children.
But companies must tread carefully as
the ethical debate plays out.

Ten years ago, the U.S. Congress launched a $3 billion taxpayer-funded initiative to uncover the links between genes and disease. Labeled by proponents as biology's moon shot and by detractors as science's next Manhattan Project, the Human Genome Project promises to rev-  *olutionize testing and treatment for thousands of genetic diseases. It also promises to spawn scores of new business opportunities. The coming flood of genetic data also raises profound ethical questions for companies. In her new book,* Future Perfect: Confronting Decisions about Genetics *(Columbia University Press, 2001), Lori B. Andrews, a professor at the Chicago-Kent College of Law and director of the Institute for Science, Law, and Technology at the Illinois Institute of Technology, examines the legal and ethical issues surrounding genomics. HBR senior editor Bronwyn Fryer recently asked Andrews what executives need to know about the opportunities and risks.*

1 We often hear about the promise of genetic testing and treatment in the medical arena. Aside from medical applications, are there other business opportunities?

2 Absolutely. The genetic gold rush is on, and it's shaping everything from entertainment to law enforcement, from architecture to retailing. DNA is already becoming the new currency of identification. Consider genetic tagging, for example. At the Sydney Olympics, the tags on official caps, shirts, and other merchandise were printed with special ink that had been treated with one athlete's DNA. When you scanned the label with a handheld device, you could tell whether the merchandise was the genuine article or a knock-off. Anything that requires positive identification – from driver's licenses to works of art – can be tagged in this way. There will also be many opportunities for product breakthoughs. One inventor is working on a new kind of roof developed from biological materials; it sheds old shingles and grows new ones.

3 And I think we'll see a lot of new services that provide people with genetic information while protecting their privacy. You might go into a gene booth at a mall, give a blood sample – anonymously – and find out on the spot whether you carry the gene for, say, cystic fibrosis. This is information you may not necessarily want a doctor to know, but it may help you make a decision about whether or not to have a child.

4 Why wouldn't you want a doctor to know you're carrying such a gene?

5 Because you don't control your own medical information. Doctors share it with insurance companies, and insurance companies can share it with employers. In an American Management Association study of large and midsize companies conducted last year, one-

In an American Management Association study of large and midsize companies conducted last year, one-third admitted to collecting genetic information about their employees.

third admitted to collecting genetic information about their employees. Seven percent said they use this information in hiring and promotion decisions, despite the fact that discriminating against someone on the basis of a genetic disease violates the Americans with Disabilities Act and the employee's privacy. But the ADA does not prohibit employers from "peeking" at their employees' genes. One California employer, for example, surreptitiously tested its African-American employees for the sickle-cell anemia gene.

6 Moreover, the laws that have been adopted in recent years to protect against genetic discrimination in insurance have huge loopholes. Thirty-three states prohibit denying people health insurance based on certain types of

genetic information. But most of those laws do not protect people from discrimination based on genetic information about their relatives. So in 25 of the 33 states, insurers can easily circumvent the reach of the laws by basing their decisions on family histories. Moreover, state prohibitions on genetic discrimination don't apply to self-funded insurance plans, yet 85% of larger companies – those that have more than 5,000 employees – are self-insured.

7 What steps should companies take to avoid accusations of discrimination? And what should companies developing new genetic technologies do to avoid ethical quagmires?

8 Since privacy can't be assured – and since genetic predictions are not foolproof – most companies should avoid using genetic information when making decisions about employees. There's no good reason for it, even when companies act out of the best intentions. An airline might argue, for instance, that to ensure flight safety, it wants pilots to undergo genetic testing for Huntington's disease, a neurological disorder that causes involuntary movements. But such tests could ground pilots years before they show any symptoms. And the American Medical Association says it is not necessary to do predictive testing; the physical exams given to pilots will catch any neurological problems before they cause flying risks. Worse yet, a healthy pilot who finds out at 30 that he has the Huntington's gene may face severe psychological trauma.

9 Companies developing genetic applications should establish an ethics advisory panel with a human face. By this I mean gathering experts not only in law, biology, and philosophy but also in the human sciences – for instance, psychologists, sociologists, anthropologists. The reason for this is that there are cultural, religious, and social taboos against using human biological materials, as we've seen from the controversy surrounding the use of fetal tissue in developing treatments for Parkinson's disease. Companies will need to disclose the use of such materials and meet the inevitable protests with some sensitivity. Witness what happened in the area of animal research. Initially, protesters were concerned about animal welfare. When companies ignored those concerns, a much more radical animal rights movement formed. Instead of avoiding difficult issues or brushing off objections, companies will have to meet them head-on.

Reprint F0104D

APRIL 2001

Discussion

1. Describe the Human Genome Project and its effects.

2. What business opportunities have developed in regard to scientific advances in the field of genetics?

3. What loopholes exist in the laws that protect against genetic discrimination in insurance?

4. Why should companies avoid using genetic information when making decisions about employees?

5. What advice does Andrews give to companies developing genetic applications?

6. Would you choose to undergo genetic testing? Explain your answer.

7. What is your opinion on allowing companies to collect genetic information about their employees?

Teamwork

Working with a group, do Internet research on the ethical ramifications of new developments in science, particularly the ethics of human cloning. This controversial issue belongs to the new field of bioethics. In your research, consider the fact that therapeutic cloning and human reproductive cloning have different purposes.

- Reproductive cloning would result in the production of a baby. For example, reproductive cloning would allow a married couple that cannot have biological children to have a child through the process of cloning.

- Therapeutic (research) cloning would lead to human embryo-derived therapies that would benefit sick or injured people. For example, therapeutic cloning could provide sources of embryo stem cells, which might be used to treat people with injuries to the spinal cord or serious diseases.

Go online to find articles from newspapers and magazines that focus on this controversy. (Seven articles are mentioned below in Writing Assignments 1.) Read several articles that provide a variety of perspectives on human cloning. After discussing the articles in your group, draw up a list of arguments and counterarguments on the topic of cloning.

Writing Assignments

1. Write a synthesis on the topic of the ethics of human cloning. Base your synthesis on several of the articles listed below or on recent journal articles. Cite your sources in the in-text citation format (Trefil 38). List your sources at the end of

the paper as Works Cited and alphabetize them according to the authors' last names. You may use this thesis: Although scientists have discovered how to clone a human being, human cloning must not be allowed because, according to the World Health Assembly, it is "ethically unacceptable and contrary to human integrity and morality."*

- Alexander, Brian. "(You)^2." *Wired* (February 2001): <http://www.wired.com>.

- Cibelli, Jose B., Robert P. Lanza, Michael D. West, and Carol Ezzell. "The First Human Cloned Embryo." *Scientific American* (January 2002): 44–48+. <http://www.scientificamerican.com>.

- Fukuyama, Francis. "Gene Regime." *Foreign Policy* (March–April 2002): 56–63: <http://www.foreignpolicy.com>.

- Kass, Leon R. Preventing a Brave New World." *New Republic* (21 May 2001): 30–39. <http://www.thenewrepublic.com>.

- Stix, Gary. "Why Clones?" *Scientific American* (February 2002): 18–19: <http://www.scientificamerican.com>.

- Talbot, Margaret. "Jack or Jill?" *Atlantic Monthly* (March 2002): 25. <http://www.theatlanticmonthly.com>.

- Trefil, James. "Brave New World." *Smithsonian* (December 2001): 38–46. <http://www.smithsonianmag.com>.

2. Working with a partner, conduct an interview with a scientist or a professional who is knowledgeable about the topic of the human genome. (See "DNA: Handle with Care" in this chapter for an example of an interview.) Use a tape recorder during the interview and write up the information as a report in three sections: introduction, interview questions and answers, and conclusion. You may use the questions listed below in your interview.

- What is the human genome?

- How is it possible to decode the genome?

- What major advances will take place in the future in the field of genetics?

- Should scientists be allowed to engage in cloning?

- What medical guidelines should be established for cloning?

3. Write an essay discussing the theory of swarm intelligence as it can be applied to business. Use the Internet search engine Google or the Internet business data-

---

*Press Release WHA19, 14 May 1997, "World Health Assembly States Its Position on Cloning in Human Reproduction," <http://www.who.int/archives/inf-pr-1997/en/97wha9.html>.

base ABI/Inform to find articles on this topic. You can also find the following articles in the library.

- Bonabeau, Eric, and Christopher Meyer. "Swarm Intelligence: A Whole New Way to Think about Business." *Harvard Business Review* 79, no. 5 (May 2001): 106–14. <http://www.hbsp.Harvard.edu>.

- Lloyd, Tom. "When Swarm Intelligence Beats Brainpower." *The Telegraph* (6 June 2001). <http://www.telegraph.co.uk>.

4. Write a research paper on the topic of the ethics of modern genetics. You may use the articles printed or mentioned in this chapter, including the expansion readings, as sources for your paper. Also find several recent sources. These books should be helpful.

Andrews, Lori B. *Future Perfect: Confronting Decisions about Genetics.* New York: Columbia University Press, 2001.

Barash, David P. *Revolutionary Biology: The New, Gene-Centered View of Life.* New Brunswick, NJ: Transaction Publishers, 2001.

Dawkins, Richard. *The Extended Phenotype: The Long Reach of the Gene.* Oxford and New York: Oxford University Press, 1999.

Fox, Michael W. *Bringing Life to Ethics: Global Bioethics for a Humane Society.* Albany: State University of New York Press, 2001.

Fukuyama, Francis. *Our Posthuman Future: Consequences of the Biotechnology Revolution.* New York: Farrar, Strauss, and Giroux, 2002.

Kass, Leon R., and James Q. Wilson. *The Ethics of Human Cloning.* Washington, D.C.: AEI Press, 1998.

Lauritzen, Paul, ed. *Cloning and the Future of Human Embryo Research.* Oxford and New York: Oxford University Press, 2001.

Tudge, Colin. *The Impact of the Gene, from Mendel's Peas to Designer Babies.* New York: Hill and Wang, 2001.

Expansion Readings

"Biology and Politics: The Great Cloning Debate." *The Economist,* 11 May 2002, 29–30.

Enriquez, Juan, and Ray Goldberg. "Transforming Life, Transforming Business: The Life-Science Revolution." *Harvard Business Review* 78, no. 2 (March–April 2000): 96–104.

"How Far to Go: Human Reproductive Cloning." *The Economist,* 4 January 2003, 11.

"Genomics: Ticket to Ride." *The Economist,* 13 January 2001, 78.

"Neuroscience: The Future of Mind Control." *The Economist,* 25 May 2002, 11.

"Neuroscience: Open Your Mind." *The Economist,* 25 May 2002, 77–79.

"Science and Technology: Copy or Counterfeit?" *The Economist,* 4 January 2003, 61–62.

Oral Presentation

Working with a partner, give a 20-minute oral presentation to the class on one of the articles listed under Expansion Readings or an article of your choice on scientific advances. Summarize the article by including the author's thesis, major points, and supporting data, and evaluate its strengths and weaknesses. Be prepared to answer questions on your topic. If you have the technical capability, use the presentation graphics program PowerPoint for your presentation. Otherwise, make at least one overhead to use on the overhead projector. (See Appendix B, Oral Presentation.)

Travels on the Web

1. The Internet offers numerous opportunities to read more about advances in science and how they will affect our future society in fields ranging from agriculture to business to health. Log on to the following Web sites to find recent information on this topic. Print out the most interesting pages and bring them to class to share with your classmates.

   • Council for Biotechnology Information: <http://www.whybiotech.com>

   • National Institutes of Health: <http://www.nih.gov>

   • *New Scientist* magazine: <http://www.newscientist.com>

   • *Scientific American* magazine: <http://www.scientificamerican.com>

   • World Health Organization: <http://www.who.int>

2. Research on decoding the human genome is being carried out by the U.S. government at the National Institutes of Health and by Celera Genomics, a private company. Log on to the following Web sites to read about the latest developments.

   • The National Institutes of Health: <http://www.nih.gov>. The National Human Genome Research Institute is part of the National Institutes of Health in Bethesda, Maryland. Click on Institutes, Centers and Offices, and select the National Human Genome Research Institute (NHGRI). Read about the research that is being done and write a brief summary of the most up-to-date information.

   • Celera Genomics: <http://www.celera.com>. Celera Genomics was founded in May 1998 to create gene maps of humans and other organisms. It has been at the forefront of research on sequencing the human genome. On Celera's Home Page, select Therapeutic Discovery. Read about Celera's projects and write a brief summary of the most recent research.

Chapter 9

Health

Preview   "For Developing Countries, Health Is Wealth"

Skimming

Skim the article quickly to find the following general information.

1. Read the title and all headings and look at any illustrations.

2. Read the first and last paragraphs, looking for the author's purpose and main idea.

3. Read the last paragraph, looking for a summary or conclusion.

4. Write a sentence containing your preliminary understanding of the main idea of the article.

Questioning

Answer the following questions and discuss your answers in class.

1. Does your native country's government provide adequate health care services for all its citizens?

2. How serious is the AIDS pandemic in your native country?

Scanning

Scan the article quickly to find the following specific information.

1. According to the World Health Organization (WHO) commission, what is the minimum yearly cost of essential health treatments in developing countries?

2. What is the average per-capita health spending in the poorest countries?

3. What is the principle of differential pricing?

4. How many lives per year could be saved by 2010 if the WHO commission's recommendations are enacted?

Vocabulary in Context

Read the following sentences and try to guess the meaning of the italicized words by using the context. Then replace the italicized words with synonyms (words or phrases that have nearly the same or similar meanings).

1. "Millions of people in developing countries around the globe lack this *blessing* and basic freedom." (Paragraph 1)

2. "For each of these conditions, *interventions* that can dramatically improve health outcomes already exist." (Paragraph 2)

3. "This sounds like a trivial amount compared with average *per-capita* annual health spending of $2,000 in high-income countries." (Paragraph 4)

4. "A sustained, cooperative effort to improve health in developing countries would yield benefits that far *exceed* its costs." (Paragraph 7)

5. Because reduced disability *translates* into higher productivity, the total benefits would be larger. (Paragraph 8)

BY LAURA D'ANDREA TYSON

FOR DEVELOPING COUNTRIES, HEALTH IS WEALTH

LIFE SAVINGS: Health-care investments of $30 to $40 per person could yield $186 billion yearly in economic benefits to the poorer nations

Laura D'Andrea Tyson is dean of London Business School.

1 Lord Chesterfield observed that good health is the first and greatest of all blessings and the first of all liberties. Millions of people in developing countries around the globe lack this blessing and basic freedom. What's more, their poor health both reflects their poverty and contributes to it. Economists have found a strong correlation between better health and faster economic growth—a correlation that holds up even after accounting for other factors that explain national differences in economic progress. Providing adequate health services to the world's poorest citizens could save millions of lives each year, reduce poverty, and promote development. Laudable as this goal is, can it be achieved? A carefully researched report from a World Health Organization commission chaired by Jeffrey Sachs of Harvard University—on which I served—concludes that the answer is yes.

2 A relatively small number of identifiable conditions—such as malaria, tuberculosis, childhood infectious diseases, maternal and perinatal nutritional deficiencies, and HIV/AIDS—are the main causes of illness and high mortality rates in developing countries. For each of these conditions, interventions that can dramatically improve health outcomes already exist. Most such interventions are not technically exacting and can be delivered by local health centers, working with state and private health-care providers and nongovernmental organizations.

3 Spending on health in the developing countries must increase significantly over the next decade, however. The WHO commission—known formally as the Commission on Macroeconomics & Health—estimates that the minimum cost of essential treatments, including those necessary to fight the AIDS pandemic, is between $30 and $40 per person per year in those countries.

4 This sounds like a trivial amount compared with average per-capita annual health spending of $2,000 in high-income countries. But it is considerably more than the average per-capita health spending of $13 per year in the poorest countries. Even if developing countries significantly increase the resources they devote to health and use such resources more efficiently, the WHO commission concludes that developed countries must contribute an additional $27 billion per year by 2007. This increase is large compared with their current contribution of about $6 billion per year, but it would amount to only about 0.1% of the gross domestic product of the developed countries, leaving ample resources for other developmental goals.

5 At the same time, the WHO commission acknowledges that efficient delivery of development assistance for health will require new organizations such as the Global Fund to Fight AIDS, Tuberculosis, & Malaria. Commission members applaud the establishment of this fund and endorse the U.N. recommendation that its resources be scaled up to $8 billion a year by 2007. The commission also urges each developing country to establish a temporary commission to formulate a strategy for increasing domestic spending on health and for extending essential health services to all citizens. The WHO has pledged to work with these national organizations to establish operational targets and a framework for the effective use of donor aid.

6 Drug companies, too, have a crucial role to play in the fight to improve the health of the poor. The WHO commission recommends that the global pharmaceutical industry formulate voluntary guidelines to ensure that essential medicines be made available to developing countries at the lowest viable commercial prices. Such guidelines should recognize the principle of differential pricing—meaning lower prices in low-income countries as the norm—and should provide for licensing of patented drugs to generic producers in developing countries. In addition, donor countries should negotiate with drug companies for the lowest prices on behalf of countries too small and poor to negotiate on their own. At the same time, developing and donor countries must work together to ensure that lower prices and generic licensing in poorer countries do not undermine market pricing and patent protection in high-income markets.

7 A sustained, cooperative effort to improve health in developing countries would yield benefits that far exceed its costs. The Commission on Macroeconomics & Health predicts that enactment of its recommendations could save about 8 million lives per year by 2010. The 8 million deaths prevented would translate into about 330 million disability-adjusted life years, a measure of more years of life and fewer years of disabilities.

8 Conservatively, each disability-adjusted life year saved would yield the economic benefit of one year's per-capita income in a developing country. The direct economic benefits of saving 330 million disability-adjusted life years would be around $186 billion each year. Because reduced disability translates into higher productivity, the total benefits would be larger. On economic and humanitarian grounds, the case is compelling for the world community to invest in the health of its poorest citizens. ∎

Glossary

ample	generous or more than adequate in amount
blessing	something that brings happiness, prosperity, or good fortune
correlation	mutual relationship; causal relationship
disabilities	physical or mental impairments or injuries
donor	one that gives, donates, or presents something
exacting	demanding; requiring precision
exceed	to go beyond, surpass; to be greater than
generic	general; having a nonproprietary name
interventions	preventions of illness
laudable	worthy of praise, commendable
mortality	death
pandemic	an outbreak of a disease occurring over a wide geographic area
patent	a license to make, use, or sell something
patented	protected by a patent
per-capita	for each person
perinatal	around the time of birth
productivity	efficiency of output and production; the calculated rate of making goods; creation of economic value or production of goods and services
translates	results in, leads to
trivial	ordinary, of little worth
undermine	to weaken or ruin
viable	financially sustainable

Comprehension

1. Explain what economists have discovered about the relationship between health and economic growth.

2. What would result from providing adequate health care services to the world's poorest citizens?

3. List the main causes of illness and high mortality rates in developing countries.

4. What is the formal name of the WHO commission that researched and wrote the report on health care in developing countries?

5. How much money do developed countries currently contribute to developing countries for health care per year?

6. How much additional money per year did the WHO commission recommend that developed countries contribute by 2007?

7. Describe the purpose of the national organizations that the WHO commission urged each developing country to establish.

8. What recommendations did the WHO commission make concerning drug companies?

9. What benefits would result from improving health in developing countries?

10. Define the meaning of the term *disability-adjusted life years*.

11. What are the direct economic benefits of saving 330 million disability-adjusted life years?

12. Does the world community have a moral obligation to invest in the health care of its poorest citizens? Justify your answer.

Analysis

Circle the letter next to the best answer(s). Justify your choices with quotations from the text.

1. What is the main idea of the article, and in which paragraph(s) is it stated?

   a. The global pharmaceutical industry should lower its prices for all consumers to ensure that people will be healthy.

   b. Developing countries that establish commissions on health services will be given grants from the WHO to support their efforts.

   c. The world community should contribute money to improve the health services in developing countries for both economic and humanitarian reasons.

   d. Reduced disability results in higher productivity in a country, which increases total benefits.

2. What is the meaning of the italicized word in this sentence in paragraph 8? "On economic and humanitarian grounds, the case is *compelling* for the world community to invest in the health of its poorest citizens."

   a. clear   c. logical

   b. appealing   d. convincing

3. We can infer the following from this sentence in paragraph 4: "Even if developing countries significantly increase the resources they devote to health and use such resources more efficiently, the WHO commission concludes that developed countries must contribute an additional $27 billion per year by 2007."

   a. Providing adequate health care services to poor countries could save millions of lives yearly.

   b. Poor countries lack sufficient financial resources to invest in improving their health care services.

c. High-income countries give more importance to health care services than do low-income countries.

d. Developed countries have an obligation to help developing countries improve their standard of living.

4. The author's writing style in this article is _____ and _____ .

   a. formal   c. technical

   b. informal   d. nontechnical

5. The tone of this article is _____ and _____ .

   a. neutral   c. authoritative

   b. persuasive   d. tentative

6. What overall method of development is used in this article?

   a. attacking the assumptions of an argument

   b. evaluating the advantages and disadvantages of a plan

   c. chronologically describing a problem

   d. supporting an argument by enumerating specific proposals

7. What techniques does the author use to get the reader's attention in the first paragraph?

   a. an indirect quotation   c. repetition of words

   b. metaphors   d. definitions of terms

Preview   "Can We Learn to Beat the Reaper?"

Skimming

Skim the article quickly to find the following general information.

1. Read the title and all headings and look at any illustrations.

2. Read the first and last paragraphs, looking for the author's purpose and main idea.

3. Read the last paragraph, looking for a summary or conclusion.

4. Write a sentence containing your preliminary understanding of the main idea of the article.

Questioning

Answer the following questions and discuss your answers in class.

1. What do you predict will be the average life expectancy by the end of the 21st century?

2. Do you want to live to the age of 100?

3. Do you know anyone who is older than 90? If so, who?

Scanning

Scan the article quickly to find the following specific information.

1. What was the average life-span early in the evolution of *Homo sapiens?*

2. How have all the gains in length of life been achieved?

3. What happens once you start to immortalize a cell?

4. How many centenarians were there in the United States in 2002?

Vocabulary in Context

Read the following sentences and try to guess the meaning of the italicized words by using the context. Then replace the italicized words with synonyms (words or phrases that have nearly the same or similar meanings).

1. "For scientists and physicians, there has been no goal more *seductive* than extending human life, and none that has been harder to achieve." (Paragraph 2)

2. "For a long time, many scientists believed that the human life-span was *infinitely* extendible." (Paragraph 3)

3. "Even before the human genome was *mapped,* scientists found genes that appeared to play a role in how cells age." (Paragraph 7)

4. Other *purported* life extenders have problems too. (Paragraph 9)

5. "Taking such putative anti-aging nostrums as human growth hormone or DHEA—a hormone *precursor*—may increase the risk of certain diseases." (Paragraph 9)

Paraphrasing

After reading the article, reread the sentences under Vocabulary in Context. Now rewrite them using your own words. Change the vocabulary and sentence structure, but do not change the author's intended meaning or paraphrase any technical terms. There are several ways of paraphrasing each sentence.

By JEFFREY KLUGER

1 GIVE THE HUMAN BODY HALF A CHANCE AND before you know it, it tries to die. If it's not cancer, it's heart disease; if it's not heart disease, it's stroke. With all the ways the body can do itself in, you would almost think it wanted to end it all. The fact is, it does.

2 Before earthly organisms even got a chance to live, they had to agree to some pretty punishing terms: you're born, you grow up, you produce some young, then you get out of the way and leave room for the generation coming along. Animals and plants have no trouble honoring the deal; humans, however, keep trying to change it, hoping to hang around longer than nature envisioned—or our bodies can manage. For scientists and physicians, there has been no goal more seductive than extending human life, and none that has been harder to achieve. Only now are we learning that it is a goal that may forever be out of our reach.

3 For a long time, many scientists believed that the human life-span was infinitely extendible. The average life-span early in the evolution of *Homo sapiens* is thought to have been just 20 years. By the beginning of the 20th century, that figure more than doubled—to a still brief 47. Since then, however, life expectancy has been exploding, with people in the developed world now able to live deep into their 70s and often beyond.

4 But life expectancy (the number of years you can expect to live before being claimed by illness or accident) is not life-span (the maximum age to which the perfectly maintained, disease-free body could remain alive before it simply wore out and broke down). All the gains in length of life have been achieved by treating diseases that used to kill us in youth or, at best, in what we now consider our middle years—and are thus gains in life expectancy. Meanwhile, life-span has remained fixed at a hard ceiling of about 125 years.

5 "If science cured every known disease of the elderly, you'd add only 15 years to current life expectancy," says Dr. Leonard Hayflick, professor of anatomy at the University of California, San Francisco, and author of *How and Why We Age*. Accidents and age-related loss of organ function would then start claiming the old—though some, at least in theory, would reach the 125-year mark.

6 But many people continue to believe that life-spans can be pushed further still. If the aged body breaks down, it must be because something in the cells directs it to do that, and if that thing could be found and shut off, couldn't we live indefinitely? The short answer is yes. The long answer is that the short answer is way too simple.

7 Even before the human genome was mapped, scientists found genes that appeared to play a role in how cells age. More significantly, they discovered a cufflike structure—dubbed a telomere—at the end of chromosomes that shortens each time a cell divides. When the telomere all but disappears, the cell stops dividing, and the cell line dies out. A naturally occurring enzyme, called telomerase, can maintain telomere length in some cells.

8 But things aren't as easy as simply dosing a cell with telomerase. Once you immortalize the cell, it will start to divide indefinitely—just the thing cancer cells do to such destructive effect. In a recent, unrelated study that hints at the problem, scientists found that an enzyme known as P53 that has the power to suppress tumors may also shorten life expectancy. As for genetic manipulation, it is theoretically possible to re-engineer senescence genes or introduce proteins that block their operation, but with what could be thousands of genes involved in aging, that may be as far beyond biologists as building a starship is beyond rocket scientists. "That would be a long way off," admits Robert Butler, head of the International Longevity Center in New York City.

9 Other purported life extenders have problems too. Taking such putative anti-aging nostrums as human growth hormone or DHEA—a hormone precursor—may increase the risk of certain diseases. Restricting caloric intake by as much as 30% has lengthened life in some caged animals. But caged animals are not feral humans, and who among the already healthy is going to slash food intake by a third anyway?

10 The quieter news is that while immortality is beyond us, that 125-year life-span is still out there beckoning. Eliminating the dietary and lifestyle habits that are setting you up for the heart attack that is going to kill you at 50 can, in a blink, extend your life by decades. Doing the same thing on a global level—and throwing in progress on disease treatment too—can cause the life expectancy of the entire species to inch further and further out. There are about 50,000 centenarians in the U.S.—a blip in a country of close to 300 million people. But over time, those tens of thousands could creep into the millions. It takes work to join their ranks, but it is work more and more people may be willing to do. ∎

Can We Learn to Beat the Reaper?

Science has been winning battles against old age, but can it win the war?

Glossary

caloric   relating to calories, units expressing energy-producing value in food when oxidized in the body

ceiling   an upper limit

centenarians   persons who are 100 years old or older

chromosome   DNA-controlling body that has most or all of the genes of the individual

dosing   giving a dose to, treating

enzyme   complex protein produced by living cells

feral   untamed, uncultivated, wild

gene   the functional unit of inheritance controlling transmission and expression of traits

genome   the genetic matter of an organism

Homo sapiens   humankind

immortalize   to free from death; to make immortal

infinitely   endlessly; extending indefinitely

life-span   the duration of existence of an individual

mapped   located on a chromosome; delineated

nostrums   questionable remedies

organ   bodily part performing a function

precursor   a substance from which another substance is formed

purported   alleged, supposed

putative   commonly accepted or supposed

reaper   a metaphor for death (the grim reaper); one who harvests a crop

seductive   attractive, tempting

senescence   aging

slash   to reduce sharply, to cut

species   the human race, human beings

suppress   to inhibit the growth or development of

telomere   the natural end of a chromosome

Discussion

1. What has been the most seductive goal for scientists and physicians?

2. What are we learning now about this goal?

3. What is the life expectancy for people in the developed world?

4. Explain the difference between life expectancy and life-span.

5. If science cured every disease of the elderly, how many years would this add to current life expectancy?

6. Why won't dosing a cell with the enzyme telomerase extend the human life-span?

7. Why is genetic manipulation not a possible way to reduce the aging process?

8. Name other methods that have been mentioned as alleged life extenders.

9. Explain what we can do to extend our lives by decades.

10. What can we do on a global level to extend the life expectancy of the entire species?

11. Do you eat a healthy diet and live a healthy lifestyle?

12. What changes would you be willing to make in your lifestyle if these changes could extend your life? Explain your answer.

Analysis

Circle the letter next to the best answer(s). Justify your choices with quotations from the text.

1. What is the main idea of the article, and in which paragraph(s) is it stated?

   a. Although life expectancy rates may increase in the future, the human life-span of 125 years is unlikely to increase.

   b. Life expectancy of the human species has been increasing steadily in every century.

   c. Medical advances in curing diseases that previously killed human beings at a young age have extended life expectancy.

   d. Genetic manipulation will eventually make it possible for humans to live longer.

2. What is the meaning of the italicized word in this sentence in paragraph 2? "Animals and plants have no trouble honoring the deal; humans, however, keep trying to change it, hoping to hang around longer than nature *envisioned*—or our bodies can manage."

   a. demanded

   b. determined

   c. imagined

   d. allowed

3. We can infer the following from this sentence in paragraph 10: "The quieter news is that while immortality is beyond us, that 125-year life-span is still out there beckoning."

    a. Although humans cannot achieve eternal life, they have the possibility to extend their life expectancy.

    b. It is impossible that the human life-span could be extended beyond 125 years.

    c. Many scientific advances will be made in the future in the area of longevity and life-span.

    d. Even though scientists are pessimistic, human beings will continue to search for eternal life.

4. The author's writing style in this article is _____ and _____ .

    a. impersonal

    b. personal

    c. idiomatic

    d. formal

5. The tone of this article is _____ and _____ .

    a. subjective

    b. objective

    c. colloquial

    d. scholarly

6. What overall method of development is used in this article?

    a. analyzing a scientific database

    b. defining a technical process

    c. enumerating the steps in a procedure

    d. explaining the solution to a problem

7. What techniques does the author use to get the reader's attention in the introduction (paragraphs 1 and 2)?

    a. quotations

    b. humor

    c. parallelism

    d. statistics

Teamwork

Working in a group, investigate the current statistics on life expectancy. Log on to the Web site of the World Health Organization at <http://www.who.int>. Click on Search and type the words *life expectancy*. After completing your research, write a report that covers the following points.

1. A comparison of life expectancy rates in developed countries and developing countries

2. The difference between male and female life expectancy rates

3. The increase in life expectancy rates since 1800

4. The projected increase in life expectancy rates in the 21st century

5. The World Health Organization's rankings of countries based on a new way to calculate healthy life expectancy using Disability Adjusted Life Expectancy (DALE)

Writing Assignments

1. In "For Developing Countries, Health Is Wealth," printed in this chapter, Laura D'Andrea Tyson writes that "a sustained, cooperative effort to improve health in developing countries would yield benefits that far exceed its costs." Make a list of the arguments used by the author to support her belief. Then write a 400-word summary of "For Developing Countries, Health Is Wealth."

2. Write a synthesis based on "For Developing Countries, Health Is Wealth," printed in this chapter, and the article "The Health of Nations" from *The Economist* (December 22, 2001, pp. 83–84). Use the Internet business database ABI/Inform to access "The Health of Nations." Search for this article by typing the words *economist* and *health* and *nations*.

   Cite your sources in the in-text citation format, giving title and page number when there is no author ("The Health of Nations" 83). List your sources at the end of the paper as Works Cited and alphabetize them according to the authors' last names. When no author is listed for a source, alphabetize it according to the first word of the title, excluding *a, an,* or *the.* (See Appendix B, Synthesis.)

3. The World Health Organization report of June 4, 2000, ranked 191 countries using a new way to calculate healthy life expectancy. DALE (Disability Adjusted Life Expectancy) calculates how many years of healthy life a person will have. According to this report, the Japanese have the longest healthy life expectancy (74.5 years) among 191 countries. After doing research, write an essay discussing the factors that have led to Japan's having the highest ranking. Consider diet, smoking, alcohol consumption, exercise, and other factors that may affect health.

4. Write a research paper on one of the following topics: (1) health care in developing countries in the 21st century or (2) life expectancy in the 21st century. You may use the articles printed or mentioned in this chapter, including the expansion readings, as sources for your paper. Also find several recent sources. These books should be helpful.

Garrett, Laurie. *Betrayal of Trust: The Collapse of Global Public Health*. New York: Hyperion, 2001.

Hayflick, Leonard. *How and Why We Age*. New York: Ballantine Books, 1996.

Price-Smith, Andrew T. *The Health of Nations*. Cambridge: MIT Press, 2002.

Riley, James C. *Rising Life Expectancy: A Global History*. Cambridge: Cambridge University Press, 2001.

Expansion Readings

Dawkins, Richard. "What Is Science Good For? A Conversation with Richard Dawkins." *Harvard Business Review* 79, no. 1 (January 2001): 159–63.

"Drugs and Developing Countries: Pill Paupers." *The Economist,* 21 December 2002, 10–11.

"Drugs for the Poor: Exotic Pursuits." *The Economist,* 1 February 2003: 52.

"The Health of Nations." *The Economist,* 22 December 2001, 83–84.

Pecoul, Bernard. "Fighting for Survival." *Harvard International Review* 23, no. 3 (Fall 2001): 60–65.

"Poverty and Sickness." *The Economist,* 22 December 2001, 10.

Oral Presentation

Working with a partner, give a 20-minute oral presentation to the class on one of the articles listed under Expansion Readings or an article of your choice on health issues in the future. Summarize the article by including the author's thesis, major points, and supporting data, and evaluate its strengths and weaknesses. Be prepared to answer questions on your topic. If you have the technical capability, use the presentation graphics program PowerPoint for your presentation. Otherwise, make at least one overhead to use on the overhead projector. (See Appendix B, Oral Presentation.)

Travels on the Web

The Internet offers numerous opportunities to read more about the issues of health and life expectancy throughout the world in the 21st century.

1. The following Web sites are excellent sources of state-of-the-art information. Find guidelines to healthy living and recent statistics on life expectancy, print out the information, and bring it to class to discuss with your classmates.

   • Centers for Disease Control and Prevention, National Center for Health Statistics: <http://www.cdc.gov/nchs>. Under Information Showcase, choose Health, United States, and Healthy People (2010).

   • *United Nations Development Program.* Select *Human Development Reports* 2002: <http://www.worldpolicy.org>

   • World Health Organization: <http://www.who.int>

2. On the following Web site, you can take a test to assess your longevity potential.

   • <http://www.livingto100.com> (The Living to 100 Life Expectancy Calculator)

   After you take this test, print out the results and bring them to class to share with your classmates.

Chapter 10
Working Women

··

> **"All It Takes Is a Dream"**
> Shilpa Mathai
> *The Middle East*
> January 2001

> **"Cracks in Mexico's Glass Ceiling"**
> Elisabeth Malkin
> *Business Week*
> July 10, 2000

> **"Rio Co-op Raises Worker Standards, Fashionably"**
> Andrew Downie
> *The Christian Science Monitor*
> November 7, 2001

Preview "All It Takes Is a Dream"

Skimming

Skim the article quickly to find the following general information.

1. Read the title and all headings and look at any illustrations.

2. Read the first and second paragraphs, looking for the author's purpose and main idea.

3. Read the last paragraph, looking for a summary or conclusion.

4. Write a sentence containing your preliminary understanding of the main idea of the article.

Questioning

Answer the following questions and discuss your answers in class.

1. How would you describe the status of women in your native country in regard to their human, social, and political rights?

2. How common is it for women to work outside the home in your native country?

3. Do you think that women who have young children should work outside the home? Explain your answer.

Scanning

Scan the article quickly to find the following specific information.

1. For how many years did Fauzia Al Araimi work to raise the initial investment outlay for her factory?

2. What type of work captured Fauzia's attention initially?

3. How much money did Fauzia have when she decided to set up her factory in Nizwa, in central Oman?

4. What does Fauzia believe are the real essentials for success in business?

Vocabulary in Context

Read the following sentences and try to guess the meaning of the italicized words by using the context. Then replace the italicized words with synonyms (words or phrases that have nearly the same or similar meanings).

1. "Her never say die attitude, steely determination and optimism *sustained* her vision." (Paragraph 4)

2. "She went to international conferences and seminars and read *voraciously* about plastics." (Paragraph 8)

3. "The *fledgling* factory had to contend with a sudden hike in raw material prices as well as stiff competition from a bigger rival that suddenly emerged on the scene." (Paragraph 10)

4. "Had such a system existed in Oman when Araimi planned to establish herself in business, the 10 years of working and saving to *amass* the necessary start-up capital could have been avoided." (Paragraph 15)

5. "Araimi hopes other young *entrepreneurs* will follow her lead." (Paragraph 17)

Paraphrasing

After reading the article, reread the sentences under Vocabulary in Context. Now rewrite them using your own words. Change the vocabulary and sentence structure, but do not change the author's intended meaning or paraphrase any technical terms. There are several ways of paraphrasing each sentence.

1 **"I** love challenges," exclaims Fauzia Al Araimi. "What's life without a fight?" Araimi is the voice of a new generation in Oman, a 21st-century woman who has shattered glass ceilings and Arab stereotypes to follow her dreams in a burqa-clad world.

2 This gritty 33-year-old entrepreneur runs a profitable plastic container manufacturing industry, the first of its kind in Oman, producing disposable plastic packaging products. Araimi's factory, Sur Plastics, is in its second year and rakes in enough work and sufficient profits to keep its machines rolling 24 hours a day, at full capacity. No mean feat considering the size of the odds stacked against her.

3 "Life has been no cakewalk for me. I always cherished the dream of starting my own enterprise, of doing something on my own. But for a middle class girl in Oman, without a business lineage and no credit rating worth writing about, that seemed an insurmountable ambition," says Araimi candidly.

Local market demand was met by imports. That was all I needed to know to get hooked on plastics.

4 However, she refused to be defeated. Her never say die attitude, steely determination and optimism sustained her vision. "I was determined to find a way out. Of course, I had to organise some finances first. The only way I could get round the problem was to work and save on the job. Which is what I did; I worked for 10 years to raise the initial investment outlay for my factory."

5 Her higher diploma in business management landed her a job in the government services. Ten long years later, Araimi had a nest egg to invest in her project: "If things hadn't materialised, all of my life savings would have

Fauzia Al Araimi, one of a generation of Omani women determined to make things happen irrespective of gender

All it takes is a

Shilpa Mathai reports from Oman on the vision of an ambitious Omani entrepreneur

disappeared in a second," she recalls. But, fortunately, that did not happen.

6 Was it plastics all the way for her? "Not at all, it was farming that captured my attention initially. I had visions of my own farm with luscious fruits and vegetables and all of Oman queuing up to get their produce at my gates," she laughs. "But the more I thought about it, the more the practicalities loomed large. The saline water in Oman is hardly conducive for agriculture and livestock farming is fraught with its own inherent risks. So that idea was shelved, and I was on the prowl trying to pin down a worthy cause."

All a woman needs to succeed is education and the will to work hard

7 Inspiration struck at a friend's office one day, when in the course of a visit she noticed a number of invoices for plastic containers from manufacturers in UAE and Saudi Arabia. "I immediately quizzed her on why the company did not use a local manufacturer and was told, to my utter astonishment, there was no one producing these articles in Oman. Local market demand was met by imports. That was all I needed to know to get hooked on plastics."

8 Araimi plunged into overdrive right away. She went to international conferences and seminars and read voraciously about plastics. It was 1997, the Year of the Entrepreneur in Oman. The Ministry of Commerce and Industry was

Oman's multi-lane highways connect all the country's major towns and cities. Nizwa, where Fauzia Al Araimi's plastics factory is located, is in central Oman but accessible to all points

R Wells

Fruit and vegetable farming on a large scale was Araimi's first choice but she switched to plastics after identifying a major gap in the market

R Wells

dream

granting soft loans, tax holidays and plenty of incentives to help small businesses in the country. "I found out from the ministry that approval had already been granted for a similar project. Undeterred, I got in touch with the person concerned who told me he was no longer interested in pursuing the project so I bought the certificate of approval for the scheme from him."

9 Armed with a kitty of RO300,000 ($770,000) Araimi decided to set up her unit in Nizwa, in central Oman. "Even though operating from a new industrial estate meant battling infrastructural problems, I also took into account the distribu-

tion logistics of targeting the whole country from a mid point. From Nizwa I can easily access the Yemeni market later. Of course, it also meant I commuted 300 kilometres a day to get to work. Now I go in only three days a week; the rest of the time I'm busy marketing our products elsewhere," says Araimi, who lives with her family in Oman's capital city, Muscat.

10 Getting the project on track was no easy matter. The fledgling factory had to contend with a sudden hike in raw material prices as well as stiff competition from a bigger rival that suddenly emerged on the scene. "But that helped us streamline our portfolio. We concentrated on a few products and events made me even more determined to succeed." In recognition of her efforts, Araimi was recently inducted into the Businessmen's Council, an

Omani women are becoming increasingly visible members of the workforce

official advisory body drawn from the upper echelons of the Omani business community.

11 "Women have always been accorded respect in Oman," she muses. "There were never any gender biases. My mother was a single parent with three daughters all those years ago. She was one of the first women to join the Royal Oman Police; her life's dictum was that all a woman needs to succeed is education and the will to work hard. She taught us to fend for ourselves in a man's world."

We are not all veiled stereotypes, reality is different

12 "My earliest memories of female entrepreneurs were the wizened Omani women selling peanuts outside my school," explains Araimi. "I'm very keen to further the cause of Omani women. We are not veiled stereotypes. That is a rather romantic cliché, but reality is different. We are as diverse as women anywhere."

13 This was a sentiment Araimi echoed in New York earlier this year at the United Nations Conference on Women, where she was part of a delegation from Oman. "I would like to see a fund set up to help aspiring entrepreneurs without a family business background. We do have a fund, the Youth Development Fund, but it furnishes only 50 per cent of the project investment outlay. Where can a young graduate go to raise the other 50 per cent? I propose a co-operative be set up, which would furnish capital in the form of a long term loan, along with the necessary guidance and technical expertise.

14 "It is often financially impractical for an upcoming enterprise to have its own specialised departments, and the fund could help reduce overheads by opening a centralised office to handle functions like marketing and finance. Actually, there are very few barriers to doing business here, Oman is very much an equal opportunities country. But it lacks a support system to nurture small enterprises."

15 Had such a system existed in Oman when Araimi planned to establish herself in business,

Omani women have been involved in commerce for generations. Many rural women run food produce and handicraft enterprises from their homes in the interior, while in the cities women are also active in business and politics

the 10 years of working and saving to amass the necessary start-up capital could have been avoided.

Money is never a limiting factor. Talent and vision are the real essentials for success

16 These are thoughts that constantly nag her as she manages her factory, handling its marketing functions, furthering the cause of women, attending Businessmen's Council meetings, while taking on various courses in a bid to constantly update her know-how, as well as playing football with her three young sons and overseeing their homework. How does she do it and

still manage to look supremely relaxed and refreshed? "My boys are very energetic and I love being with them," she laughs. "It's nothing really, you can do it all if you manage your time well. I'm just lucky I have a supportive husband."

17 Araimi hopes other young entrepreneurs will follow her lead. "I hope people realise that money is never a limiting factor. Talent and vision are the real essentials for success. I love my work and now that the factory has found its feet, I have several other ideas," she confesses. "I want Sur Plastics to expand overseas, I want to introduce new product lines and I hope to do an MBA in marketing to keep up with developments. I have lots of dreams left. I guess I'll always be wanting to do something." ■

Glossary

amass	to accumulate, collect
biases	prejudices
burqa	long one-piece hooded cloak worn by Arab women
cakewalk	an easy task
candidly	frankly, honestly, sincerely
cliché	something that has become overly familiar; a well-known and worn-out phrase or expression
conducive	tending to promote or assist
dictum	a formal pronouncement of a principle or opinion
disposable	designed to be used once and then thrown away
echelons	levels
entrepreneurs	people who organize and manage a business, assuming the risks for the sake of a profit
fend	to try to get along without help
fledgling	new, young, or just started
fraught	weighed down, burdened
gender	the male and female sex
glass ceiling	intangible barrier within the hierarchy of a company that prevents women or minorities from obtaining upper-level positions
gritty	courageously persistent
hooked on	attracted strongly to
immersed	fully involved, engrossed
incentives	things or ideas that incite action; motivators
infrastructural	relating to the system of public works of a country, state, or region; underlying foundation
inherent	belonging by nature; intrinsic
insurmountable	incapable of being overcome
landed	secured, gained
lineage	family, ancestry
logistics	the handling of the details of an operation; procurement, maintenance, and transportation of personnel, equipment, and materials
nag	to bother, worry
nurture	to further the development of
odds	disadvantages that are greater than advantages
outlay	expenditures

queuing up	lining up, waiting in a line
rakes in	gains rapidly
saline	salty
shattered	broke into pieces, demolished
shelved	put aside
steely	firm and strong as steel
stereotypes	standardized mental pictures that represent a prejudicial attitude or oversimplified opinion
streamline	to make simpler or more efficient
sustained	supported
undeterred	not discouraged or inhibited
upcoming	approaching
voraciously	eagerly, with a huge appetite

Comprehension

1. Describe the business that Fauzia Al Araimi owns.

2. Where did Fauzia work for 10 years before she had enough money to start her business?

3. Why did Fauzia give up her idea of owning a farm?

4. How did Fauzia decide to go into the manufacturing of plastic containers?

5. What does Fauzia say about the role of women in Oman?

6. What type of fund does Fauzia suggest be set up in Oman for business entrepreneurs?

7. Why is Fauzia able to manage her factory, further the cause of women, take courses, and play with her three children?

8. What are Fauzia's dreams for the future?

9. Fauzia has achieved extraordinary business success in a male-dominated culture. What factors have contributed to her success?

Analysis

Circle the letter next to the best answer(s). Justify your choices with quotations from the text.

1. What is the main idea of the article, and in which paragraph(s) is it stated?

   a. Women in Oman have opportunities to own businesses, but few women are successful because many barriers to their success exist.

   b. Fauzia Al Araimi, who became a successful businesswoman through determination, hard work, and vision, is a role model for Omani women.

   c. If a person receives an excellent education and has money, he or she can succeed in the business world.

   d. Raising capital is one of the most difficult parts of starting a business in Oman.

2. What is the meaning of the italicized word in this sentence in paragraph 3? "I always *cherished* the dream of starting my own enterprise, of doing something on my own."

   a. nurtured

   b. believed in

   c. remembered

   d. maintained

3. We can infer the following from these sentences in paragraph 12: "We are not veiled stereotypes. That is a rather romantic cliché, but reality is different."

   a. Because Omani women are all different, they cannot be easily understood.

   b. The veils that Omani women wear protect them from reality.

   c. Many people have oversimplified mental images of Omani women.

   d. Omani women face discrimination and prejudice in everyday life.

4. The author's writing style in this article is ＿＿＿＿＿ and ＿＿＿＿＿ .

   a. journalistic

   b. academic

   c. bureaucratic

   d. colorful

5. The tone of the article is ——————— and ——————— .

   a. straightforward

   b. ambiguous

   c. pessimistic

   d. optimistic

6. What overall method of development is used in this article?

   a. analyzing a personal experience by describing causes and effects

   b. enumerating the steps in a commercial process

   c. debating the value of an economic proposal

   d. comparing and contrasting approaches

7. The author has an energetic writing style. What techniques give her style this energy?

   a. direct quotations

   b. long sentences

   c. complex vocabulary

   d. strong verbs

CRACKS IN MEXICO'S GLASS CEILING

A finance whiz is paving the way for other women to rise

MARIA ASUNCION ARAMBURUZABALA

BORN May 2, 1963, in Mexico City.

EDUCATION Accounting degree from Autonomous Technological Institute of Mexico.

CAREER Vice-president of brewer Grupo Modelo. Structures private equity investment deals backed by family fortune, including recent acquisition of a 20.62% stake in media giant Televisa's holding company. Sits on boards of Modelo, Teléfonos de México, and now Televisa.

PERSONAL Divorced; enjoys cooking and the ocean.

DATA: BUSINESS WEEK

María Asunción Aramburuzabala, a vice-president of brewer Grupo Modelo, does her homework. When a chance to buy into Mexican media giant Grupo Televisa presented itself in April, she arrived at the company's offices armed with reams of numbers. For three hours, Aramburuzabala combed through the financials of each division with Televisa CFO Alfonso de Angoitia. "I was very surprised," he says. "She had already done a very detailed study." Nine weeks after that first meeting, Aramburuzabala got what she wanted: a 20.62% stake in Televisa holding company Grupo Televicentro along with three seats on its board.

With that deal, Aramburuzabala became a full member of the all-male club that is Mexican big business. Her family is one of the four that control Modelo, one of Mexico's largest publicly traded companies. Yet among the family-run giants that still dominate large swaths of Mexican industry, custom dictates that the corporate mantle pass from father to son. In cases where there are no male heirs, a son-in-law is next in line for the throne. When Aramburuzabala,

37, took over managing her family's interests, "people thought I was a little rich girl wanting to play at business and that I would soon get tired and stop," she recalls. But her purchase of the Televisa stake proves otherwise.

INTERNET PUSH. It has been a long time coming, but the feminist revolution is reaching the boardrooms of Mexico's family-run companies. Aramburuzabala is helping speed things along. She has no intention of being a passive investor in Televisa. Although she is pleased with the way CEO Emilio Azcárraga Jean has restructured the once bloated company, Aramburuzabala expects to add her input to strategic decisions. She won't tell what she paid for the 20.62% stake, which is split among several members of her family, but analysts estimate it's worth about $536 million.

"People thought I was a little rich girl wanting to play at business"

What attracted her to Televisa was its combination of old and new media. The company already dominates in television, radio, and publishing and is now making a big push into the Internet. It launched a Spanish-language portal, esmas.com, on June 1 and plans to take stakes in other Internet companies, as well as setting up its own Net incubator. J. P. Morgan & Co. analyst José Linares estimates the value of Televisa's various Internet ventures at $2.2 billion.

Aramburuzabala doesn't need Televisa to keep busy, though. She manages a family fortune that *Forbes* estimates at $1 billion. The money comes from her family's share in Modelo, maker of Corona beer. In the 1990s, Modelo sold a combined noncontrolling 50.2% stake to Anheuser-Busch Cos. in three separate transactions totaling $1.64 billion, and the Aramburuzabala clan suddenly had money to invest. So for the past three years, Aramburuzabala has been running a sort of private equity fund, investing mainly in real estate.

BAD TIDINGS. Still, it wasn't until six years ago, when her father was dying of cancer, that she immersed herself in the family business. In 1996, she persuaded her family's partners to let her take over two bankrupt yeast companies. Within a year, she had put them back in the black by merging divisions and launching products. When the layoffs began, Aramburuzabala would show up at the plant at 3 a.m. to talk to workers on the night shift. "It was tough," she recalls. At Modelo, she earned the respect of her colleagues as part of the small team that handled the fraught negotiations with Anheuser-Busch.

As Aramburuzabala breaks new ground for businesswomen in Mexico, there are other signs of change. Women are starting their own companies in record numbers while multinationals have promoted some of their female executives to top positions. For instance, Compaq Computer Corp.'s Mexican subsidiary has long had a woman chief executive, Barbara Mair. Since taking over in 1993, the 38-year-old Mair has pumped up sales from $65 million to $500 million last year. Despite her own success, Mair believes that Mexican women continue to limit themselves in their career choices. "They don't feel it's possible," she says.

Expect to hear more about Aramburuzabala. She is already scouting around for new investments. "I love business," she says. "It's a passion." That enthusiasm will surely open doors for other women.

Elisabeth Malkin in Mexico City

Discussion

1. How did Maria become a full member of the all-male club that is Mexican big business?

2. Why was Maria attracted to Televisa?

3. What has Maria been doing for the past three years?

4. What are the signs of change for businesswomen in Mexico?

5. Describe the similarities and the differences between Fauzia al Araimi (the subject of the article "All It Takes Is a Dream," printed earlier in this chapter) and Maria Aramburuzabala. Consider each woman's personal and professional lives.

6. Both Fauzia and Maria had to struggle to become successful in business. Whose struggle seems to have been more difficult? Why?

7. Maria Aramburuzabala has changed the Mexican custom that dictates that family businesses are passed from father to son or son-in-law. What is the custom in your native country in regard to inheritance of family businesses?

8. What are the major obstacles facing women who want to be owners of companies and managers in the business world?

9. Name some women from your native country who are successful in business, and describe their companies.

Rio co-op raises worker standards, fashionably

By Andrew Downie
Special to The Christian Science Monitor

RIO DE JANEIRO

1 ON A hillside slum above the oceanfront condos and blue seas of Rio de Janeiro, a few women sit hunched over sewing machines, their feet pumping pedals and their hands carefully working strips of cloth under chattering needles.

2 Though located in a *favela*, the Cooparoca women's sewing cooperative in Rocinha is the antithesis of the stereotypical sweatshop, where workers are paid pennies to sew baseballs or T-shirts for multinationals, which then sell them at a huge profit in the US and Europe.

3 The top earner here might make $600 a month – more than eight times Brazil's monthly minimum wage of $71. A part-timer may earn only $20, or just take classes. The choice is up to the individual.

4 "I worked in a shop before, and I hated it," says Lucélia Carvalho, Cooparoca production manager. "It's like one big family here. Everything is dis-cussed, and you don't have a boss on your back all the time," Ms. Carvalho says. "The money is better here, but I don't do it for the money, I do this because there is a good atmosphere."

5 Far from the stereotypical poorly-lit dungeon churning out tatty garments, Cooparoca – the name stands for Rocinha Cooperative of Women's Artisans and Seamstresses – is located in a pleasant three-story building that is as spacious and airy as it is possible to be in one of Latin America's most populous *favelas*, or slums.

6 EVEN more surprising than the conditions are the clothes. The women here produce garments for M. Officer, a Brazilian fashion house so cool, it was among the first to hire supermodel Giselle Bundchen, the girlfriend of "Titanic" star Leonardo di Caprio.

7 Cooparoca's partnership with M. Officer has proven that favela workers are capable of making haute couture clothes to the exacting standards demanded by top designers – and has made the coop a well-known name in the Brazilian fashion industry. In the past few years, Cooparoca has worked with German designer Karl Lagerfeld and Brazilian pop star Fernanda Abreu, and has given clothes to supermodels such as Naomi Campbell.

8 The firm is expected to double last year's turnover and bring in $100,000 in 2001, most of it from M. Officer contracts, says coop coordinator Maria Teresa Leal.

9 Ms. Leal started the coop in 1981, after noticing how enthusiastic – and creative – Rocinha's northeastern immigrants were about fashion. She convinced big textile companies to donate surplus cloth and materials, and gathered women into a cooperative to make cushions, pompoms, and crocheted covers. In addition to teaching women how to sew, the coop holds classes on women's health and contraception.

10 After a few years of selling the products informally to friends, Cooparoca was formally registered in 1987, and won grants from the United Nations Development Program and a government credit line that enabled the organization to buy the precarious hillside shack that later became its headquarters.

11 The big break came in 1994, when a friend agreed to let Leal show off Cooparoca's designs at a Rio fashion show. The only problem was that the women had no experience making clothes, and with just a couple of weeks to learn they produced outfits that were ill-fitting and poorly finished.

12 The critics loved it.

13 "They said we had been influenced by the Belgian deconstructionist designers that were trendy at the time," says Leal. "But really, we didn't know how to construct. It was madness; we didn't know what we were doing, and we had no money. But it worked. The next day, the editors of Vogue and Elle were at my house. I think it was just one of those occasions when you are in the right place at the right time."

14 Since then, Cooparoca has gone from strength to strength. In 1997, it was given 41 industrial sewing machines by the Banco do Brasil and three other Brazilian companies, as well as receiving grants from UNESCO, the Rio state government, and a host of local businesses.

15 The deals helped bring Cooparoca to the attention of the fashion world. The contract signed last year with M. Officer, the chic Sao Paulo fashion house that has been at the forefront of the Brazilian fashion boom, enabled the coop to increase its workforce almost tenfold. Today, it employs 80 people. The youngest is 18, and the oldest is 65.

16 Leal is the brains behind the organization, but the workers run their own show. Big decisions are made democratically, and the seamstresses set their own production targets and may work from home, allowing them to care for children while they work. Each woman is paid on a piece-rate basis and decides in advance how many garments she will sew per week. The only demand is that workers meet their stated target.

17 THAT democratic atmosphere was important to Carlos Miele, M. Officer's innovative head. Mr. Miele, the first designer to use disabled models in catwalk shows, admired the concept behind Cooparoca and wanted to contribute to its growth.

18 The designer asked Cooparoca seamstresses to produce the custom-made denim frills, patchwork squares, and crocheted rings that adorn his clothes. He recently showed off their work in London and is considering offers to sell Cooparoca's multicolored lamp covers at Barney's in New York. If sales continue to grow, Miele hopes to provide jobs for 120 more people in Rocinha.

19 "We have a society that is about excluding people, and my work is about including people," Miele says. "All I did was give them a chance, and now I am happy because I get a great product – and they are happy because they get work."

Discussion

1. What makes the Cooparoca women's sewing cooperative in Rocinha, a *favela* (slum) in Brazil, different from other types of sewing and clothing manufacturing shops?

2. How did Maria Teresa Leal, coordinator of the Cooparoca, make a success out of the cooperative?

3. What was ironic about the clothes designed and made by the Cooparoca for a fashion show in Rio de Janeiro in 1994?

4. Describe the democratic atmosphere at the Cooparoca.

5. What types of women's cooperatives exist in your native country?

6. The Rocinha Favela has a Web site that is in Portuguese. Log on to <http://www.Rocinha.com.br> to look at photographs of this unusual place. If you know Portuguese, print out several pages, translate the information into English, and share it with your classmates.

Teamwork

Working with a group, discuss the degree to which women in the country in which you are studying have achieved equality with men. Then conduct a survey of 20 women business students to determine what factors motivate women to enter the business field. First decide on the methodology of your survey (telephone or face-to-face interview) and then develop a questionnaire with at least 10 questions. For example, ask your survey participants questions about their age, nationality, native language, education, major field, specific career goals, and motivation. After conducting the survey, write a brief report, including the survey's purpose, methodology, results, and the conclusions you have drawn from the questionnaire answers. Present your survey results in a table if possible.

Writing Assignments

1. Write an essay discussing the changing role of women in a specific area of the world. Do research to answer these questions: What is the illiteracy rate for women? What is the school enrollment rate for females? What percent of women have college degrees? How many women work? What is the life expectancy for women?

   For your research, use the Internet business database LexisNexis Academic. Select Site Map, choose Business, click on Business News, and do a Guided News Search. You can also use the Internet business database ABI/Inform. Cite your sources in the in-text citation format (Thomas 43). List your sources at the end of the paper as Works Cited and alphabetize them according to the authors' last names. Some relevant articles are listed below.

- "How Women Beat the Rules." *The Economist,* 2 October 1999, 48. (Saudi Arabia)

- Itoi, Karen. "Women Warriors." *Newsweek,* 3 April 2000, 64. (Japan)

- Power, Carla. "Women of the New Century." *Newsweek,* 8 January 2001, 14. (Europe)

- ———. "The New Arab Woman." *Newsweek,* 12 June 2000, 22. (Middle East)

- Thomas, Karen. "The New Arab Woman." *The Middle East* (January 2000): 43–45. (Middle East)

2. Write a synthesis about the problems facing working women and the advances they have made in the business world. Base your synthesis on the women in the articles in this chapter: Fauzia Al Araimi in Oman ("All It Takes Is a Dream"), Maria Aramburuzabala in Mexico ("Cracks in Mexico's Glass Ceiling"), and Maria Teresa Leal in Brazil ("Rio Co-op Raises Workers' Standards, Fashionably"). You may also include among your sources the expansion readings from this chapter. Cite your sources in the in-text citation format (Malkin 166). List your sources at the end of the paper as Works Cited and alphabetize them according to the authors' last names.

3. Working with a partner, conduct an interview with a woman who owns her own business or has a managerial position in a company. (See "DNA: Handle with Care" in chapter 8 for an example of an interview.) Use a tape recorder during the interview and write up the information as a report in three sections: introduction, interview questions and answers, conclusion.

You may use the questions listed below in your interview.

- What type of business are you in?

- What academic degrees do you have?

- Who were your role models?

- Who was your mentor?

- What previous jobs have you had?

- What are your future goals?

4. Write a research paper on the topic of the changing role of women in the business world. You may use the articles printed or mentioned in this chapter, including the expansion readings, as sources for your paper. Also find several recent sources. These books should be helpful.

Hewlett, Sylvia Ann. *Creating a Life: Professional Women and the Quest for Children.* New York: Talk Miramax Books, 2002.

Kelly, Rita Mae, ed. *Gender, Globalization, and Democratization.* Lanham, MD: Rowman and Littlefield Publishers, 2001.

Moore, Dorothy P. *Careerpreneurs: Lessons from Leading Women Entrepreneurs on Building a Career without Boundaries.* Palo Alto, CA: Davies-Black Publishers, 2000.

Smith, Dayle M. *Women at Work: Leadership for the Next Century.* Upper Saddle River, NJ: Prentice-Hall, 2000.

Sweetman, Caroline, ed. *Gender, Development, and Money.* Oxford: Oxfam, 2001.

Walter, Lynn, ed. *Women's Rights: A Global View.* Westport, CT: Greenwood, 2001.

Expansion Readings

Joekes, Susan. "Diminished Returns." *Harvard International Review* 21, no. 4 (Fall 1999): 54–58.

Hewlett, Sylvia Ann. "Executive Women and the Myth of Having It All." *Harvard Business Review* 80, no. 4 (April 2002): 66–73.

Meyerson, Debra A., and Joyce K. Fletcher. "A Modest Manifesto for Shattering the Glass Ceiling." *Harvard Business Review* 78, no. 1 (January–February 2000): 126–36.

"Natalie Wraga." *The Economist,* 23 November 2002, 81.

Yim, Soojin. "Gender Gap." *Harvard International Review* 22, no. 1 (Winter 2000): 12–13.

Oral Presentation

Working with a partner, give a 20-minute oral presentation to the class on one of the articles listed under Expansion Readings or an article of your choice on working women. Summarize the article by including the author's thesis, major points, and supporting data and evaluate its strengths and weaknesses. Be prepared to answer questions on your topic. If you have the technical capability, use the presentation graphics program PowerPoint for your presentation. Otherwise, make at least one overhead to use on the overhead projector. (See Appendix B, Oral Presentation.)

Travels on the Web

The Internet offers numerous opportunities to read more about the changing role of women throughout the world. Log on to the following Web sites to find information on women's growing participation and representation in political life, economic development, and business. Print out an article and bring it to class to share with your classmates.

- Catalyst: <http://www.catalystwomen.org>

- International IDEA: Institute for Democracy and Electoral Assistance: <http://www.idea.int/gender>. Click on Gender and Political Participation.

- United Nations: <http://www.un.org>. Click on Index and select Statistics or Women.

- United Nations Development Fund for Women: <http://www.unifem.undp.org>

- *Working Mother* magazine: <http://www.workingmother.com>

- The World Bank: <http//:www.worldbank.org>. Select Data & Statistics. Then choose Data by Topic and click on Gender. You can also click on GenderStats under Popular Resources.

Chapter 11
Expatriate Employees

"Expat Training"
Gary Wederspahn
T+D
February 2002

"An American Expat's View"
David Beadles
T+D
February 2002

"Women Working Overseas"
Tracey Wilen
T+D
May 2001

....
Preview   "Expat Training"
....

Skimming

Skim the article quickly to find the following general information.

1. Read the title and all headings and look at any illustrations.

2. Read the first and second paragraphs, looking for the author's purpose and main idea.

3. Read the last paragraph, looking for a summary or conclusion.

4. Write a sentence containing your preliminary understanding of the main idea of the article.

Questioning

Answer the following questions and discuss your answers in class.

1. Have you ever thought about working as an expatriate in a foreign country?

2. What countries would you prefer to work in if you were an expatriate employee?

3. What type of cross-cultural training should an expatriate employee have?

Scanning

Scan the article quickly to find the following specific information.

1. What happened to Unidata after several years of acrimonious infighting?

2. What positive characteristics of U.S. citizens abroad are mentioned by host nationals?

3. In a 1999 survey of 300 companies by Cendant International Assignment Services, what percent reported failed expatriate assignments?

4. According to Michael Marquardt in "Successful Global Training," what percent of American businesspeople going abroad receive no cultural training or preparation?

Vocabulary in Context

Read the following sentences and try to guess the meaning of the italicized words by using the context. Then replace the italicized words with synonyms (words or phrases that have nearly the same or similar meanings).

1. "Cross-border business failures make the best *case* for intercultural training." (Paragraph 1)

2. "Failure not only *undermines* the mission of their organizations, but also hinders expats from making local allies." (Paragraph 5)

3. "It's neither accurate nor fair to *exaggerate* the poor image of U.S. citizens abroad." (Paragraph 8)

4. "Non-U.S. expatriates also carry *problematic* cultural baggage." (Paragraph 9)

5. "Therefore, it's worthwhile to equip expatriates and business travelers of all nationalities with sufficient intercultural *savvy*." (Paragraph 9)

6. "In many cases, their marriages are shaken, careers threatened, and self-concepts *debilitated*." (Paragraph 10)

Paraphrasing

After reading the article, reread the sentences under Vocabulary in Context. Now rewrite them using your own words. Change the vocabulary and sentence structure, but do not change the author's intended meaning or paraphrase any technical terms. There are several ways of paraphrasing each sentence.

PASSPORT
Expat Training

Don't leave home without it.

By Gary Wederspahn

1 Organizations worldwide often react to economic downturns and uncertainty abroad by cutting training for expatriates and international business travelers. That shortsighted response is unwise and counterproductive. But don't take my word for it. Cross-border business failures make the best case for intercultural training.

2 **Unidata.** The European company Unidata, formed to challenge IBM's domination of the global computer market, was a high-profile alliance of Dutch, German, and French computer producers. That alliance formed many multicultural businesses and technical teams. After several years of acrimonious infighting, the entire venture was dissolved without launching a single product.

3 **Siemens and Westinghouse.** These two powerhouses planned to team up and sell worldwide a range of industrial automation and control systems. The project, however, never survived negotiations. The stated cause: lack of common ground between partners.

4 **Renault and Volvo.** According to *Ward's Automotive International,* the deal between these two automotive giants failed due to "overwhelming cultural differences."

5 Expatriates and international business travelers know the importance of making a positive impression. Failure not only undermines the mission of their organizations, but also hinders expats from making local allies.

Expatriate dis-plomacy

6 Saudi Arabians, Turks, and Egyptians have told me that they dislike the tendency of U.S. business travelers to rush starting a project before they've invested time and effort in building personal relationships. Intercultural experts Philip R. Harris and Robert T. Moran, in their book *Managing Cultural Differences,* summarize feedback from Arab businesspeople regarding how they perceive many Westerners. To them, Westerners

• act superior, as if they know the answer to everything

• aren't willing to share credit for joint efforts

• are unable or unwilling to respect and adjust to local customs and culture

• prefer solutions based on their home cultures rather than meeting local needs

• resist working through local administrative, legal, channels, and procedures

• manage in an autocratic and intimidating way

• are too imposing and pushy.

7 Reactions from people in other countries strongly indicate that more intercultural training of U.S. businesspeople is required. The May 1999 *Forbes* article "Damn Yankees" reveals the negative opinions of U.S. businesspeople held by citizens of 11 countries. "What drives me crazy," says one Colombian executive, "is the American need for information, right now! Americans are also too straightforward, too direct."

8 It's neither accurate nor fair to exaggerate the poor image of U.S. citizens abroad. Many host nationals also mention their positive characteristics: optimism, industriousness, inventiveness, decisiveness, enthusiasm, and friendliness.

9 Non-U.S. expatriates also carry problematic cultural baggage. For example, the Dutch are thought to be blunt, Germans inflexible, Japanese vague and indirect, and Latin Americans casual towards deadlines. Therefore, it's worthwhile to equip expatriates and business travelers of all nationalities with sufficient intercultural savvy.

Cultural maladjustment

10 Despite best intentions to establish rapport with the locals, expatriates in the stressful throes of cultural adaptation aren't in good condition to develop such relationships. In many cases, their marriages are shaken, careers threatened, and self-concepts debilitated.

11 Settler International, a worldwide relocation assistance company, reports that the divorce rate among expatriate couples is 40 percent higher than their domestic counterparts, and the school dropout rate of their children is 50 percent higher than in their home countries. Adjusting to an unfamiliar environment, cultural values, and social customs is stressful. A 1999 survey by Cendant International Assignment Services found that of 300 companies contacted, 63 percent reported failed expatriate assignments.

12 Symptoms of culture shock significantly hinder expatriates' ability to establish friendships with local people. The problems include

• negative feelings about the local culture and people, including irritability, hostility, and defensiveness

• homesickness, nervousness, depression, uncharacteristic mood swings, anxiety, and anger

• withdrawal or exaggerated dependence, aggressiveness, domineering behavior, and inappropriate attention-seeking

• self-damaging behavior, such as sexual adventurism and alcohol or drug abuse

• indecisiveness, inflexibility, close-mindedness, hypersensitivity to criticism, impatience, and boastfulness

• ridicule or excessive criticism of local people.

13 Proper assessment, selection, counseling, training, and support can prevent or lessen most of those unfortunate reactions.

PASSPORT

Starting the discussion

14 Michael Marquardt, in his *Info-line* "Successful Global Training," writes that 70 percent of American businesspeople going abroad receive no cultural training or preparation; 59 percent of HRD executives say their companies offer no cross-cultural training; 5 percent didn't even know of the existence of such training.

15 Clearly, organizations need to do more to prepare expatriates for establishing rapport with their local colleagues and neighbors. Here's how you can start a cross-cultural training discussion at your organization.

16 **Assess the need.** If some of your senior executives aren't convinced that employees need cross-cultural training, conduct a survey of all employees who have cross-border relationships and responsibilities, especially current and former expatriates who can share their firsthand experiences.

17 **Fine-tune the focus.** Hold focus groups to determine which employees have the greatest need and which projects and countries have the highest priority. Limiting your request for training resources to the most important requirements makes it easier to justify intercultural training to senior management.

18 **Debrief the damage.** Analyze all incidents of failed overseas assignments and business ventures. Audit them for preventable cross-cultural causes. Calculate the financial and human costs. Debrief senior international decision-makers.

19 **Raise the awareness level.** Enlighten employees and managers of the cross-cultural challenges and opportunities facing your organization:

- Obtain reprint permission of articles (such as this one) for your in-house publications.
- Ask intercultural specialists to make presentations at high-visibility meetings and sack-lunch seminars.
- Publicize the successes of your expatriates and international business travelers.
- Invite providers of intercultural services to showcase parts of their programs.

20 You can also post links on your intranet to online sources of free information on the cultures of most countries.

Gary Wederspahn *is an intercultural trainer, consultant, speaker, and writer. He has designed and conducted cross-cultural training for hundreds of expatriates and global executives. This article is based partly on his new book,* Intercultural Services: A Worldwide Buyer's Guide and Sourcebook *(Butterworth Heinemann); gary@intercultural-help.com.*

Glossary

acrimonious	harsh in words and manner
assessment	evaluation
audit	to examine and review
autocratic	absolute, with unlimited authority
baggage	beliefs that get in the way
blunt	abrupt in speech or manner; insensitive
case	a convincing argument
counterproductive	tending to hinder the attainment of a desired goal
debilitated	weakened
debrief	to ask questions to obtain useful information
domineering	controlling
downturns	declines in business activity
exaggerate	to overstate, overemphasize
expatriates	people who are living in a foreign land
focus groups	groups that investigate attitudes through conversations among participants
imposing	forceful
intimidating	frightening by arrogant treatment or threats
launching	introducing, initiating
priority	something meriting attention before competing alternatives; preferential rating
problematic	posing a problem, difficult to solve
protocol	a code prescribing adherence to correct etiquette
pushy	aggressive
rapport	relation marked by harmony or accord
ridicule	mockery, making fun of
savvy	practical knowledge
shortsighted	lacking foresight or the ability to see future effects
throes	hard or painful struggles
undermines	weakens or ruins

Comprehension

1. How do organizations worldwide often react to economic downturns and uncertainty abroad?

2. What argument is supported by the three examples of Unidata, Siemens and Westinghouse, and Renault and Volvo?

3. List some of the perceptions that people from around the world have of U.S. business travelers.

4. Why is it worthwhile to equip expatriates and business travelers of all nationalities with sufficient intercultural knowledge?

5. What statistics does the author give to prove that adjusting to an unfamiliar environment, cultural values, and social customs is stressful?

6. List some symptoms of culture shock and explain what organizations can do to prevent or lessen most reactions to culture shock.

7. What statistics support the author's statement that "Clearly, organizations need to do more to prepare expatriates for establishing rapport with their local colleagues and neighbors"?

8. What methods does the author suggest to start a discussion on cross-cultural training at an organization?

9. In your experience, have you found that "Westerners are unable or unwilling to adjust to local customs and culture"? Explain your answer.

10. What is the meaning of the term *culture shock*? Have you ever suffered from culture shock? If so, explain the causes and effects.

Analysis

Circle the letter next to the best answer(s). Justify your choices with quotations from the text.

1. What is the main idea of the article, and in which paragraph(s) is it stated?

   a. Although being an expatriate employee involves challenges, business-people can benefit from such assignments by expanding their knowledge of other cultures.

   b. In American companies, employees are not given enough cross-cultural training before being sent to work abroad, so many organizations fail to achieve their mission.

   c. Many business travelers from around the world fail in their overseas assignments because they are affected by culture shock.

   d. Companies should offer their expatriate employees intercultural training to prevent cross-border business failures that result from cultural differences.

2. What is the meaning of the italicized word in this sentence from paragraph 12? "Symptoms of culture shock significantly *hinder* expatriates' ability to establish friendships with local people."

  a. hold back

  b. test

  c. destroy

  d. strengthen

3. The following inference can be drawn from this statement in paragraph 6: "Saudi Arabians, Turks, and Egyptians have told me that they dislike the tendency of U.S. business travelers to rush starting a project before they've invested time and effort in building personal relationships."

  a. Saudi Arabians, Turks, and Egyptians are usually not concerned about starting projects on time.

  b. U.S. business travelers attach less importance to building personal relationships than do Saudi Arabians, Turks, and Egyptians.

  c. U.S. business travelers attach the same importance to building personal relationships as do Saudi Arabians, Turks, and Egyptians.

  d. U.S. businesspeople tend to worry too much about meeting deadlines for business projects.

4. The author's writing style in this article is _____ and _____ .

  a. personal

  b. impersonal

  c. conversational

  d. bureaucratic

5. The tone of the article is _____ and _____ .

  a. factual

  b. ironic

  c. critical

  d. approving

6. What overall method of development is used in this article?

   a. describing a problem and suggesting a solution

   b. analyzing a technical procedure

   c. developing an argument chronologically

   d. enumerating the characteristics of a plan

7. What techniques does the author use to get the reader's attention in the introduction (paragraphs 1–5)?

   a. concrete examples

   b. current statistics

   c. strong adjectives

   d. technical definitions

An American Expat's View

You're not in Kansas anymore.

By David Beadles

1 "Remember, this isn't America; we do things differently here in Europe."

2 If I hear that phrase again on the job, I'm likely to froth in a fit of fury. After working for three years across six different European countries for three different companies (two in the past six months), that's one phrase I've heard more than a few times. But the truth is, it's true. The frustrating thing is, people assume I don't know that.

3 Believe it or not, the European business world doesn't think much of "the American manifest destiny." Yes, the United States is the world's economic and military powerhouse. Indeed, Europe does thank America for its assistance in WWII. And, when Bill Gates speaks, the world does listen. When you're outside of U.S. borders, however, those feats don't hold much relevance. Unfortunately, most Americans working abroad don't seem to be aware of that fact. Thus, I continue to suffer from my compatriots' missteps.

4 I'll never forget the American systems planner visiting our Brussels office for a mere three days who insisted on bringing her own Starbucks coffee. Her European colleagues snickered in the back smoking room, saying something like, "Americans don't know coffee. We've been brewing the best beans for centuries. Then along comes a retail fad, and they think they know it all. The least she could have done was try the exquisite beverage from our 10.000 euro Italian espresso machine."

5 Was such a small thing really an issue? Indeed it was. It served to alienate the woman from many colleagues at the outset of her brief stay, potentially threatening the success of her project.

6 I could go on with other stories, some in which I'm the buffoon. On the other hand, I've participated in numerous projects in which the American perspective was just right.

7 My best advice: If you're working abroad, prepare yourself for the adventure. Don't just read a few travel articles on the Web; learn the region's history. Find out what the locals like to do and eat, and their biggest peeves. Once

> My best advice: If you're working abroad, prepare yourself for the adventure. Don't just read a few travel articles on the Web; learn the region's history.

you're there, open yourself up to the experience. Listen to what people have to say, wait, and listen some more. Non-native English speakers may take a little more time to get their point across, so be patient.

8 Three years ago, my then-boss (we'll call him Joe) traveled abroad for the first time—to Amsterdam. Joe's your typical American executive: fast thinking, talking, and acting. If he's not multitasking between his cellular phone, his email, and the meeting simultaneously taking place in his office, then he might as well be idle.

9 Joe and I attended our first team business dinner, which was quite the event: a five-course extravaganza with the finest of wines. Before we'd finished the second course, Joe was pacing the room. Towards the end of the meal, just as our European colleagues

began sharing their expectations and hopes for our new venture, Joe was outside hailing a taxi. His actions that night foreshadowed a behavior pattern that had him out of the organization within 10 months.

10 I'm not sure whether it's American arrogance or merely a need to feel comfortable outside of the realm of familiarity, but Americans do seem to create their own roadblocks to success in the international workplace. The frightening thought is how many companies continue to send employees abroad to work on critical projects, without a day of cultural awareness or linguistic training.

11 As I see it, Americans can go about working outside of their national borders in two ways. One, throw themselves into the middle of the situation and figure things out—and, quite often, they succeed. But, there's another, subtler method that proves more effective: Do their homework. It's simple and widely respected.

12 That preparation will come in handy the next time a colleague tries to educate you on the fundamental differences between European and American protocol. If you've done your research, then you'll be in a position to agree or offer your own insight: "Yes, I know. In fact, you put mayonnaise on your french fries. But you really call them fried potatoes, don't you?"

David Beadles, *originally from Washington, D.C., is a telecom marketeer with past working stints in Geneva, Munich, and Potsdam, Germany. He's in Brussels now.*

Discussion

1. What work experience has the author had in Europe?

2. What is frustrating to the author?

3. How did the American systems planner who was visiting the Brussels office alienate her colleagues?

4. What advice does the author give to people working abroad?

5. What mistake did the author's boss make when he traveled abroad for the first time to Amsterdam?

6. What frightening thought does the author mention?

PASSPORT

Women Working Overseas

By Tracey Wilen

1 In the mid-1980s, Nancy Adler, an organizational behavior professor with McGill University's Faculty of Management, conducted a monumental study. She investigated whether commonly held myths about women in international business were true—such as women aren't interested in international business, women aren't willing to travel overseas because of family responsibilities and other reasons, and women aren't viewed as credible overseas due to local perceptions of women. Her study revealed that many of those ideas were indeed myths, often held by male managers and HR people. In fact, women were interested in and willing to conduct business overseas. And since the study, many more women are doing just that. Although Adler's study brought the falsity of such myths to light, many still exist—despite the dramatic increase of women in business, women-owned businesses, and women conducting business overseas.

2 The U.S. Department of Labor (www.dol.gov), the National Association of Women Business Owners (www.nawbo.org), and the Small Business Administration (www.sba.gov), published these facts:

◄») www.dol.gov
◄») www.nawbo.org
◄») www.sba.gov

● Women account for more than 46 percent of the workforce in America, expected to increase to 48 percent by 2005.
● In 2000, women made up 45.3 percent of executive, administrative, and management positions.
● Businesses owned by women number 8 million in the United States and employ one out of every four workers. Women-owned U.S. businesses are growing at double the rate of all businesses.
● Thirty-three percent of women business owners report that they exported in their first or second year of operation, and most were successful on their first transaction.

3 More women are traveling overseas to conduct business for their corporations or their own business ventures. Still, some guidebooks suggest that women shouldn't participate in international business. Many travel guides don't address women's issues in international business or, worse, suggest that women shouldn't be sent on foreign business assignments due to role differences.

4 I conducted my own research from 1992 to 1998 that indicates women can participate and are successful in international business despite the various reactions and views they encounter around the world. There is one area that businesswomen find critical to their success abroad: establishing credibility during the initial stages of business.

much authority I have [to represent] the corporate office. Due to that, I take extra steps to make sure that the proper introductions are made in advance to limit concerns that [some locals] might have about my credibility.

7 To help businesswomen working overseas, here are some pointers for establishing credibility:

8 **Be visible.** Attend and host meetings between your company and your international counterparts whenever possible. International travel is often associated with a firm's decision makers, so being present adds to your credibility.

9 **Get introduced.** Introductions are important, particularly for women. If you're doing business with a firm for the first time, have yourself introduced by a higher-ranking person in your company who already knows the people

Men often derive **credibility** from their gender and **status** within a company; women's credibility is more often derived from their **skills**.

Establishing your credibility

5 Men often derive credibility from their gender and status within a company; women's credibility is more often derived from their skills. Many women say they have to work harder to establish credibility because of their gender. Perhaps this statement from a Los Angeles businesswoman explains the situation best:

6 *When I travel outside of the United States for the corporate office, I'm viewed as foreign first and female second. However, I feel I'm still met with some degree of skepticism as to what my role is and how*

with whom you'll be dealing. If you can't have that person introduce you, ask him or her to send a fax or email in advance outlining your title, responsibilities, and background.

10 **Include a distinct title on your business cards.** Identifiers such as *manager* or *director* define your position clearly. If there's any doubt about your title, an overseas co-worker may assume automatically that you have a lesser role than the male members of your team. To avoid such confusion, some women wear a school ring, graduate school pendant, or corporate pin designating

tenure to artfully advertise their background or experience.

11 Businesspeople in some cultures may look and respond more to the men on your team because outside of the United States, women generally hold fewer executive positions. Prepare by advising colleagues of tactics that will help you and other female team members, such as making seating arrangements that place women in a position of authority.

12 If someone appears confused about your name and rank, offer another business card even if you've already given one. That subtle tactic reinforces your title and ensures acknowledgment of your participation as an active member at the meeting.

13 **Lead business discussions.** If there's only one woman and everyone is of equal rank on your team, the woman should take the lead to help establish her credibility, and team members

should advise team members not to answer questions directed to her. A good response is, "Jane is the best person to answer that question."

14 **Be professional.** Present yourself in a sincere, confident, and professional manner—in appearance and speech—to create a good first impression. Be yourself. Don't come on too strong, but don't defer when it's appropriate for you to respond. Deferring to age and position, however, is always acceptable for both sexes.

15 **Be aware of women's roles in other countries.** Understanding the status of women in their own environments gives you insight into how those cultures may perceive you.

The role of the manager

16 Managers can be effective in international business by helping enhance their teams' credibility. A manager can

portant that all team members, including managers, understand their roles in any meetings. If a colleague isn't participating appropriately for his or her role, call for a break to explain that the group becomes less effective when it's not cohesive.

18 **Reinforce the authority of female team members during meetings.** For example, if a woman isn't receiving the appropriate respect, the manager can bring attention to her role and authority.

19 Despite commonly held myths about women in international business, women are traveling and conducting business internationally in increased numbers, and they're successful in their business dealings. Adler and her fellow researcher, Dafna Izraeli, predict that global competition will completely eliminate the archaic patterns that have underrepresented and underutilized women in management, especially international business. In fact, it's already occurring.

Tracey Wilen *is in business management at Cisco Systems. This article is based on her book* International Business: A Basic Guide for Women; *twilen@cisco.com.*

Understanding the **status of women** in their own environments gives you **insight** into how those cultures may **perceive you**.

should defer to her to help reinforce her authority. Some American men may need to be made aware that their tendency to jump in and answer questions, especially when a woman is speaking, can undermine her authority and the team's effectiveness. A woman leader

introduce staff members by title and outline each person's area of expertise, act as moderator to refer questions to the appropriate team member, and highlight staff achievements.

17 **Don't act out of role.** It's im-

Discussion

1. What did Nancy Adler's study on women in international business reveal?

2. According to the author's research, what is one area that businesswomen find critical to their success abroad?

3. Explain the difference between how men derive credibility and how women derive credibility.

4. List the six pointers that Tracey Wilen gives to help expatriate businesswomen establish credibility.

5. Why is it important for expatriate businesswomen to be aware of women's roles in other countries?

6. How can managers be effective in international business?

7. What is the meaning of the term *patriarchy,* and what are the characteristics of a patriarchal society?

Teamwork

Working with a group, discuss the difficulties that managers have in choosing appropriate employees for overseas assignments. Consider the special characteristics and skills that expatriate employees should have. Then draw up a list of questions that managers could use when interviewing employees who are applying for these assignments abroad.

After you have developed at least ten questions, do a role play with the members of your group. Two students will take the roles of the company managers who are interviewing job applicants, and one student will take the role of the employee who wants to work abroad. After you have practiced the role play, present it to the class.

Writing Assignments

1. Imagine that you have been assigned to work in Japan for two years as an expatriate employee of a large U.S. technology company. You and your family received only two days of cross-cultural training before leaving for Japan, and you have not adjusted to the new culture. Write a letter to your boss in which you explain the challenges you and your family are facing after three months in Japan and ask to be sent back to the United States because of difficulties you are experiencing both at work and at home. The style of the letter should be clear and conversational. The tone should be colloquial and negative. (See Appendix B, Business Letter.)

2. Imagine that you are the boss in the United States who received the business letter described in writing assignment 1. Write a memorandum in reply to the employee. The style of the memorandum should be informal and concise. The tone should be balanced and authoritative. (See Appendix B, Memorandum.)

3. In "Women Working Overseas," Tracey Wilen presents statistics on working women in the United States. Write a short report on the current status of U.S. professional women. Check the following Web sites the author gives to get current statistics on U.S. working women. In your report, discuss the changes that have occurred since Wilen's article was published in May 2001.

   • U.S. Department of Labor: <www.dol.gov>.

   • National Association of Women Business Owners: <www.nawbo.org>.

   • Small Business Administration: <www.sba.gov>.

4. Write a research paper on the topic of the challenges facing expatriate employees. You may use the articles printed or mentioned in this chapter, including the expansion readings, as sources for your paper. Also find several recent sources on this topic. These books should be helpful.

   Axtell, Roger E. *Do's and Taboos around the World.* New York: John Wiley, 2000.

   Dresser, Norine. *Multicultural Manners: New Rules of Etiquette in a Changing Society.* New York: John Wiley, 1995.

   Harris, Philip R., and Robert T. Moran. *Managing Cultural Differences.* Houston: Gulf Publishing Company, 1996.

   Selmer, Jan, ed. *Expatriate Management: New Ideas for International Business.* Westport, CT: Quorum Books, 1995.

   Wederspahn, Gary. *Intercultural Services: A Worldwide Buyer's Guide and Sourcebook.* Woburn, MA: Butterworth-Heinemann, 2001.

   Wilen, Tracey. *International Business: A Basic Guide for Women.* <www.xlibris.com>, 2001.

Expansion Readings

Black, J. Stewart, and Hal B. Gregerson. "The Right Way to Manage Expats." *Harvard Business Review* 77, no. 2 (March–April 1999): 52–63.

"International Assignments: Nasty, Brutish, and Short." *The Economist,* 16 December 2000, 70–73.

Oral Presentation

Working with a partner, give a 20-minute oral presentation to the class on one of the articles listed under Expansion Readings or an article of your choice on expatriate employees. Summarize the article by including the author's thesis, major points, and supporting data and evaluate its strengths and weaknesses. Be prepared to answer questions on your topic. If you have the technical capability, use the presentation graphics program PowerPoint for your presentation. Otherwise, make at least one overhead to use on the overhead projector. (See Appendix B, Oral Presentation.)

Travels on the Web

The Internet offers numerous opportunities to read more about employment abroad, how to identify global career opportunities, and how to succeed in overseas assignments.

1. Log on to one of the following Web sites to read about this topic. Write a summary of the information you have read, and bring it to class for discussion with your classmates.

   - Meridian Resources (Profit from Global Knowledge)
     <http://www.meridianglobal.com>.
     Select Training and, under Expatriate Cycle, click on Working and Living Internationally.

   - Expatica.com (News and Community for the Expatriate)
     <http://www.expatica.com>.
     Select Human Resources and Expatica Jobs.

   - United States Department of State: <http://www.state.gov>.
     Select Travel and Living Abroad and Business Center.

2. The online site of the *Wall Street Journal* (WSJ.com) is the source of a wide variety of information for college students studying business. Log on to the following WSJ.com Web site to read about global careers: <http://www.dowjones.com>.

   Choose Electronic Publishing. Then, under Internet Publishing, click on CollegeJournal.com. The CollegeJournal site offers such topics as Success at Work, Career Paths, and Global Careers. If you choose Global Careers, you can access Country Profiles for "tips on social and business customs in 26 major countries from Window on the World Inc." This information is useful for any businessperson who will be working as an expatriate. Print out the information on the countries where you might be interested in working and bring it class to share with your classmates.

3. More than ten years ago, three women expatriates from Europe created a company called Paguro, which offers support services to expatriate families. Log on to Paguro.net at <http://www.paguro.net>. Read about Paguro and then make a list of the services offered to individuals and corporations by this Web site.

4. Use the Internet business database LexisNexis Academic to locate current information on expatriate training. Select Site Map, choose Business, and click on Business News. Do a Guided News Search by typing the words *expatriates* and *training*. Print out an interesting article and bring it to class for discussion.

Chapter 12
Contract Negotiation

<table>
<tr>
<td>

"Good Negotiation Equals Good Contracts"
Steven P. Cohen
Contract Management
August 2001

</td>
<td>

"You Say Tomato"
Lalita Khosla
Forbes
May 21, 2001

</td>
</tr>
</table>

Preview   "Good Negotiations Equals Good Contracts"

Skimming

Skim the article quickly to find the following general information.

1. Read the title and all headings and look at any illustrations.

2. Read the first and second paragraphs, looking for the author's purpose and main idea.

3. Read the last paragraph, looking for a summary or conclusion.

4. Write a sentence containing your preliminary understanding of the main idea of the article.

Questioning

Answer the following questions and discuss your answers in class.

1. What is the meaning of negotiation?

2. Have you ever negotiated a contract?

3. How skilled are you at bargaining to get what you want?

Scanning

Scan the article quickly to find the following specific information.

1. What is the definition of a successful negotiation?

2. What happens if a negotiator ignores one facet of the negotiation process?

3. Why does it make sense to view each negotiation as an episode in an ongoing relationship?

4. What is the foundation of successful negotiations?

5. Who are stakeholders?

Vocabulary in Context

Read the following sentences and try to guess the meaning of the italicized words by using the context. Then replace the italicized words with synonyms (words or phrases that have nearly the same or similar meanings).

1. "A well-written contract should be *unambiguous;* it should not hold surprises for the people charged with fulfilling its terms." (Paragraph 1)

2. "The agreement process—negotiation—must *contemplate* the long-term commitments the parties are making." (Paragraph 3)

3. "Parties can practice negotiating with each other, and develop the habit of reaching agreement by working first on *mundane* issues such as the negotiation time and place, agenda items, and issues to be covered." (Paragraph 10)

4. "A negotiation process that anticipates as many issues as possible increases the *likelihood* of smooth contract fulfillment." (Paragraph 11)

5. "*Soliciting* the support of employees with different priorities and mindsets is challenging but critical." (Paragraph 12)

6. "The issues that parties fight over and resolve during negotiation are less likely to become problems when the contract is implemented." (Paragraph 15)

Paraphrasing

After reading the article, reread the sentences under Vocabulary in Context. Now rewrite them using your own words. Change the vocabulary and sentence structure, but do not change the author's intended meaning or paraphrase any technical terms. There are several ways of paraphrasing each sentence.

Good Negotiation EQUALS *Good Contracts*

A contract negotiated with fulfillment in mind will generally have fewer problems later.

BY STEVEN P. COHEN

1 "Wait a minute! We never agreed to that!" How often have these chilling words overturned a contract manager's supposedly predictable world? A disagreement about one or more party's obligations under a contract sends folks scurrying to the documentation to figure out whose interpretation is accurate. A well-written contract should be

About the Author

STEVEN P. COHEN is president of The Negotiation Skills Company, Inc., in Pride's Crossing, MA. The company trains corporate employees how to best negotiate to achieve their desired results. Cohen also serves as an independent executive mentor to corporate leaders across the globe. Send comments on this article to cm@ncmahq.org.

unambiguous; it should not hold surprises for the people charged with fulfilling its terms.

2 A contract documents the existence of an agreement between parties. However, that strictly accurate definition barely begins to cover the role a contract plays in making an agreement real. Unless the process that yields the agreement, most commonly known as negotiation, is considered fair by the negotiating parties and their constituents, the agreement reached may not be durable. If the agreement is not workable, the contract in which it is recorded can be nearly impossible to manage.

Beyond a Checklist

3 A successful negotiation can be defined as one that has yielded a mutually agreeable result each party

will implement without having a gun held to their heads. The agreement process—negotiation—must contemplate the long-term commitments the parties are making. In organizing and proceeding with a negotiation, the parties must take steps to ensure that

- the process itself fosters agreement;

- the items agreed upon are mutually understood;

- the negotiating parties have the authority and responsibility to reach agreement; and

- fulfilling the promises exchanged in the negotiation process can be monitored to each party's satisfaction.

4 Negotiation is not a straightforward process. For example, an airplane pilot has a checklist that he goes through step by step before a plane can even leave the parking place. There are right and wrong answers on that list, and unless all the answers turn up "right," the plane should not take to the air.

5 By contrast, a negotiator has no list of answers that are always right or wrong. There is no specific order that every single negotiation must follow— although there may well be a series of steps common to some negotiation processes. Consequently, a good negotiator must be cognizant of multiple factors simultaneously. Rather than looking for a mandatory series of steps or considerations for each negotiation, it is important to enter into the negotiation process focused on many issues at the same time. If a negotiator ignores one facet of the process, it may haunt him later on, particularly during the implementation of the resulting contract.

6 Keeping the long-term consequences in mind is fundamental for the development of an agreement that makes sense five minutes, five months, or even five years after the hands are shaken and the contract signed. Multitasking is no easy job. Preparation can make it possible to develop a checklist of issues that may arise (or should not be ignored) during negotiations. It can also help protect a negotiator from surprises, even from folks he has dealt with many times before. Taking people for granted is full of risks, no matter how well a negotiator thinks he knows them. One never knows whether a new boss, client, or customer has begun to exert influence on another party, hence it's prudent to pay attention to one's negotiating partner.

An Ongoing Relationship

7 A large percentage of negotiations take place among parties who have ongoing business together. The same is true in personal life, where we negotiate with family members and friends all the time. It makes sense to

Top 10 Rules *for Negotiating a Successful Contract*

1. **Set goals.** Realize and commit to your goals. Understand exactly how achieving your goals benefits you and your company after the contract is signed.

2. **Find the decision maker.** Negotiate with the person who is responsible for seeing the deal through and who can sign off on all agreements made.

3. **Stay focused.** As you negotiate, keep asking yourself, "What is the point of this statement, this conversation, this meeting?" Don't waste your time or that of the people with whom you are negotiating.

4. **Seek information.** Think of negotiation like a game of cards; every time a new card is dealt to you, it changes your capacity to reach your goals—and changes the balance of power. Each bit of information you learn in the negotiation process is like a newly-dealt card.

5. **Respect your opponents.** Treat the people with whom you negotiate with respect. If you attack someone else's self-image, you are jeopardizing your chance of reaching a mutually agreeable resolution. Everyone wants to be understood. Seek first to understand before seeking to be understood.

6. **Seek opportunities.** Don't ignore folks who are not drop-dead decision-makers. When you're faced with someone who doesn't have the power or authority to solve your problems, remember they may be acting as a filter for their superiors. Reaching an agreement with them will turn them into your allies in working to convince their decision-makers.

7. **Ignore prejudices.** Don't let cultural differences become obstacles to fair negotiation. In the global marketplace, you will be dealing with people from different corporate, ethnic, regional, and national cultures. Focus on the issues about which you are negotiating, not the styles or approaches of others with whom you are working.

8. **Be firm.** When someone says or does something you find troublesome, don't just sit and take it. Be clear about what bothers you. If a negotiator gets away with the "small stuff" without being challenged, he will use a bulldozer on you when more serious issues arise.

9. **Exude confidence.** Don't approach negotiations with a victim attitude. If you do, you will be sure to emerge as a victim.

10. **Prepare.** In real estate, the three most important things are said to be "location, location, location." In negotiation, these things are "preparation, preparation, preparation." Don't set yourself up to be surprised.

—Steven Cohen

view each negotiation as an episode in an ongoing relationship; that gives the parties a sense of context and it increases their consciousness of the joint decision-making process's long-term consequences. In ongoing relationships, the negotiation process is often more efficient because the parties have an easier time communicating due to their familiarity with one another's style.

8   In business, as well as personal life, negotiators need to assess how important the relationship is in the context of other elements of the decision-making process. Sometimes a negotiator has to consider changing clients or suppliers to achieve a better result for the company. In those circumstances, the relative importance of the relationship is diminished. For example, if the quality of components delivered by a long-term supplier has declined, the relationship cannot be used to justify accepting lower quality than the ultimate product requires. A negotiator may offer the long-term supplier an opportunity to "clean up his act" to continue the relationship, but the ultimate decision must still be based on issues of quality.

9   Negotiating is not a competitive sport. In an ongoing relationship, sometimes one party may gain more than others in a particular negotiation, but over the long term the process may yield fundamental equality or equipoise, with each party benefiting. It is often harder, however, to focus on understanding and pursuing one's own interest rather than aiming to crush another party. A negotiator's job is to maximize the gains he derives from the process. Negotiators recognize that parties may have different goals; the best negotiators find ways to maximize the likelihood that as many of those goals as possible will be addressed in the ultimate agreement. One may get a better price than another party would prefer to pay, but it is important to remember that the goal is a better price and not simply beating up the other side.

10   In a new relationship, confidence-

Who Really Makes the Decisions?

A typical frustration among negotiators is to develop what they believe is a great deal, only to have it shot down by someone in the other party. Negotiators need to understand if the people they are dealing with are the "drop-dead decision-makers," or individuals who have the authority to deliver on whatever agreement is reached. It can be important to find out who signs the contract, who has to sign off on various elements, or which department is responsible for delivery.

For instance, a negotiator was once involved in negotiating with a major national company. Eventually, he and the other party's negotiator reached a deal they both considered fair. Each time the other firm's negotiator submitted a "final" document, a different level of the corporate hierarchy weighed in with objections to elements of the deal important to that part of the company. When the negotiator admitted that the decision-making process had to be approved by five levels at corporate headquarters, the first negotiator walked away from the deal. Thus, it is crucial to investigate what is behind the "face" of one's negotiation partner. If his company won't back up the negotiator's agreement, it's also unlikely to fulfill the agreement once it's signed.

—Steven Cohen

building measures may help to convince the other party to buy into the deal and sign the contract. Parties can practice negotiating with each other, and develop the habit of reaching agreement by working first on mundane issues such as the negotiation time and place, agenda items, and issues to be covered. If one party arrives with one agenda and the other arrives with a different agenda, they are literally not on the same page. The stage has not been set for mutual understanding, much less agreement. By agreeing on what may seem to be inconsequential issues, negotiators set a pattern for success that is likely to continue through the process and lead to an executable contract.

11   Preparation is the foundation of successful negotiations. Focusing on the elements that can contribute to or detract from an agreement enables the parties to develop a contract free of surprises. Surprises are often the greatest threat to comfortable contract management. A negotiation process that anticipates as many issues as possible increases the likelihood of smooth contract fulfill-

ment. Good preparation gives a negotiating party a chance to deal with issues before they become problems.

Who are the Stakeholders?

12   Before working with an external party, however, negotiators must ensure that their own team players are working together. If the very people who must implement the contract don't buy into it, the negotiator's ability to confidently present a solution to the external party may be seriously undermined. Soliciting the support of employees with different priorities and mindsets is challenging but critical.

13   Yet even among these differences, negotiators can draw strengths. A benefit of having different mindsets within a company is that people from different areas can often help the negotiator develop assumptions about external negotiation partners. If a negotiation partner's decisions are driven by marketing considerations, one's own marketing department may be able to improve the negotiator's assumptions about what factors drive the other party's decisions.

14   To prepare for negotiation, negotia-

tors must understand who their stakeholders are. Stakeholders are parties who will derive some sort of consequence from the negotiation process and its results. Some stakeholders have an immediate demonstrable interest in things like specifications, price, or delivery. Others may appear more tangential to the agreement, such as customers of customers, suppliers of suppliers, or regulatory agencies that may not belong "at the table." Nonetheless, they may have strong interests and influences on fulfilling the contract. Once the stakeholders are identified, negotiators must determine what interests, goals, or objectives drive their decisions. By understanding these issues, the negotiator has a greater chance of getting the stakeholders to buy into the agreement.

15   With a sense of who the stakeholders are, negotiators can determine each party's constituent stakeholders. The next step is to pay close attention to how stakeholders position themselves and with whom they align. The goal is to be aware of any parties that

might be able to throw a monkey wrench into fulfilling the contract if the agreement threatens their interests. Listing the factors that drive stakeholders' decisions will give negotiators a better sense of what needs to be considered to develop a contract that will work. The issues that parties fight over and resolve during negotiation are less likely to become problems when the contract is implemented.

16   During the preparation process, look for connections between stakeholders and among their interests and goals. Keep in mind that although money is a priority for every party involved in the negotiations, it is more important to examine what money may mean to different parties—and what other assets they might consider as an alternative to cash in the negotiation process. For example, egos, deadlines, or cash flow may be issues that take some of the heat off price as a stand-alone factor.

Plan for the Future

17 Negotiations leading to a manageable contract must include elements that

address how promises made will be monitored. Planning for this can make a tremendous difference in how smoothly the contract terms are fulfilled. In some cases, each party may accept the others as appropriate monitors of promises kept. There are other cases where contracts specify industry standards, trade associations, or other external mechanisms to measure the adequacy of contract fulfillment. Still other agreements specify the processes that may be used for dispute settlement, such as mediation, arbitration, or litigation. A contract written in contemplation of possible problems will generally have fewer problems during its life. Successful negotiations, after all, don't end when the contract is signed; the parties must also fulfill the agreement's details. *CM*

Glossary

align	to line up on the side of or against a cause
buy into	to accept, believe
charged with	given a task or responsibility
cognizant	aware, knowledgeable about something
constituents	the people involved in or served by the negotiation
contemplate	to consider
context	the interrelated conditions in which something occurs; environment
diminished	lessened, decreased
dispute	argument, controversy
durable	lasting; able to exist for a long time
equipoise	a state of equilibrium
facet	any of the definable aspects that make up a subject
fosters	encourages; promotes the growth or development of
haunt	to have a harmful effect on; to trouble
implement	to carry out; to ensure fulfillment by concrete measures
inconsequential	unimportant; irrelevant
likelihood	probability
mandatory	obligatory; containing a command
mindset	mental attitude or inclination
monitored	watched, kept track of
monkey wrench	something that disrupts
multitasking	the concurrent performance of several jobs
mundane	commonplace, ordinary
negotiation	the action or process of arriving at an agreement through discussion and compromise
ongoing	continuing; being actually in process
priority	something given attention before competing alternatives
prudent	wise; shrewd in the management of practical affairs
soliciting	approaching with a request; asking for
tangential	incidental, peripheral
unambiguous	clear and understandable
undermined	weakened or ruined

Comprehension

1. Why is it important that the process of contract negotiation be considered fair by the negotiating parties and their constituents?

2. What must the parties ensure when organizing and proceeding with a negotiation?

3. Why is negotiation not a straightforward process?

4. Why is the negotiating process more efficient in ongoing relationships?

5. Why is negotiating not a competitive sport?

6. What are the advantages of preparation for negotiation?

7. Why do negotiators need to understand whether the people they are dealing with are the "drop-dead decision-makers"?

8. Why should negotiators determine the interests, goals, or objectives of their stakeholders?

9. What determines how smoothly the contract terms are fulfilled?

10. List the personality traits that an effective negotiator should have.

Analysis

Circle the letter next to the best answer(s). Justify your choices with quotations from the text.

1. What is the main idea of the article, and in which paragraph(s) is it stated?

   a. Detailed preparation is a critical element in contract negotiation because it determines the success or failure of the negotiations.

   b. The team that gets the best contract is usually the team that worked the hardest and was the most inflexible.

   c. It is much easier to negotiate with people with whom you have worked before and have an ongoing relationship.

   d. Successful contract negotiation depends on preparation for the negotiation, fairness in the negotiation process, and monitoring of the final agreement.

2. What is the meaning of the italicized word in this sentence from "Top 10 Rules for Negotiating a Successful Contract"? "If you attack someone else's self-image, you are *jeopardizing* your chance of reaching a mutually agreeable resolution."

   a. extending

   b. endangering

   c. ensuring

   d. enhancing

3. We can infer the following from this statement in paragraph 9: "Negotiating is not a competitive sport."

   a. Good negotiations do not end with a losing team and a winning team.

   b. It is impossible to be the winner of a contract negotiation.

   c. Intense competition between negotiating teams should be avoided.

   d. Training and practice do not improve negotiating skills.

4. The author's writing style in this article is _____ and _____ .

   a. formal

   b. informal

   c. technical

   d. nontechnical

5. The tone of the article is _____ and _____ .

   a. subjective

   b. objective

   c. argumentative

   d. balanced

6. What overall method of development is used in this article?

   a. analyzing a policy and criticizing its weakness

   b. clarifying a complex process

   c. identifying the effects of a future course of action

   d. arguing against an accepted theory

7. Why does the author compare a negotiator with an airplane pilot in paragraph 4?

   a. to develop an argument that negotiators are like pilots

   b. to support his argument that preparation for negotiation is important

   c. to show that negotiators, unlike pilots, do not have to follow a mandatory series of steps

   d. to prove that both negotiators and pilots must be able to handle stress

You Say Tomato

In dealing with foreigners, Americans sometimes come across as intrusive, manipulative and garrulous. This can get partnerships off to a bad start.

BY LALITA KHOSLA

1 IN NEGOTIATING WITH FOREIGN BUSINESS PEOPLE, small things matter. During seemingly endless negotiations with the Japanese Ministry of Trade and Industry (MITI), Minnesota Mining and Manufacturing's (3M) Harry Heltzer and a few of his colleagues left the table and began preparing tea. Later, their prospective partners, executives of the Sumitomo Trading Co., asked why Heltzer and his crew had behaved so uncharacteristically. Heltzer, who later rose to be 3M's chief executive, smiled and explained: You guys know how to haggle with MITI; we just wanted to be out of your way.

2 That little gesture of trust made a deep and lasting impression on the Sumitomo people; 40 years later the Sumitomo 3M joint venture is one of the most successful in Japan and contributes more than 10% of 3M's total profits.

3 Americans aren't always so sensitive to foreign tastes and habits. More recently, for instance, at Hewlett-Packard a group of engineers in California began designing software with HP's engineers in Grenoble, France. A rift nearly destroyed the project.

4 HP engineers in San Jose sent long, detailed e-mail to their counterparts in Grenoble. The engineers in Grenoble viewed the lengthy e-mail as patronizing and replied with quick, concise e-mail. That made the U.S. engineers believe that the French were withholding information. The process spiraled out of control. People started blaming personalities. A cultural logjam rolled into place.

5 HP turned to Charis Intercultural Training, a consulting firm based in Pleasanton, Calif., to help improve the relationship. "We went in as cultural sleuths," says Charis President Marian Stetson-Rodriguez. Charis quizzed members of each team, asking about their preferred communication styles. After six months of cultural training, the relationship improved.

6 Helping business people avoid intercultural faux pas has become a $100-million business for companies like Charis and San Francisco-based Meridian Resources. Intel, for instance, uses Charis to provide 55 training classes to instruct Intel employees on cultural nuances.

7 Here are a few hints from the people at Charis and Meridian. By remembering these subtle points, your partnerships may avoid running into trouble:

Helping business people avoid intercultural faux pas has become a $100-million business

▶Italians, Germans and French don't soften up executives with praise before they criticize. Americans do, and to the Europeans that seems manipulative.

▶Israelis, accustomed to fast-paced meetings, have no patience for American small talk.

▶British executives often complain that their U.S. counterparts chatter too much. Our penchant for informality, egalitarianism and spontaneity sometimes jars people.

▶Europeans often feel they are being treated like children when Americans insist they wear name tags.

▶Indian executives are used to interrupting one another. If Americans listen without asking for clarification or posing questions, the Indians may feel the Americans aren't paying attention.

▶When negotiating with Malaysian or Japanese executives, periodically allow for 6 seconds of silence. If you are negotiating with an Israeli, don't pause.

▶Think twice before asking some foreigners questions like "How was your weekend?" That sounds intrusive to foreigners who tend to regard their business and private lives as totally compartmentalized.

▶For more hints and suggestions, visit www.meridian global.com and click on Web Tools. **F**

Discussion

1. The word *tomato* is not prounced in the same way in American English and British English. Americans say *tomato* with a long *a* (like the vowel sound in *may*). The British say *tomato* with a short *a* (like the vowel sound in *ma*). Explain how the title "You Say Tomato" relates to the content of the article.

2. Describe the problem that arose between Hewlett-Packard engineers in California and Hewlett-Packard engineers in Grenoble, France.

3. How did Charis Intercultural Training improve the relationship?

4. What suggestions would you make to others about negotiating with people from your native culture?

5. Do you find that Americans are sensitive to cultural differences?

6. Have you had any experience in negotiating a business contract? If so, explain the results.

Teamwork

Working with a group, divide into two negotiating teams, one of which is from the United States and the other from a different country. The purpose of the negotiation is to establish ground rules for future negotiations about a business contract. Ground rules include dates, times, location, agenda items, and other practical matters concerning the negotiating sessions. Each team should draw up a list of ground rules and special requests in regard to the negotiating situation.

After each team has developed its list of ground rules, practice doing a role play with the members of the other team and then present the role play to the class.

Writing Assignments

1. An abstract is a short summary (usually between 50 and 150 words) of a longer document. A descriptive abstract presents the topics covered in the document; it is similar to a table of contents. An informative abstract provides the reader with the major points, findings, and conclusions. Make an outline of the article "Good Negotiation Equals Good Contracts," printed in this chapter. Then write a 150-word informative abstract of the article.

2. Today some contract negotiations are conducted by e-mail. In your library periodicals collection, locate the past issues of the *Harvard Business Review* and read the article titled "The Electronic Negotiator" by Regina Fazio Maruca and Kathleen Valley (*Harvard Business Review* [January–February 2000, 78, no. 1:

16–17]). After reading the article, make an outline of the article and then write a summary of it. Attach a copy of the article to your summary.

3. Imagine you are the chief negotiator of a team that has to negotiate a business contract with another company. Write a memorandum to your negotiating team in which you explain the principles you intend to follow to achieve a successful contract. The style of the memorandum should be formal and personal, and the tone should be positive and businesslike. (See Appendix B, Memorandum.)

4. Write a research paper on the topic of global negotiation. You may use the articles printed or mentioned in this chapter, including the expansion readings, as sources for your paper. Also find several recent sources. These books should be helpful.

Brett, Jeanne M. *Negotiating Globally: How to Negotiate Deals, Resolve Disputes, and Make Decisions across Cultural Boundaries.* San Francisco: Jossey-Bass, 2001.

Cleary, Patrick J. *The Negotiation Handbook.* Armonk, NY: Sharpe, 2001.

Fisher, Roger, William Ury, and Bruce Patton. *Getting to Yes: Negotiating Agreement without Giving In.* New York: Penguin Books, 1991.

Thompson, Leigh L. *The Mind and Heart of the Negotiator.* 2d ed. Upper Saddle River, NJ: Prentice-Hall, 2001.

Expansion Readings

Kolb, Deborah M., and Judith Williams. "Breakthrough Bargaining." *Harvard Business Review* 79, no. 2 (February 2001): 89–97.

Maruca, Regina Fazio, and Kathleen Valley. "The Electronic Negotiator." *Harvard Business Review* 78, no. 1 (January–February 2000): 16–17.

Sebenius, James K. "The Hidden Challenge of Cross-Border Negotiations." *Harvard Business Review* 80, no. 4 (April 2002): 76–85.

———. "Six Habits of Merely Effective Negotiators." *Harvard Business Review* 79, no. 4 (April 2001): 87–95.

Oral Presentation

Working with a partner, give a 20-minute oral presentation to the class on one of the articles listed under Expansion Readings or an article of your choice on contract negotiation. Summarize the article by including the author's thesis, major points, and supporting data and evaluate its strengths and weaknesses. Be prepared to answer questions on your topic. If you have the technical capability, use the presentation graphics program PowerPoint for your presentation. Otherwise, make at least one overhead to use on the overhead projector. (See Appendix B, Oral Presentation.)

Travels on the Web

The Internet offers numerous opportunities to read more about contract negotiation in the business world.

1. The following Web sites offer training courses and advice on negotiation techniques and strategies. Log on to these Web sites, find an article on negotiation, and bring the article to class to share with your classmates.

   - The Negotiation Skills Company: <http://www.negotiationskills.com>.
     Select Articles/Newsletters.

   - The Negotiation Center: <http://www.negotiations.org>.
     Select Explore Topics and then click on Culture and Negotiation or Corruption and Negotiation.

2. Log on to CFO Magazine at <http://www.CFO.com> and select Browser Archives. Under M & A, choose Negotiation, which contains an article by Harvard law professor Roger Fisher, an expert in the field of negotiations. The article, titled "Getting the Other Side to Say Yes," is a CFO interview from September 14, 2001. After printing out the article, write a summary of it and bring the article and summary to class to share with your classmates.

3. Use the Internet business database LexisNexis Academic to locate current information on labor-management contract negotiations, which are called collective bargaining. Select Site Map, choose Business, and click on Business News. Do a Guided News Search by using the terms *negotiations* and *bargaining*. Print out an interesting article and bring it to class for discussion.

Chapter 13
Management

"How We Went Digital without a Strategy" Ricardo Semler *Harvard Business Review* September–October 2000	"Separating Sheep from Goats as Start-ups Fall to Earth" Jennifer L. Rich *The New York Times* March 11, 2001

Preview   "How We Went Digital without a Strategy"

Skimming

Skim the article quickly to find the following general information.

1. Read the title and all headings and look at any illustrations.

2. Read the first and second paragraphs, looking for the author's purpose and main idea.

3. Read the last paragraph, looking for a summary or conclusion.

4. Write a sentence containing your preliminary understanding of the main idea of the article.

Questioning

Answer the following questions and discuss your answers in class.

1. What well-known managers have you heard of?

2. What are the responsibilities of a manager?

3. What qualities should an effective manager have?

Scanning

Scan the article quickly to find the following specific information.

1. Over the last 10 years, how did the number of Semco employees change?

2. What is the name of the South American Web portal that Semco developed for the building industry?

3. What is Ricardo Semler's business philosophy?

4. What has the turnover rate been at Semco in the past six years?

5. What spirit is nurtured at Semco?

Vocabulary in Context

Read the following sentences and try to guess the meaning of the italicized words by using the context. Then replace the italicized words with synonyms (words or phrases that have nearly the same or similar meanings).

1. "For the 20 years I've been with the company, I've *steadfastly* resisted any attempt to define its business." (Paragraph 1)

2. "Nearly 2,000 executives from around the world have trekked to São Paulo to study our operations. Few, though, have tried to *emulate* us." (Paragraph 2)

3. "It was a nightmare to manage, it resulted in poor or *haphazard* service, and it was ridiculously inefficient." (Paragraph 13)

4. "We're also partnering with a company called eTradeshow to host *virtual* construction fairs within the portal." (Paragraph 18)

5. "Proposals have to meet two simple *criteria* that govern all the businesses we launch." (Paragraph 27)

6. "But I'm beginning to see troubling signs that the traditional ways of doing business are reasserting their *hegemony*." (Paragraph 30)

Paraphrasing

After reading the article, reread the sentences under Vocabulary in Context. Now rewrite them using your own words. Change the vocabulary and sentence structure, but do not change the author's intended meaning or paraphrase any technical terms. There are several ways of paraphrasing each sentence.

How We Went *Digital* Without a *Strategy*

Over the last decade, Semco has successfully extended its business from manufacturing to services to the Internet. Here's what it has learned: transformation is easy – if you throw away your plans and let your people lead you.

by Ricardo Semler

1 I OWN A $160 MILLION South American company named Semco, and I have no idea what business it's in. I know what Semco does – we make things, we provide services, we host Internet communities – but I don't know what Semco is. Nor do I want to know. For the 20 years I've been with the company, I've steadfastly resisted any attempt to define its business. The reason is simple: once you say what business you're in, you put your employees into a mental straitjacket. You place boundaries around their thinking and, worst of all, you hand them a ready-made excuse for ignoring new opportunities: "We're not in that business." So rather than dictate Semco's identity from on high, I've let our employees shape it through their individual efforts, interests, and initiatives.

2 That rather unusual management philosophy has drawn a good deal of attention over the years. Nearly 2,000 executives from around the world have trekked to São Paulo to study our operations. Few, though, have tried to emulate us. The way we work – letting our employees choose what they do, where and when they do it, and even how they get paid – has seemed a little too radical for mainstream companies.

3 But recently a funny thing happened: the explosion in computing power and the rise of the Internet reshaped the business landscape, and the mainstream shifted. Today, companies are desperately looking for ways to increase their creativity and flexibility, spur their idea flow, and free their talent – to do, in other words, what Semco has been doing for 20 years.

4 I don't propose that Semco represents the model for the way businesses will operate in the future. Let's face it: we're

How do you get a sizable organization to change without telling it to? It's easy – but only if you're willing to give up control.

a quirky company. But I do suggest that some of the principles that underlie the way we work will become increasingly common and even necessary in the new economy. In particular, I believe we have an organization that is able to transform itself continuously and organically – without formulating complicated mission statements and strategies, announcing a bunch of top-down directives, or bringing in an army of change-management consultants. As other companies seek to build adaptability into their organizations, they may be able to learn a thing or two from Semco's example.

Transformation Without End

5 Over the last ten years, Semco has grown steadily, quadrupling its revenues and expanding from 450 to 1,300 employees. More important, we've extended our range dramatically. At the start of the '90s, Semco was a manufacturer, pure and simple. We made things like pumps, industrial mixers, and dishwashers. But over the course of the decade, we diversified successfully into higher-margin

---

Ricardo Semler is the majority owner of Semco in São Paulo, Brazil. He is the author of two previous HBR articles, "Managing Without Managers" (September–October 1989) and "Why My Former Employees Still Work for Me" (January–February 1994), and the book Maverick *(Warner Books, 1993).*

---

services. Last year, almost 75% of our business was in services. Now we're stretching out again – this time into e-business. We expect that more than a quarter of our revenues next year will come from Internet initiatives, up from nothing just one year ago. We never planned to go digital, but we're going

6 digital nonetheless.

You may wonder how that's possible. How do you get a sizable organization to change without telling it – or even asking it – to change? It's actually easy – but only if you're willing to give up control. People, I've found, will act in their best interests, and by extension in their organizations' best interests, if they're given complete freedom. It's only when you rein them in, when you tell them what to do and how to think, that they become inflexible, bureaucratic, and stagnant. Forcing change is the surest way to frus-

7 trate change.

Enough lecturing. Let me give you a concrete example of how our transformation has played out. Ten years ago, one of the things we did was manufacture cooling towers for large commercial buildings. In talking with the property owners who bought these products, some of our salespeople began to hear a common refrain. The customers kept complaining about the high cost of maintaining the towers. So our salespeople came back to Semco and proposed starting a little business in managing cooling-tower maintenance. They said, "We'll charge our customers 20% of whatever savings we generate for them, and we'll give Semco 80% of those revenues and take the remaining 20% as our commis-

8 sion." We said, "Fine, give it a shot."

Well, the little business was successful. We reduced customers' costs and eliminated some of their hassles, and they were happy. In fact, they were so happy that they came back and asked if we'd look after their air-conditioning compressors as well. Even though we didn't manufacture the compressors, our people didn't hesitate. They said yes. And when the customers saw we were pretty good at maintaining compressors, they said, "You know, there are a lot of other annoying functions that we'd just as soon off-load, like cleaning, security, and general

9 maintenance. Can you do any of those?"

At that point, our people saw that their little business might grow into quite a big business. They began looking for a partner who could help bolster and

extend our capabilities. They ended up calling the Rockefeller Group's Cushman & Wakefield division, one of the largest real-estate and property-management companies in the United States, and proposing that we launch a 50–50 joint venture in Brazil. Cushman wasn't very keen on the idea at first. People there said, "Property management by itself isn't a very lucrative business. Why don't we talk about doing something that involves real estate? That's where the money is."

10 We spent some time thinking about going into the real-estate business. We didn't have any particular expertise there, but we were willing to give it a try. When we started asking around, though, we found that no one in the company had much interest in real estate. It just didn't get anyone excited. So we went back to the Cushman folks and said, "Real estate sounds like a great business, but it's not something we care about right now. Why don't we just start with property management and see what happens?" They agreed, though not with a lot of enthusiasm.

11 We ponied up an initial investment of $2,000 each, just enough to pay the lawyers to set up a charter. Then we set our people loose. In no time, we had our first contract, with a bank, and then more and more business came through the door. Today, about five years later, the joint venture is a $30 million business.

12 It's also the most profitable property-management business within Cushman & Wakefield. The reason it has been so successful is that our people came into it fresh, with no preconceived strategies, and they were willing to experiment wildly. Instead of charging customers in the traditional way – a flat fee based on a building's square footage – they tried a partnership model. We'd take on all of a property owner's noncore functions, run them like businesses, and split the resulting savings.

13 One customer, for example, had been using 126 subcontractors for all sorts of maintenance and security tasks. It was a nightmare to manage, it resulted in poor or haphazard service, and it was ridiculously inefficient. We took over all 126 tasks, from changing lightbulbs to managing the car fleet to maintaining elevators, and we treated each as a separate business. We tore every task apart to see how it could be done better, and we made a series of improvement proposals

to the client, ranging from relatively simple operating changes (reducing security personnel by installing video cameras) to highly technical systems installations (revamping the ATM architecture to dramatically reduce downtime). We outlined the investment and the expected gain and shared the cost reduction. The client reaped big savings and service improvements and got a single point of contact for doing everything necessary to run the building. And Semco made a heck of a lot more money than it would have by charging a flat fee.

14 Most manufacturers would probably consider a shift from making cooling towers to managing buildings pretty radical. Before making such a leap, they'd do a lot of soul-searching about their core businesses and capabilities. They'd run a lot of numbers, hold a lot of meetings, do a lot of planning. We didn't bother with any of that. We just let our people follow their instincts and apply their common sense, and it worked out fine.

Going to the Net

15 Our recent move into the digital space has proceeded in much the same way, with our people again taking the lead. In fact, some of the eight Internet ventures we've launched grew directly out of our earlier service initiatives. As our facility-management business expanded, for example, we extended it, through a joint venture with Johnson Controls, to managing retail facilities. As our people began to work closely with store managers, they began to notice the huge costs retailers incur from lost inventory. One employee came forward and asked for a paid leave to study opportunities in that area. We gave him a green light, and within a year he had helped us set up a joint venture with RGIS, the largest inventory-tracking company in the world. Less than two years later, the venture had become the biggest inventory-management business in South America. Now it is branching out into Web-enabled inventory control, helping on-line companies coordinate the fulfillment of electronic orders.

16 Our work in property management also brought us face to face with the disorganization and inefficiency of the construction business. Here, too, our people saw a big business opportunity, one that would build on the unique capabilities of the Internet. A number of the members

Semco is able to transform itself continuously and organically – without formulating complicated mission statements and strategies, announcing top-down directives, or bringing in an army of change-management consultants.

of our joint ventures with Cushman & Wakefield and Johnson Controls banded together, with Semco's support, to set up an on-line exchange to facilitate the management of commercial construction projects. All the participants in a building project – architects, banks, construction companies, contractors, and project managers – can now use our exchange to send messages, hold real-time chats, issue proposals and send bids, and share documents and drawings. They can collaborate even if they're using different software, because the Web platform automatically does all the translation. The exchange is revolutionizing the construction process here in Brazil.

17 That business, which we're operating as a 50–50 joint venture with the U.S. Internet software company Bidcom, has itself become a springboard for further new initiatives. One of the most exciting is the creation of a South American Web portal for the entire building industry. The portal, called Edify, provides a single point of access for all the people, goods, and services required for a construction project. It's a place where contractors can hire tradesmen, hardware stores can sell lumber and fixtures, homeowners can buy insurance and cable television service, and real-estate agents and interior decorators can promote their offerings. We make money by charging transaction fees on all the business that takes place through the portal.

18 We're also partnering with a company called eTradeshow to host virtual construction fairs within the portal. As our people began to work closely with construction companies, they realized that many sectors of the South American building trade – flooring and masonry, for example – aren't large enough to pay the costs of physical trade shows. As a result, new ideas and products have been slow to enter the markets. We saw that on-line shows would be highly attractive to these sectors, providing them access not only to new products but to potential new partners all around the world. We'll be holding 60 different fairs on the site. In addition, we'll be

hosting virtual versions of major international trade shows in such industries as automobiles, computers, and medical equipment. Visitors will be able to walk through a 3-D representation of the trade-fair space, collect business cards and brochures, watch presentations, and chat with sales representatives. These shows will generate fees for us while driving more traffic to the portal.

Management Without Control

19 Semco's ongoing transformation is a product of a very simple business philosophy: give people the freedom to do what they want, and over the long haul their successes will far outnumber their failures. Operationalizing that philosophy has involved a lot of trial and error, of taking a few steps forward and a couple back. The company remains a work in progress – and I hope it stays that way forever.

20 As I reflect on our experience, though, I see that we've learned some important lessons about creating an adaptive, creative organization. I'll share six of those lessons with you. I won't be so presumptuous as to say they'll apply to your company, but at least they'll stir up your thinking.

21 **Forget about the top line.** The biggest myth in the corporate world is that every business needs to keep growing to be successful. That's baloney. The ultimate measure of a business's success, I believe, is not how big it gets, but how long it survives. Yes, some businesses are meant to be huge, but others are meant to be medium-sized and still others are meant to be small. At Semco, we never set revenue targets for our businesses.

Rather than force our people to expand a business beyond its natural limits, we encourage them to start new businesses.

We let each one find its natural size – the size at which it can maintain profitability and keep customers happy. It's fine if a business's top line stays the same or even shrinks as long its bottom line stays healthy. Rather than force our people to expand an existing business beyond its natural limits, we encourage them to start new businesses, to branch out instead of building up.

22 **Never stop being a start-up.** Every six months, we shut down Semco and start it up all over again. Through a rigorous budgeting and planning process, we force every one of our businesses to justify its continued existence. If this business didn't exist today, we ask, would we launch it? If we closed it down, would we alienate important customers? If the answers are no, then we move our money, resources, and talent elsewhere. We also take a fresh look at our entire organization, requiring that every employee – leaders included – resign (in theory) and ask to be rehired. All managers are evaluated anonymously by all workers who report to them, and the ratings are posted publicly. It has always struck me as odd that companies force new business ideas and new hires to go through rigorous evaluations but never do the same for existing businesses or employees.

23 **Don't be a nanny.** Most companies suffer from what I call boarding-school syndrome. They treat their employees like children. They tell them where they have to be at what time, what they need to be doing, how they need to dress, whom they should talk to, and so on. But if you treat people like immature wards of the state, that's exactly how they'll behave. They'll never think for themselves or try new things or take chances. They'll just do what they're told, and they probably won't do it with much spirit.

24 At Semco, we have no set work hours, no assigned offices or desks, no dress codes. We have no employee manuals, no human resource rules and regulations. We don't even have an HR department. People go to work when they want and go home when they want. They decide when to take holidays and how much vacation they need. They even choose how they'll be compensated. (See the sidebar "Eleven Ways to Pay.") In other words, we treat our employees like adults. And we expect them to behave like adults. If they screw up, they take the blame. And since they have to be rehired

every six months, they know their jobs are always at risk. Ultimately, all we care about is performance. An employee who spends two days a week at the beach but still produces real value for customers and coworkers is a better employee than one who works ten-hour days but creates little value.

25 **Let talent find its place.** Companies tend to hire people for specific jobs and then keep them stuck in one career track. They also tend to choose which businesses people work in. The most talented people, for instance, may be assigned automatically to the business unit with the biggest growth prospects. The companies don't take into account what the individual really wants. The resulting disconnect between corporate needs and individual desires shows up in the high rates of talent churn that afflict most companies today.

26 We take a very different approach. We let people choose where they'll work and what they'll do (and even decide, as a team, who their leaders will be). All entry-level new hires participate in a program called Lost in Space. They spend six months to a year floating around the company, checking out businesses, meeting people, and trying out jobs. When a new hire finds a place that fits with his personality and goals, he stays there. Since our turnover rate in the past six years has been less than 1% – even though we've been targeted heavily by headhunters – we must be doing something right.

27 **Make decisions quickly and openly.** The best way for an organization to kill individual initiative is to force people to go through a complicated, bureaucratic review and approval process. We strive to make it as easy as possible for Semco employees to propose new business ideas, and we make sure they get fast and clear decisions. All proposals go through an executive board that includes representatives from our major business units. The board meetings are completely open. All employees are welcome to attend – in fact, we always reserve two seats on the board for the first two employees who arrive at a meeting. Proposals have to meet two simple criteria that govern all the businesses we launch. First, the business has to be a premium provider of its product or service. Second, the product or service has to be complex, requiring engineering

skills and presenting high entry barriers. Well-considered proposals that meet those standards get launched within Semco. Even if a proposed business fails to meet both criteria, we'll often back it as a minority investor if its prospects look good.

28 **Partner promiscuously.** To explore and launch new businesses quickly and efficiently, you need help; it's pure arrogance to assume you can do everything on your own. I'm proud to say that we partner promiscuously at Semco. Indeed, I can't think of a single new business we've started without entering into some kind of alliance, whether to gain access to software, draw on a depth of experience, bring in new capabilities,

---

Eleven Ways to Pay

At Semco, we let employees choose the way they are paid. There are 11 compensation options.

1. *Fixed salary*
2. *Bonuses*
3. *Profit sharing*
4. *Commission*
5. *Royalties on sales*
6. *Royalties on profits*
7. *Commission on gross margin*
8. *Stock or stock options*
9. *IPO/sale warrants that an executive cashes in when a business unit goes public or is sold*
10. *Self-set annual review/ compensation in which an executive is paid for meeting self-set goals*
11. *Commission on difference between actual and three-year-value of company*

And because the options can be combined in different ways, there is a vast number of possible permutations. We've found that by being flexible about rewards, we encourage our employees to innovate and take risks. In the end, people understand it's in their best interest to choose compensation packages that maximize both their own pay and the company's returns.

or just share risk. Partnerships have provided the foundation for our experiments and our expansion over the years. Our partners are as much a part of our company as our employees.

Staying Free

I travel a lot in my job, and recently I've been spending time in Silicon Valley. I've been visiting Internet companies, talking with technology visionaries, and participating in panel discussions on the future of business. The new companies and their founders excite me. I see in them the same spirit we've nurtured at Semco – a respect for individuals and their ideas, a distrust of bureaucracy and hierarchy, a love for openness and experimentation.

But I'm beginning to see troubling signs that the traditional ways of doing business are reasserting their hegemony. Investors, I fear, are starting to force young start-ups into the molds of the past – molds that some thought had been broken forever. CEOs from old-line companies are being brought in to establish "discipline" and "focus." Entrepreneurs are settling into corner offices with secretaries and receptionists. HR departments are being formed to issue policies and to plot careers. Strategies are being written. The truly creative types are being caged up in service units and kept further and further from the decision makers.

It's sad and, I suppose, predictable. But it isn't necessary. If my 20 years at Semco have taught me anything, it's that successful businesses do not have to fit into one tight little mold. You can build a great company without fixed plans. You can have an efficient organization without rules and controls. You can be unbuttoned and creative without sacrificing profit. You can lead without wielding power. All it takes is faith in people. ▽

Reprint R00511

Glossary

afflict	to distress, trouble, injure
alienate	to make unfriendly, hostile, or indifferent; estrange
arrogance	a feeling or an impression of superiority manifested in an overbearing manner
bureaucratic	characterized by specialization of functions, adherence to fixed rules, and a hierarchy of authority
churn	frequent turnover, rotation of personnel
commission	a fee paid to an employee for transacting business or performing a service
criteria	standards on which a judgment or decision may be based
dictate	to impose, pronounce, or specify authoritatively
digital	relating to computers, information technology, e-commerce, and the Internet
emulate	to imitate; to strive to equal
expertise	the skill of an expert
haphazard	marked by lack of plan, order, or direction; random
headhunters	recruiters of personnel, especially at the executive level
hegemony	domination; predominant influence or authority over others
hierarchy	classification of a group of people according to ability or professional standing
inventory	the quantity of goods or materials on hand; stock
keen on	enthusiastic about, fond of; eager
launch	to introduce, originate
mainstream	a prevailing current or direction of activity or influence
ponied up	paid money
preconceived	formed prior to actual knowledge or experience
presumptuous	arrogant; overstepping due bounds of courtesy or propriety
quirky	peculiar, unusual, idiosyncratic
radical	extreme; marked by a considerable departure from the usual
reaped	obtained
revamping	remaking, renovating, reconstructing
springboard	a point of departure
stagnant	not advancing or developing
steadfastly	firmly, with determination
strategy	a careful plan or method; a clever scheme

trekked	made a journey involving difficulties
turnover	change in personnel
virtual	unreal but similar to in effect or essence
wielding	exerting one's authority by means of

Comprehension

1. Why has Ricardo Semler resisted any attempt to define the business of Semco?

2. What is unusual ("radical") about the way Semco works?

3. Why does Ricardo Semler believe that the way Semco works will become increasingly common and even necessary in the new economy?

4. How did Ricardo Semler get Semco to change from just a manufacturing company to a services and Internet company?

5. What would most manufacturers do before changing from making cooling towers to managing buildings?

6. Describe Semco's Internet ventures.

7. What is the ultimate measure of a business's success?

8. What happens every six months at Semco?

9. What makes Semco an unusual place to work?

10. Describe the Lost in Space program at Semco.

11. Why does Ricardo Semler believe that decisions should be made quickly and openly?

12. What has Ricardo Semler learned from his 20 years at Semco?

13. How would you like to work at Semco? What are the advantages and the disadvantages?

Analysis

Circle the letter next to the best answer(s). Justify your choices with quotations from the text.

1. What is the main idea of the article, and in which paragraph(s) is it stated?

   a. Ricardo Semler believes that the freedom and creative opportunities his company provides to employees will become more and more important in the new economy.

   b. When employees are restrained by rigid rules, they are of less benefit to their organization and become stagnant.

   c. Offering 11 different compensation plans is one of the most unusual aspects of Semco.

   d. Semco serves as a model for many companies around the world, even though its management methods are unusual.

2. What is the meaning of the italicized word in this sentence in "Eleven Ways to Pay"? "There are 11 compensation options. . . . And because the options can be combined in different ways, there is a vast number of possible *permutations*."

   a. rewards

   b. problems

   c. solutions

   d. variations

3. We can infer the following from this statement in paragraph 19: "The company remains a work in progress—and I hope it stays that way forever."

   a. Semler has strongly encouraged progressive and unusual ideas in his company because he believes in creativity.

   b. Expansion of a profitable business through partnerships is always a good management strategy.

   c. Achieving well-defined and measurable goals is emphasized by Semco's top management.

   d. Semler believes that his company should continue to develop by being dynamic, flexible, and open to change.

4. The author's writing style in this article is _____ and _____ .

   a. impersonal

   b. personal

   c. conversational

   d. academic

5. The tone of the article is _____ and _____ .

   a. subjective

   b. objective

   c. humorous

   d. serious

6. What overall method of development is used in this article?

   a. analyzing a technical proposal

   b. enumerating steps in an administrative process

   c. chronologically describing a problem

   d. justifying a method through analysis of causes and effects

7. In the conclusion to the article ("Staying Free"), what techniques does the author use?

   a. contrasting ideas

   b. parallelism

   c. direct quotations

   d. definitions

Business

THE BUSINESS WORLD

JENNIFER L. RICH

Separating Sheep From Goats As Start-Ups Fall to Earth

PETROPOLIS, Brazil

1   BALANCING a small laptop computer on his knees, the Brazilian banker Luiz Cezar Fernandes struggled to pull a tobacco-filled pipe from the front pocket of his light-blue slacks. He tamped down the tobacco and lit the pipe before returning his attention to the computer, where he had been jumping from site to site on the Internet.

2   "Look at how quickly that site downloads," he said, eyes twinkling as he puffed on the pipe. "Have you ever seen anything that fast?"

3   Sitting in what would soon be the lounge of his new offices, Mr. Fernandes, a soft-spoken man with a round face and a white beard, was marveling over the one-megabyte-a-second wireless Internet connection that had just been installed in his laptop.

4   Elsewhere in the office, workers added cheerful red paint to the exposed beams and laid concrete slab tiles on the sun-drenched patio. Outside, sheep bleated in the pasture. The sheep.

5   For investment bankers who want to walk away from their high-tension lives but cannot live without working, Mr. Fernandes has found a solution. He is running CL Convergence, a Brazilian consulting firm that salvages troubled Internet businesses.

6   When **Crédit Lyonnais,** the French bank, recently asked Mr. Fernandes to come out of retirement to run CL Convergence, he said yes, but on one condition: the office must be on his sheep ranch — Fazenda Marambaia — 55 miles up in the hills behind Rio de Janeiro.

7   After losing a fight among shareholders at a bank that he had founded, Mr. Fernandes retired to the ranch with his third wife two years ago, after more than 30 years as one of Brazil's highest-profile bankers.

8   "I don't want to be one of those people that gets old and deaf and gets run over by a car on a street corner in Rio," said Mr. Fernandes, a youthful, 55-year-old grandfather of two.

9   Eager to have Mr. Fernandes, Crédit Lyonnais accepted his terms. They brought in a third partner, a Brazilian auditing and consulting firm called **Trevisan,** and shooed the ranch's milking cows out of the barn. With the livestock banished to a paddock across the pasture, architects drew plans to deodorize and convert the space into what may be one of the most technologically advanced offices in Brazil.

10   Because of the wireless Internet connections, up to 120 employees can take their work out to the gardens (designed by the landscape artist Burle Marx). Mr. Fernandes also installed fiber optic cable and ordered modular furniture from a manufacturer in Germany. CL Convergence is spending about $3 million on the offices.

11   "When you work 12 to 14 hours a day, it's important to be happy with your environment," Mr. Fernandes said.

12   For now, though, the company's 20 or so employees — mostly recent graduates from local schools, work from a temporary office in his helicopter hangar. From there, they analyze business models and predict the future of the country's financially troubled Internet companies, aiming to identify their potential for salvation and prosperity.

13   The idea is to give companies deemed worth saving a stamp of approval that will entice international venture capitalists back to Brazil again. Over the last year, venture capital investment has all but dried up in Brazil, as investors have been scared away by costly losses.

14   "The same irrationality that drove the market to buy things that would never have value, has made them not want to look at anything anymore," Mr. Fernandes said. "There needs to be someone to come in and say, 'This is really going to work.' "

15   THE company is willing to take risks. Rather than assessing an upfront fee, CL Convergence will charge only success fees or take an equity stake in the companies it represents. In exchange, companies that hire Mr. Fernandes must agree to move their bookkeeping and other back-office operations to his ranch. That way, he said, CL Convergence can monitor the bottom line more effectively.

16   From its offices in São Paulo, Trevisan will provide auditing and consulting support, while Crédit Lyonnais will be called for any investment banking needs.

17   José Irigoyen, head of Latin American capital markets at Crédit Lyonnais in New York, said: "The only way this model will work is to have very low overhead costs. And we'll be sharing the customer's interest, which can only be done if big organizations come together."

18   Mr. Fernandes estimates that the company, which pays him nothing for the use of the ranch, will save $2 million to $3 million a year on overhead.

19   Mr. Fernandes hopes that venture capitalists, upon returning to Brazil, will need to have companies like his to baby-sit their investments. But some experts said it remained unclear whether his instincts would prove correct.

20   "These types of companies are going to be necessary," said Bob Wollheim, the chief executive of **Ideia.com,** a Brazilian company that helps incubate Internet start-ups. But Mr. Wollheim said that making the concept work on a sheep farm "might be difficult."

21   In its first few weeks of operation, however, CL Convergence has had brisk business. The phones in the helicopter hangar have been ringing constantly. Mr. Fernandes said he had received 42 visits from potential clients and signed four contracts. (He declined to give additional details.)

22   "Imagine if we were located on Avenida Paulista or Rio Branco," he said, referring to main business arteries in São Paulo and Rio de Janeiro. "We would never have a minute's peace."

23   To reach the ranch, potential clients must drive 90 minutes from Rio or pay about $700 round trip for the 12-minute ride on one of the ranch's two helicopters. The relative difficulty of visiting helps screen out those who are not serious, Mr. Fernandes said.

24   And as far as business is concerned, Mr. Fernandes is nothing if not serious. He said that after leaving his São Paulo home when he was 12, because of a fight with his father, he used a state program for under-age runaways to get a job as an errand boy at a local bank. By the time he was 21, and with the equivalent of an eighth-grade education, Mr. Fernandes and some partners had founded Banco Garantia, which eventually became Brazil's largest domestically owned investment bank before it was bought by Credit Suisse First Boston in 1998.

25   By 1983, though, Mr. Fernandes left Garantia to found Banco Pactual, Brazil's largest domestically owned asset management firm. After a dispute among partners over the future of the bank, Mr. Fernandes left in 1999, ostensibly to retire and assume the life of a gentleman rancher. Petropolis, an affluent mountain hideaway founded in the 1840's by the Brazilian emperor Dom Pedro II and still home to some of the emperor's descendants, appeared a logical choice.

26   MR. FERNANDES actually bought Fazenda Marambaia in 1987, and, unable to resist the instinct to turn a profit, converted what had been a summer retreat for moneyed Brazilian families into a profitable ranch.

27   "I pictured having a pasture full of those cute little white fluffy sheep," Mr. Fernandes said. But he was dissuaded from that idea because the wool on the sheep soaks up water during the summer rainy season, and they cannot move about easily to graze.

28   Instead, Mr. Fernandes maintains a purebred flock of around 2,200 hairless black sheep — meat producers — that he sells to breeders and local restaurants.

Wiping his face and pulling out his pipe after a lunch of stuffed lamb, Mr. Fernandes does not seem to regret the decision. ☐

A Brazilian banker runs a high-tech consulting firm from a bucolic retreat.

Discussion

1. On what condition did Luiz Cezar Fernandes agree to come out of retirement to run CL Convergence?

2. Why did Fernandes retire to his sheep ranch in Petropolis in 1999?

3. Describe the work environment where Fernandes manages CL Convergence.

4. What kind of work do the employees at CL Convergence do?

5. Who are the partners of CL Convergence, and what is their work model?

6. Describe the education and professional experience of Fernandes.

7. What did Fernandes do with Fazenda Marambaia after he bought it in 1987?

8. Both Ricardo Semler and Luiz Cezar Fernandes are Brazilian businessmen who run companies. In what other ways are they similar, and in what ways are they different?

9. Would you rather work at Semco or at CL Convergence? Explain your answer.

Teamwork

Working in a group, develop a help wanted advertisement for Semco to place in *The Economist*. Describe the nature of the company, the position that has to be filled, the qualifications that an applicant should have, and the compensation packages for employees of Semco. Design the advertisement so that it is clear, readable, and appealing.

After you have developed the advertisement, practice doing a role play of the job interview. One student will take the part of the Semco manager, and one will take the part of the job applicant. Then perform your role play for the class.

Writing Assignments

1. Conduct an interview with an owner or manager of a business. (See "DNA: Handle with Care" in chapter 8 for an example of an interview.) Use a tape recorder during the interview and write up the information as a report in three sections: introduction, interview questions and answers, and conclusion.

You may use the questions listed below in your interview.

- What academic degrees do you have?

- How did you get your start in this type of business?

- How many employees do you have?

- What divisions of the business have you worked in?

- What are your future goals for the company?

- What is your philosophy of management?

2. Write a synthesis based on the two articles printed in this chapter: "How We Went Digital without a Strategy" by Ricardo Semler and "Separating Sheep from Goats as Start-ups Fall to Earth" by Jennifer L. Rich. Cite your sources in the in-text citation format (Semler 51). List your sources at the end of the paper as Works Cited and alphabetize them according to the authors' last names. You may develop your own thesis or use the following one: Managers of companies have to develop unique philosophies and methods to be effective in the 21st century.

3. According to "The Best (and worst) Managers of the Year" (*Business Week* [January 13, 2003]: 58–92), the following individuals were among the top 25 managers of 2002: Steve Ballmer, Microsoft (U.S.); Ken Kutaragi, Sony Computer Entertainment (Japan); Fujio Mitarai, Canon (Japan); Jorme Ollila, Nokia (Finland); Lee Scott, Wal-Mart (U.S.); and Margaret C. Whitman, eBay (U.S.).

    After doing research, write a report on one of these managers. Write an abstract (a short summary) as the first section. Use this format for your report.

> I. Abstract (50 words)
> II. Introduction (background and thesis)
> III. Education
> IV. Professional Experience
> V. Key Accomplishments

To read "The Best (and worst) Managers of the Year," use the Internet business database ABI/Inform. Under Search Methods, click on Publication, type in *Business Week,* and select the January 13, 2003, issue.

4. Write a research paper on the topic of the management of change. You may use the articles printed or mentioned in this chapter, including the expansion readings, as sources for your paper. Also find several recent sources. These books should be helpful.

Aaker, David A. *Developing Business Strategies.* 6th ed. New York: John Wiley, 2001.

Dauphinais, William, Grady Means, and Colin Price, eds. *Wisdom of the CEO: 29 Global Leaders Tackle Today's Most Pressing Business Challenges.* New York: John Wiley, 2000.

Gerstner, Louis V., Jr. *Who Says Elephants Can't Dance? Inside IBM's Historic Turnaround.* New York: HarperBusiness, 2002.

Magretta, Joan. *What Management Is: How It Works, and Why It's Everyone's Business.* New York: Free Press, 2002.

Poisant, Jim. *Creating and Sustaining a Superior Customer Service Organization.* Westport, CT; London: Quorum Books, 2002.

Rockefeller, David. *Memoirs.* New York: Random House, 2002.

Rosen, Robert, Patricia Digh, Marshall Singer, and Carl Phillips. *Global Literacies: Lessons on Business Leadership and National Cultures.* New York: Simon and Schuster, 2000.

Semler, Ricardo. *Maverick: The Success Story behind the World's Most Unusual Workplace.* New York: Warner Business Books, 1993.

Welch, Jack. *Jack: Straight from the Gut.* New York: Warner Business Books, 2001.

Expansion Readings

Bardaracco, Joseph L., Jr. "We Don't Need Another Hero." *Harvard Business Review* 79, no. 8 (September 2001): 120–26.

Collingwood, Harris, and Diane L. Coutu. "Jack on Jack." *Harvard Business Review* 80, no. 3 (March 2002): 88–94.

Doutu, Diane L. "Edgar H. Schein: The Anxiety of Learning." *Harvard Business Review* 80, no. 3 (March 2002): 100–106.

Goffee, Robert, and Gareth Jones. "Why Should Anyone Be Led by You?" *Harvard Business Review* 78, no. 5 (September–October 2000): 62–70.

Kaplan, Robert E. "Know Your Strengths." *Harvard Business Review* 80, no. 3 (March 2002): 20–21.

Orbanes, Phil. "Everything I Know about Business I Learned from Monopoly." *Harvard Business Review* 80, no. 3 (March 2002): 51–57.

"Personal Histories: Leaders Remember the Moments and People That Shaped Them." *Harvard Business Review* 79, no. 11 (December 2001): 27–38.

"A Survey of Management." *The Economist,* 9 March 2002, 3–20.

Zaleznik, Abraham. "The Twice-Born Leader." *Harvard Business Review* 79, no. 9 (October 2001): 152.

Oral Presentation

Working with a partner, give a 20-minute oral presentation to the class on one of the articles listed under Expansion Readings or an article of your choice on management styles. Summarize the article by including the author's thesis, major points, and supporting data and evaluate its strengths and weaknesses. Be prepared to answer questions on your topic. If you have the technical capability, use the presentation graphics program PowerPoint for your presentation. Otherwise, make at least one overhead to use on the overhead projector. (See Appendix B, Oral Presentation.)

Travels on the Web

The Internet offers numerous opportunities to do research about management.

1. Use the Internet business database ABI/Inform to find articles on the topic of management from the *Harvard Business Review* and the *Sloan Management Review.* Click on Search Methods, select Publication, and type the words *harvard business review* or *sloan management review.* ABI/Inform provides abstracts (short summaries) of the articles in these journals. After you have read several interesting abstracts, go to periodicals section of the library to read the complete articles. Make a copy of one article and bring it to class to share with your classmates.

2. Do research on the Internet on one of the following well-known managers: Mary Kay Ash, Mary Kay Cosmetics; Bill Gates, Microsoft; Roberto Goizueta, Coca-Cola; Sam Walton, Wal-Mart; Jack Welch, General Electric. Use the search engine Google or your favorite search engine to find an article that describes the accomplishments of one of these managers. Write a summary of the article, and attach a copy of the article to your summary.

3. Log on to Amazon.com (<http://www.amazon.com>) and look for the following books by or about the managers listed in the preceding task. After reading the customer reviews of the books, choose one book to read. Write a critical review of the book.

    - Ash, Mary Kay. *Mary Kay, You Can Have It All: Lifetime Wisdom from America's Foremost Woman Entrepreneur.* Rocklin, CA: Prima Publishers, 1996.

    - Gates, Bill. *Business @ the Speed of Thought: Using a Digital Nervous System.* New York: Warner Books, 1999.

    - Greising, David. *I'd Like the World to Buy a Coke: The Life and Leadership of Roberto Goizueta.* New York: John Wiley, 1998.

    - Walton, Sam. *Sam Walton: Made in America, My Story.* New York: Bantam Books, 1992.

    - Welch, Jack. *Jack: Straight from the Gut.* New York: Warner Business Books, 2001.

4. Log on to the search engine Google or your favorite search engine and type in the words *Ricardo Semler* and *Maverick.* Then read the various book reviews of Semler's autobiography *Maverick: The Success Story behind the World's Most Unusual Workplace* to decide whether you would like to read this book. For example, you could log on to the Web site of Michael Gray, CPA, at <http://www.profitadvisors.com> to read Gray's review of March 30, 1998. Print out a copy of the review that you read and bring it to class to share with your classmates.

14
Entrepreneurship

. . . .

"Dream Deferred: The Story of a High-Tech Entrepreneur in a Low-Tech World" Monique Maddy *Harvard Business Review* May–June 2000	**"Smart and Smarter"** Daniel Lyons *Forbes* March 18, 2002

. . . .
Preview   "Dream Deferred: The Story of a High-Tech
. . . .   Entrepreneur in a Low-Tech World"

Skimming

Skim the article quickly to find the following general information.

1. Read the title and all headings and look at any illustrations.

2. Read the first and second paragraphs, looking for the author's purpose and main idea.

3. Read the last paragraph, looking for a summary or conclusion.

4. Write a sentence containing your preliminary understanding of the main idea of the article.

Questioning

Answer the following questions and discuss your answers in class.

1. What is the meaning of the word *entrepreneur?*

2. What qualities should an entrepreneur have?

3. Can you envision yourself as an entrepreneur in the future?

Scanning

Scan the article quickly to find the following specific information.

1. How much venture capital had Monique Maddy raised at the time of Adesemi's downfall?

2. After attending Georgetown University, where did Monique study for a master's degree in international development and economics?

3. Because of her research, what did Monique decide to focus Adesemi's initial efforts on?

4. What percent of the world's 6 billion people have access to the Internet?

5. What caused a huge drain on Monique's time and energy?

6. How has Monique spent her time in the months since Adesemi was liquidated?

Vocabulary in Context

Read the following sentences and try to guess the meaning of the italicized words by using the context. Then replace the italicized words with synonyms (words or phrases that have nearly the same or similar meanings).

1. "No entrepreneur wants to fail, of course, but it is part of the bargain when you *opt out of* a traditional career." (Paragraph 4)

2. "Even more, I had grown frustrated by its [the UN's] lack of *tangible* impact." (Paragraph 9)

3. "First, I had to start in one country only—more than that would be *prohibitively* expensive." (Paragraph 12)

4. "One little start-up simply could not afford to offer a wide *array* of communications services at once." (Paragraph 13)

5. "Because of the major *deficiencies* of the telecommunications infrastructure, our engineers insisted that our network would have to be completely wireless to ensure reliability." (Paragraph 18)

6. "Adesemi had successfully launched 400 wireless pay phones throughout Dar es Salaam and developed an *intricate* distribution channel for its phone cards." (Paragraph 21)

7. "Licensing problems that had *plagued* us for years in Tanzania began to spin out of control." (Paragraph 24)

8. "Diversity is a tremendous strength, and such a *heterogeneous* workforce should have been a real boon to Adesemi." (Paragraph 36)

Paraphrasing

After reading the article, reread the sentences under Vocabulary in Context. Now rewrite them using your own words. Change the vocabulary and sentence structure, but do not change the author's intended meaning or paraphrase any technical terms. There are several ways of paraphrasing each sentence.

Dream Deferred

THE STORY OF A HIGH-TECH ENTREPRENEUR IN A LOW-TECH WORLD

by Monique Maddy

Adesemi was a tough little American start-up in Africa that many believed would ultimately blanket the third world with affordable wireless telecommunications. In the end, it could not overcome the built-in obstacles to doing business in emerging markets, but its founder learned four essential lessons that will guide her when she ventures forth again.

THE LAST TIME I SAW AFRICA, my heart was still filled with hope. I remember the moment clearly: as my plane lifted off from Abidjan, Ivory Coast, to take me to a meeting in Seattle with potential investors, I looked down at the continent where I was born. I thought, "My company can succeed here. Tough times are ahead, but my dream is still attainable." Then, for the rest of the flight, I played a mind game quite common to entrepreneurs—I allowed myself to imagine what that long-sought-after success would actually look and feel like. My company, Adesemi, would blanket the entire developing world with affordable wireless telecommunications services, bringing desperately needed communications to billions of people. And I would be rich and famous.

2 One month later, my company – and my dream – crashed to earth, an event that was as shocking as it was personally and financially devastating. It was shocking because we had come so far and achieved so much. In fact, at the time of Adesemi's downfall, we had raised more than $15 million in venture capital and launched the world's first fully integrated "virtual" phone system – incorporating voice mail, pagers, and hundreds of wireless pay phones – in one of its poorest nations, Tanzania. We had even come close to hitting breakeven, with $2 million in annual revenue, and we were finally on the verge of explosive growth.

3 Those accomplishments, however, weren't enough to save us. In the time it took our board to vote for liquidation – two hours – our dreams were history. After six years of begging for money from investors who were terrified of emerging-market risk, negotiating with mistrustful local partners, and constantly smoothing and soothing a culturally divergent workforce, I was left with an Adesemi that was a shadow of the third-world powerhouse we had envisioned. I had flown across the Atlantic and back more than 200 times, thrown together countless last-minute deals with recalcitrant suppliers, and endured the Kafka-esque bureaucracy of the third world. It had all been too little, too late.

4 And yet, today, six months after Adesemi's demise, I don't regret my experience. No entrepreneur wants to fail, of course, but it is part of the bargain when you opt out of a traditional career. That doesn't mean I'm happy about what happened to my company. Losing Adesemi was something of a public death. But it was worth it for what I learned about

---

Monique Maddy was the founder and CEO of Adesemi Communications International, a company launched in 1993 to bring information technologies to lower- and middle-income people in emerging-market countries. She now lives in Cambridge, Massachusetts.

starting a business, particularly in an emerging market. I still believe it is possible to do good in the world and do well at the same time. But I know now that such a goal takes nothing short of a deep-pocketed, visionary investor and the political commitment of the emerging

> "I knew that in order to make a real difference, I would have to venture out on my own."

markets themselves to economic change – not to mention a generous portion of good old-fashioned luck. I'm convinced that if we – Adesemi's core group – could somehow bring about the sustained convergence of those elements while applying the lessons we've learned, we could achieve our goal of bringing the benefits of digital communications to emerging-market countries. So I'm not ready to say my dream is dead. It's only deferred.

5 A Dream Is Born

I doubt that anyone wakes up one day and just decides to be an entrepreneur. I didn't, that's for sure. In fact, when I was ten, I firmly decided that I wanted to work for the United Nations. It had such a noble mission, I thought: peace and economic prosperity for everyone. That was a goal I would gladly devote my life to. I knew too well what economic privation looked like.

6 I was born in Liberia, a country with about 2.9 million people and a gross national product of $2.8 billion. In many ways, Liberia was one of Africa's less troubled nations, at least before its bloody civil war, the seeds of which were sown in a violent military coup in 1980. But still, when I was growing up, the average Liberian was extremely poor, earning only $250 a year. My family was one of the lucky few. My father first drove a taxi, then worked as an accountant, and eventually started a small restaurant in a mining town. That made us middle class, a rare breed in Liberia.

7 My father had high hopes for me

and my siblings, and he was convinced they could be realized only if we were well educated. And so, in 1968, when I was six and my older brother eight, he sent us to boarding school in England. Sending young children, particularly girls, away to boarding school was almost unheard of in Liberia. Many people thought my father was crazy; others thought he was cruel. Even my mother wasn't entirely at peace with the idea, but she trusted his judgment. So off we went.

8 After I finished elementary school abroad, I briefly returned to Liberia for middle school. But after that, I was gone for good. I attended a private high school in New Jersey. For college, I chose Georgetown University, then received my master's in international development and economics at Johns Hopkins University, hoping it would propel me quickly to a job with the UN. It did. One week after graduation in 1986, I started at the UN's New York headquarters. Six months later, I was assigned to Indonesia for a training program. Soon after, I was off to the UN's office in Angola, where I worked in the general management department for two years. Next, I was transferred to the Central African Republic, where I managed UN projects that were intended to promote entrepreneurship.

9 Two more years went by. I continued to believe in the UN's mission, but I had grown weary of the organization's bureaucracy and politics. Even more, I had grown frustrated by its lack of tangible impact. I wanted to make a real difference, and I was beginning to get the sense that to do that, I would have to venture out on my own. Graduate school in management seemed like a good first step, so the next fall, I enrolled at Harvard Business School.

10 HBS gave me ample opportunities to learn about the hazards of entrepreneurship, yet by my second year there, I was more convinced than ever that I could most effectively spread economic prosperity to the third world through my own efforts. I began to hammer out a business plan. My company would create the

first continentwide communications network in Africa, providing phones, television, and Internet services to lower- and middle-income people. After Africa, the company would go on to conquer the rest of the third world.

11   While consulting firms and investment-bank recruiters crawled all over campus, I started raising money for Adesemi (the name means "of royal descent" in various West African languages). Using HBS's alumni network, I talked my way into a number of telecommunications companies and ended up getting a $50,000 grant from several, including Motorola, Sprint, GE, and Lockheed. That figure was matched by a grant from the UN. I used the money to launch a research project. I needed to know where I should start Adesemi, what kind of technology I should buy, what competitors I could expect, and how much it would all cost.

Wake-Up Call

12   The research project made a few things clear very quickly. First, I had to start in one country only – more than that would be prohibitively expensive. Tanzania seemed like a good choice. At the time, it was aggressively privatizing its economy and vigorously courting foreign investors, particularly to help improve the telecommunications infrastructure. In a country with almost 30 million people, there were only 120,000 phone lines, including those allocated to business.

13   My research also suggested that I needed to narrow the focus of my strategic plan. One little start-up simply could not afford to offer a wide array of communications services at once. Growth would have to be incremental. Therefore, I decided to focus Adesemi's initial efforts on pay phones for customers on the lower rungs of the economic ladder. Specifically, Adesemi would install pay phones throughout the country and sell beepers connected to individual voice mailboxes. A customer's beeper would go off whenever he had a voice mail message; he would retrieve the message by dialing in from the nearest Adesemi pay phone. This system may seem painfully circuitous by the standards of developed nations. But it offered a brave new world for millions of Tanzanians who had no way to quickly communicate with people at a distance.

14   My research also told me that I could not start my company alone. I just did not know enough about telecommunications or engineering. I was already in Tanzania when, desperate and hopeful, I called Côme Laguë, a sectionmate from HBS. Côme had been a consultant at Monitor, the strategy consulting firm, specializing in the telecommunications industry. He has a great analytical mind and an affable, relaxed personality. Best of all, he was on safari in Africa. I convinced him to visit me in Dar es Salaam.

15   At first he had no plans to stay, but one day he took a long walk around the city. Everywhere he looked, he saw long lines at phone booths. He was in.

16   Our immediate challenge was money, and at first it came quite easily. Back in Boston, I bumped into another HBS classmate at a Newbury Street café. He happened to be looking for ways to invest his family's money, so I talked his ear off about Adesemi. A few weeks later, he invested $200,000 in seed money. In return, we gave him 20% of the company.

17   Côme and I returned to Tanzania, where we expected to use our cash to close a deal with a local partner who already had eight pay phones up and running. But while we had been off looking for money, our "partner" had joined forces with another company like ours. We were on our own. We resolved to act fast: we started applying for licenses and hiring telecommunications engineers and other local staff with general management capabilities.

> Adesemi's phone system was aimed at people on the lower rungs of the economic ladder. A beeper would alert a customer to the arrival of a voice mail message, which the customer would retrieve by using an Adesemi pay phone.

18   The overseas start-up process made us realize that we needed more capital – a lot more. Because of the major deficiencies of the telecommunications infrastructure, our engineers insisted that our network would have to be completely wireless to ensure reliability. That meant it would be a lot more costly to build. It was time to look for big-league investors.

19   Through an old friend, I was introduced to a private communications company called Landmark Communications in Norfolk, Virginia. Landmark saw an investment in Adesemi as a relatively inexpensive means of learning more about doing business in emerging-market countries. The company offered to invest $750,000 if we could raise $250,000 elsewhere. We did, by going back to the HBS

classmate who was our first investor and turning to another HBS friend as well.

20 But in what was now becoming a familiar scenario, our infusion of money only allowed us to see that we needed more. Our chief technology officer concluded that it would take an additional $3.5 million to complete the first phase with 400 wireless pay phones. Côme and I therefore rededicated our efforts to full-time fund-raising. First, we landed a favorable $1 million lease of our wireless equipment from the manufacturer. The rest was raised in the form of equity capital from two Boston-based angel investors whom we had met through yet another HBS contact. At last we were set to go.

21 Fast-forward a year. Adesemi had successfully launched 400 wireless pay phones throughout Dar es Salaam and developed an intricate distribution channel for its phone cards. Response from the public was swift and extremely positive. Almost immediately, we were processing more than 50,000 calls a day. To capitalize on our first-mover advantage, we decided to quickly launch the voice mail services and expand our network across the country.

22 To accomplish that, however, we needed to raise an additional $7 million. We were in a better position to go hunting this time; the company was generating $1.5 million per year in revenue. But venture capital was not particularly fast in coming. After almost a year, and numerous and very intense meetings, we ended up raising half the amount from the venture capital firm HarbourVest Partners in Boston. The rest came from the British Commonwealth Development Corporation and the Dutch Development Finance Corporation, government-owned enterprises devoted to economic development in emerging markets.

23 By 1998, we were able to buy our beepers from Taiwan, finance a global marketing campaign, and launch Adesemi's fully integrated virtual phone service to the rest of Tanzania. By then, we had 75 employees and revenue of about $2 mil-

lion. The future looked bright. A glowing article about Adesemi appeared in the *Wall Street Journal*, and we were soon bombarded with requests for the Adesemi virtual phone service from countries as dis-

"We were bombarded with requests for our phone service, and the future looked bright."

parate as India, Brazil, Russia, and Ivory Coast.

24 Unfortunately, the future was not to be. Licensing problems that had plagued us for years in Tanzania began to spin out of control. Central to our business model had been the assumption that Adesemi would receive a commission on the thousands of additional phone calls it generated each day on the network of the national phone company, Tanzania Telecommunications Company Limited (TTCL). Such an arrangement is the industry norm throughout the world. But no matter how much we pleaded or cajoled, TTCL refused to pay us any commission. We realized that in Tanzania, the high returns we had forecast wouldn't materialize for a long time, if ever. And there were immediate opportunities for good returns elsewhere. We knew we had to move quickly to other countries where the regulatory environments were more favorable. We identified several options, of which Ivory Coast and Sri Lanka were the most promising. To pursue the opportunities in those two countries and one other would necessitate $20 million more.

25 At first, it appeared that our existing investors would invest enough money to allow us to expand immediately into at least one new country. We hoped that once we had operations in at least three countries, we could attract an external, strategic investor who would provide an additional $10 million to $15 million. HarbourVest and Landmark agreed to put up several million dollars. But the two quasi-government agencies stalled. Over the course of a year, they insisted that the management team be scaled back to Côme and

myself, that we relocate to the basement of my apartment, and that we run countless financial scenarios in the hopes that we could find a way to use "profits" in Tanzania to transform Adesemi into a $100 million company without any additional investment. Finally, they decided they wanted out. Commonwealth Development Corporation called its original loan, forcing Adesemi to surrender its Tanzanian assets, against which the loan was secured, and to liquidate.

Hard Lessons

26 Not long ago, I was asked to speak at a conference on the role of technology in emerging-market countries. Many other speakers there boldly asserted that technology was sure to revolutionize communications and hence the economies of those countries. There would be no more third world in the twenty-first century, some said, thanks to the Internet and the impact it was already having on the global economy. It all sounded very simple. I didn't know whether to laugh or cry. The fact is, only 2% of the world's 6 billion people have access to the Internet. The revolution has hardly begun. Yes, change may come to emerging-market countries thanks to technology. But it will take time. Entrepreneurs can change the world as long as they don't try – as I did – to do it on a shoestring.

27 There will, I believe, be a next time for me. But when I return to the emerging markets as an entrepreneur, I will do so applying the hard lessons I learned during Adesemi's rise and fall. Those lessons, by the way, may leave the impression that I believe I share none of the blame for what happened to Adesemi. I wish I could say that were true. But when you decide to start a company and run it, you must accept responsibility for its fate. In the final analysis, what went wrong with Adesemi was lack of experience. I simply underestimated the sheer magnitude and complexity of what I was getting into.

28 Now I know better. Anyone thinking about – or in the process of –

launching a high-growth business in an emerging market should consider the following points.

Do-Gooders and Do-Wellers

29 Understand that there are two breeds of emerging-market venture capitalists, and accept the fact that they are separate and unequal. Adesemi raised money from two kinds of sources – VCs who are do-gooders and VCs who are do-wellers. Do-good investors and lenders are typically quasi-government agencies (though some are multinational banks) that provide equity capital and loan capital for ostensibly idealistic purposes: generating economic prosperity in emerging-market countries and stimulating further influx of capital from other investors. Do-gooders generally don't embrace the fundamental idea of reward for risk that underlies entrepreneurism. They tend to see third world countries as their turf, and they want to promote growth at their own pace – putting little money into enterprises like Adesemi and therefore allowing little opportunity for real return. In other words, do-gooders lend money to start-ups but don't necessarily trust them to do the right thing with it. To complicate matters, do-good VCs are staffed by career bureaucrats who stand to gain nothing if their agencies' investments do well. An agency may even be penalized if one of its start-ups shows a huge return: the government, or whoever is funding the agency, may be less inclined to give the VC more money to invest.

30 The do-gooders understand emerging markets – they know the competition and how consumers act – and they are familiar with government rules and regulations. But they are terrified of risk and deeply enmeshed in bureaucracy and their own rigid methods of investment and analysis. They are not necessarily looking for big paybacks on their investments. They are more preoccupied with adhering to their established procedures.

31 Do-wellers are another animal entirely – they're your classic, hungry, "show me the money" investors, who believe business is a high-stakes game. They may like worthy causes, but "doing good" is not a front-and-center concern. They see untapped opportunity in the third world, and they want to join forces with the first companies to seize it. Those firms are staffed by savvy financiers who understand that high risk is par for the course. Without it, there's very little chance of high reward. And high reward is what they are after.

32 Because of their limited experience in emerging-market countries, do-wellers frequently are not as well versed in the intricacies of doing business in these areas. Often they have trouble understanding how horrendous the bureaucratic morass in certain emerging-market countries can be. But the do-wellers are patient and willing to pour money into investments that look as though they might score big.

33 In hindsight, it's easy to see the distinction between – and implications of – the two kinds of capital available to emerging-market companies like Adesemi. For several years, I was blissfully unaware of the critical differences between venture capital sources. Money was money – I was happy to get any. And I never would have guessed that Adesemi would be brought down by the very investors – the do-gooders – that I intuitively trusted to act in the best interests of our target markets. After all, those were the people – or so I thought – who shared my dream of changing the world. I was wrong.

34 The lesson I learned, sadly, is that start-ups in the third world should stay away from do-good investors. Of course, few entrepreneurs have the luxury of turning down money. But I would say that taking money from do-good quasi-government institutions simply isn't worth it in the long run. They understand neither the concept of risk nor the concept of the long run.

The Challenge of Diversity

35 Every smart, ambitious MBA today wants to work for a start-up, but very few want to work for a start-up in Dar es Salaam, Tanzania. Those who do usually want and expect the kind of generous relocation, housing, and compensation packages offered by large multinationals. Adesemi, therefore, had to pick its managers and staff from a very small pool of people. It also had to hire under intense time pressure and financial constraints. In the first phase, the company needed about eight managers and dozens of staff people who would eventually be assigned to various locations throughout Tanzania. Côme and I hired people mainly through word of mouth and advertising, and we ended up with a crew of highly skilled and very talented adventurers from countries all over the world – Norway, Britain, Czech Republic, and New Zealand, to name a few. We also hired 50 people in Tanzania. Eventually, although we were an American company, there was not one American among our overseas staff.

36 Diversity is a tremendous strength, and such a heterogeneous workforce should have been a real boon to Adesemi. In recent years, management gurus and business academics have heralded the creativity and innovation spawned by heterogeneous teams. People who come at a business problem with different mindsets, it is said, are likely to generate new, exciting solutions. I myself believed such a notion – back in the comfort of my HBS classrooms.

37 But in practice, Adesemi's diversity was also a huge headache. One

> "I never would have guessed that Adesemi would be brought down by its do-good investors."

reason was that people on our staff had different attitudes toward work – or, more specifically, toward the concept of empowerment. To me, it was obvious that each of Adesemi's employees had to show a great deal of initiative. After all, the company was in its early stages of growth and nothing was routine. Moreover, its operations were far-flung, and I was constantly on the road talking to investors. I wanted – and needed – people to act like mini-CEOs themselves.

38 Instead, cultural habits got in the way. Our Tanzanian employees, whose attitudes had been shaped by colonial rule and then socialism, expected to be told exactly what to do every minute of the day. Then they did just that and no more. And it was not uncommon for some of our employees from Scandinavia to take off for five weeks at a time – the typical length of a vacation for their friends at home.

39 There was another, just as frustrating, reason that cultural diversity wreaked havoc among the Adesemi team: call it balkanization. Employees of the same nationalities formed cliques that disliked and frequently disrespected the other nationalities' cliques. Political correctness – with its rhetoric about honoring differences – was nowhere to be found. I am convinced, in fact, that today North Americans are the only people who practice political correctness.

40 Adesemi's balkanized employees made an art of flinging stereotypes at one another. The British were accused of being snobby and of withholding information. The Tanzanians were called inept. The Scandinavians were regarded as cold and aloof. I was considered an American – despite my African birth – and therefore arrogant and bossy. It did not help that in societies where age and seniority still matter substantially more than individual merit or accomplishment, Côme and I were younger than most of the people we were managing.

41 Moreover, people made little effort to learn about or accommodate other employees' cultural sensitivities. I will never forget when one of our British employees returned from vacation and a Tanzanian employee remarked, "Madame, you have put on a lot of weight." The British woman gasped, but the Tanzanian woman only smiled. In her culture, such comments about weight are considered complimentary. The British boss did not understand, and the two employees rarely spoke again.

42 The misunderstandings spawned by the cultural diversity of the Adesemi team caused a huge drain on my time and energy. As the CEO, and as someone who had lived in many countries, I was constantly called upon to settle disputes or simply to smooth feathers. I was forever placating warring factions. My main method was to reinterpret people for each other and to remind them of Adesemi's higher purpose. Sometimes it worked, but often it only resulted in a temporary calm before another storm. Our heterogeneity was part of our strength. But next time I will create an extremely high-level position for a person who will focus on helping employees overcome or work around cultural misunderstandings. A start-up does not have the luxury of waiting for the ingredients in its pot to melt.

Marriages of Convenience

43 Think of local partners as next-door neighbors. You may not always like them, but you will definitely need them. Every company that launches a business in an emerging market hears that local alliances will be central to its success. Ours was no exception. I first heard this imperative in business school, in a class entitled "Management in Developing Countries." Later, our investors all advised the same thing. Local partners would give Adesemi an intimate

"In many emerging-market countries, few things are what they appear to be."

knowledge of customer habits and key government and industry players. These partners would give us direct access to decision makers. They were, in short, insurance against the vagaries of doing business on unfamiliar turf.

44 But that first partner of ours, the one who ran off with another suitor, helped us learn quickly that local partners can give you as much pain as gain. Luckily, even though we had signed a memorandum of understanding with him, we had not yet awarded him any equity in exchange for the services he was supposed to provide.

45 The partner who replaced him was a businessman in Dar es Salaam who sold computers and telecommunications equipment. He was supposed to help us secure operating licenses, nail down tax exemptions, and identify local staff. Ultimately, we discovered he wasn't nearly as connected as he had claimed to be and couldn't really help us. But by that time, we had given him 5% of the business and a seat on our local board of directors.

46 After our relationship with him fell apart, he began to speak against our company publicly, and we began to worry about our reputation in the local market. We moved quickly to land yet another local partner who would keep our name clean in the eyes of the public and the government. He was an elder statesman who was highly respected because of

Four Hard-Earned Insights on Third-World Start-Ups

My experience with Adesemi taught me a number of lessons that apply to any entrepreneur considering launching a high-growth business in an emerging-market country. Here are four of the most significant:

1. Start-ups in the third world should steer clear of do-good lenders – organizations that provide equity capital and loans to companies in order to generate economic prosperity in impoverished areas. Though these lenders understand emerging markets, often they're terrified of risk and deeply enmeshed in bureaucracy. Entrepreneurs should concentrate instead on do-well investors who are looking to make money and who

understand risk, even though such lenders tend to be perplexed by the intricacies of doing business in emerging-market countries. The do-wellers may be difficult to attract at first, but once they're in, they're committed to the enterprise.

2. A diverse workforce is a strength for a company in an emerging market, but cultural misunderstandings can also drain a CEO's time and energy. Appoint a seasoned HR guru to improve cross-cultural tolerance and understanding. Everyone in the company will benefit.

3. A new venture in an emerging-market country needs local partners. Ideally, local partners should be required to invest their own

money – otherwise they won't have long-term stakes in the success of the venture. And entrepreneurs should be careful to conduct serious due diligence on potential partners. Don't get stuck with local partners who can't deliver the goods.

4. A new venture in the third world needs a patient and visionary investor with deep pockets who is willing to ride out the bumps that will inevitably appear in the road. It's very difficult to explain to an impatient investor what it's like to be an entrepreneur in the third world, dealing with officials who stonewall and dissemble. I believe that Adesemi would have been a success if it had found the right investor.

---

the role his family had played in gaining Tanzania's independence. His presence on our board protected us from rumors, but it came at a cost – a small stake in the company.

47 I still believe that people doing business in emerging-market countries need local partners. But the truth is, the parties need each other most in the very beginning. That's when the local partner has a lot to gain in the form of capital and technology and the start-up needs political contacts, customers, services, established marketing channels, and new employees. But once the venture is established, the relationship can easily lose its purpose and utility. Both sides can feel as if they are in a marriage that doesn't make sense anymore. But they're stuck together forever, usually by contract.

48 A local partner should always be required to invest his own money in a new venture so that he has a long-term stake in the business. Also, a start-up should conduct serious due diligence on the local partners it plans to marry. Remember the rules of supply and demand. There are scads of local businesspeople eager

to join forces with credible foreign entrepreneurs and investors. When seeking a partner, remember you are in the driver's seat.

Wanted: A Visionary Investor

49 Don't discount the exhaustion factor of doing business in the third world. In many emerging-market countries, few things are what they appear to be: the real decisions in government agencies are rarely made by the people who are officially said to make them, and printed regulations are infrequently followed or enforced. It's difficult – particularly in the high-technology industry – to find someone who actually understands the policies and regulations, which are generally imported by consultants. And governments are mired in a bureaucratic quicksand that you cannot escape unless you are willing to engage in corruption and bribery, which we were not, both for legal and ethical reasons.

50 There are a thousand stories from Adesemi's six years that could illustrate the numbing effect of bureaucracy on business in emerging markets, but one story stands out

because of the significant role it played in the company's downfall. It's the story behind the Tanzanian phone company's refusal to pay us commissions. It begins in 1995, not long after our second partner obtained an operating license for us from TTCL. With that piece of paper in hand, we installed $3 million worth of equipment. Then a letter arrived from TTCL saying our license was not valid because it had been signed by the wrong authority within the phone company.

51 Côme and I sprang into action, calling everyone we knew in the government to track down exactly who was supposed to grant our operating license. The matter should have been easy to resolve, but all we got was a runaround. Officials at the communications regulatory agency told us that the national phone company had to sign our license; the phone company told us the license had to be issued and signed by the regulatory agency. The back-and-forth went on for almost two years, literally preventing us from launching our operations. We were bleeding cash at about $50,000 a month – a

52 fatal rate for a company of our size and resources.

Connections and pure luck saved us temporarily. While I was back in the United States in 1996 trying to raise new capital, I had breakfast with John McArthur, the former dean of HBS. Desperate to appear optimistic, as entrepreneurs are wont to do, I tried to put a good face on Adesemi's situation, describing how we had successfully installed the wireless pay-phone network and placed booths throughout Dar es Salaam that were ready to be activated. But I did tell him that we were having serious problems with our license and that Côme and I were getting nowhere with our appeals to the government. Perhaps our only hope for resolution, I said, was that the World Bank, Tanzania's biggest lender, might step in on our behalf.

53 It just so happened that John was doing consulting work with the president of the World Bank, Jim Wolfensohn, and he offered to mention Adesemi's dilemma to him. My hopes surged, but several weeks went by without a word from the World Bank, and I began to despair. After all, where would the president of the World Bank find the time to worry about a tiny start-up in Tanzania?

54 Then, one day when I was sitting at my desk in Cambridge, Jim Wolfensohn called. I quickly described our problem; he assured me it would be taken care of promptly. The next week, a World Bank–financed consultant arrived to negotiate a settlement between Adesemi and the government. While extremely welcome, the solution provided only temporary relief. We were allowed to turn our system on, but the government still refused to pay us a commission on the traffic and revenue we were generating for its network.

55 To make matters worse, we soon found out that the World Bank had recently lent the local phone company money, on highly concessionary terms, to build its own network of pay phones. In other words, U.S. dollars, which partially fund the World Bank, were subsidizing our competition. We contacted the World Bank to point this out, and they sent another consultant to Tanzania to ask the government to give us an equitable deal. The government refused. It was, essentially, taking money from the World Bank with one hand and brushing off the World Bank with the other. It was at that point that we knew we had to take our business to other countries.

56 Adesemi's licensing saga is paradigmatic. Doing business in the third world takes a lot of waiting, pushing, cajoling, and behind-the-scenes hustling. Until you've had to live with those things, it's hard to imagine the dissembling and stonewalling that go on as part of day-to-day operations. And you can't imagine how hard it is explaining all that to investors anxiously awaiting their payback. That's why every entrepreneur doing business in the third world needs a patient and visionary investor – a person or institution willing and able to wait out the turbulence and frequent political obstructions. I still believe that if we'd had someone with deep enough pockets and deep enough patience, we would have made Adesemi a success in Tanzania and in the other countries we were targeting. And if we had succeeded, the social impact in those areas and the payback to that investor would have been huge.

My Little Boat

57 In the months since Adesemi was liquidated, I have been regrouping and reflecting. I am also working on my next project. As for Adesemi, Côme and I are serving as part-time consultants to the company, which exists as a shell and still holds a significant interest in the second-largest telecommunications company in Ghana (founded by Adesemi during its fourth year in business). Commonwealth Development Corporation now operates what is left of Adesemi Tanzania Limited and apparently intends to invest no more capital in it, which means the infrastructure will gradually disintegrate and operations will eventually cease.

58 I am also reading a lot, and return again and again to one book in particular, *First You Have to Row a Little Boat*, by Richard Bode. I have taken great solace in Bode's observation that in the effort to reach an intended destination, one should resist the urge to fight the prevailing winds. Instead, one should sail the wind.

59 Adesemi was my little boat. Just as my goal of bringing telecommunications to emerging markets seemed nearly within reach, the wind shifted, making it impossible for me to proceed as I had planned. Soon I'll be ready to resume the journey as a more seasoned sailor and, with luck, in a steadier craft. When I do, I will continue to sail the wind in the hope that with the lessons I've learned over the past six years, I will be able to chart a new route to my ultimate destination. ▽

Reprint R00307

Glossary

adhering	sticking, holding fast
allocated	apportioned for a specific purpose; designated
array	a large number; a group of elements forming a complete unit
attainable	able to be gained; achievable
balkanization	breaking up of a group into smaller, hostile units
blanket	to cover uniformly
bombarded	attacked vigorously
boon	benefit
bribery	the practice of giving money or favors to influence someone in a position of trust
cajoled	persuaded with flattery in the face of reluctance
circuitous	not being direct in action; having a circular course
cliques	exclusive groups of persons held together by common interests
coup	a brilliant, sudden, highly successful act
deep-pocketed	having substantial financial resources
deferred	delayed, put off, postponed
deficiencies	inadequacies, shortages
demise	end of existence, death
devastating	destructive, overwhelming; brought to ruin
divergent	diverse, differing from each other
due diligence	careful investigation to avoid harm
enmeshed	caught or entangled in
entrepreneurship	the act of organizing, managing, and assuming the risks of a business or enterprise
gurus	experts; persons with knowledge or expertise; teachers and intellectual guides
hazards	risks, sources of danger
heralded	greeted with enthusiasm
heterogeneous	consisting of diverse elements; mixed
hindsight	perception of the nature of an event after it has happened
imperative	rule, guide
incremental	characterized by minute increases in quantity
infusion	pouring in something that gives new life
intricacies	complexities

Kafka-esque	a feeling of being trapped in a maze of grotesque happenings (derived from the name of the German writer Franz Kafka)
liquidation	bankruptcy, insolvency; the settlement of debt by payment
magnitude	great size or extent, enormity
morass	chaos; something that traps, confuses, impedes
opt out of	to decide against something
ostensibly	to all outward appearances; apparently, supposedly
paradigmatic	serving as an example or a pattern
par for the course	normal, not unusual
plagued	worried or distressed; disturbed or annoyed persistently
privation	deprivation; lack of what is needed for existence
prohibitively	tending to restrain or preclude action
recalcitrant	difficult to manage; defiant of authority or restraint
scaled back	reduced
scenario	sequence of events
shoestring	a small amount of money or capital inadequate to meet the needs of a business
solace	source of relief or consolation; alleviation of anxiety
spawned	produced, generated
tangible	substantially real; capable of being precisely identified
visionary	one who is marked by foresight and imagination
wreaked havoc	brought about or caused confusion and disorder

Comprehension

Introduction

1. How did Monique Maddy imagine the success of her company Adesemi?

2. Why was it shocking that Adesemi failed?

3. How is it possible to do good in the world and do well at the same time?

A Dream Is Born

4. Describe Monique's education.

5. When Monique worked for the UN (United Nations), where was she assigned?

6. How did Monique plan to spread economic prosperity to the third world?

Wake-Up Call

7. After doing a research project, what did Monique learn?

8. Where did Monique get the venture capital to start Adesemi?

9. Why did Adesemi have to surrender its Tanzanian assets and liquidate?

Hard Lessons

10. In the final analysis, what went wrong with Adesemi?

11. Explain the two breeds of emerging-market venture capitalists.

12. What lesson did Monique learn from her experience with Adesemi?

The Challenge of Diversity

13. Why was Adesemi's diversity a huge headache for Monique?

Marriages of Convenience

14. How did Monique's experience with local partners compare to what she learned in Harvard Business School?

Wanted: A Visionary Investor

15. What are common problems that start-ups face in many emerging-market countries?

16. What does every entrepreneur doing business in the third world need?

My Little Boat

17. What is Monique's plan for the future?

18. How realistic is Monique's plan for the future?

Analysis

Circle the letter next to the best answer(s). Justify your choices with quotations from the text.

1. What is the main idea of the article, and in which paragraph(s) is it stated?

   a. Monique Maddy wanted to provide complete telecommunications services to poor people in Africa, but she failed to establish a company that could do so.

   b. The challenges of starting a telecommunications business in developing countries are so great that it is unlikely that an entrepreneur will achieve success in the long run.

   c. Being an entrepreneur demands more risk taking but offers greater rewards than does working as an employee in a traditional company.

   d. Monique Maddy, who learned valuable lessons from her experience in starting a telecommunications business in Tanzania, believes that she will one day achieve her dream.

2. What is the meaning of the italicized word in this sentence in paragraph 9? "I wanted to make a real difference, and I was beginning to get the sense that to do that, I would have to *venture out* on my own."

   a. decide

   b. proceed

   c. manage

   d. investigate

3. We can infer the following from this statement by Monique Maddy in paragraph 26: "Entrepreneurs can change the world as long as they don't try—as I did—to do it on a shoestring."

   a. Monique is doubtful that inexperienced entrepreneurs can change the world.

   b. Monique regrets trying to enter an emerging market as an entrepreneur without sufficient experience.

   c. Monique believes that having plenty of capital is essential to the success of entrepreneurs in emerging markets.

   d. Monique believes that entrepreneurs need emerging-market venture capitalists that have plenty of money and the patience to wait for the return on their investments.

4. The author's writing style in this article is _____ and _____ .

   a. sophisticated

   b. simple

   c. idiomatic

   d. scholarly

5. The tone of the article is _____ and _____ .

   a. subjective

   b. objective

   c. emotional

   d. balanced

6. What overall method of development is used in this article?

   a. justifying a proposal

   b. debating two sides of an issue

   c. enumerating characteristics of a system

   d. narrating a series of events

7. In the conclusion to the article ("My Little Boat"), what techniques does the author use?

   a. ironic humor

   b. indirect quotation

   c. questions

   d. metaphoric language

Discussion

1. Would you characterize Monique Maddy as an idealistic, optimistic dreamer; a realistic, pragmatic businesswoman; or a visionary, risk-taking entrepreneur?

2. How did Monique benefit from going to Harvard Business School?

3. What would you have done differently from Monique in starting a telecommunications business in a developing country?

4. If you became an entrepreneur, what kind of business would you focus on? Explain your choice.

OUTFRONT
Smart and Smarter

With Chinese labor, no factories and no engineers, two U.S. entrepreneurs are making the cheapest DVD players on the planet. Sony doesn't like it one bit.

BY DANIEL LYONS

1   THESE DAYS SONY'S BIGGEST VILlain isn't some freakish alien from *Men in Black II* (its upcoming summer flick). It's two guys operating out of a 40,000-square-foot headquarters/warehouse in Ontario, Calif. Last November David Ji and Ancle Hsu sold almost 1 million low-price Apex Digital DVD players through Wal-Mart alone—and thereby surpassed Sony in North American unit sales, claiming 23% of the market, compared with 13.6% for the $58 billion (sales) Japanese giant.

2   In dollar volume of DVD players, Sony is ahead, with an 18% share in North America, versus 12% for Apex in the fourth quarter of 2001, reports NPD Techworld, a market research firm. But it must hurt that Apex Digital stole a march on Japanese companies by being first to produce a DVD player that could play MP3 files, the controversial format used to pirate music on the Internet. While other hardwaremakers were afraid of legal battles over record-company rights, Ji and Hsu plunged ahead. (A microchip that allowed hackers to sidestep encoding that prevents copying a DVD onto a videocassette brought threats of suits from Macrovision and the Motion Picture Association; Apex replaced the chip.)

3   Apex has been early to market with other gizmos, like a new Kodak format for showing photos on a DVD player, and a new audio format from Microsoft. "We don't have the bureaucracy and overhead that Japanese companies have," says Hsu, Apex's chief operating officer.

4   The folks at Sony pooh-pooh Apex Digital as a low-quality competitor. "The question is, will these folks be around for the long haul?" says William Cubellis, marketing director for Sony's home entertainment division. Critics gripe that Apex Dig-ital and the Chinese manufacturers it uses sometimes fail to pay licensing fees for technologies that go into DVD players. Hsu and Ji admit they haven't always paid up but insist they want to make good. They are in negotiations now with different licensing groups.

5   Who are these guys? Hsu, born in Taiwan, and Ji, raised in Jiangsu province on the mainland, met while working at a scrap metal company in Los Angeles after each emigrated to the States in the 1980s. In 1992 they teamed up to form their own scrap metal company, selling to recyclers in China. Since then they have made and sold car-stereo speakers, herbal supplements and even disposable rubber gloves.

6   But they struck the big time when they decided to manufacture DVD players in 1999. They first planned to assemble the machines in the U.S., then learned it was cheaper to let Chinese partners do that. The first model, introduced two years ago, cost $179, when rival players cost twice that. Since then Apex Digital has driven prices as low as $70, teaming up with Best Buy, Circuit City, Wal-Mart, Kmart and others. Apex Digital did around $120 million in sales in 2000, about $500 million last year. This year, Apex predicts it will rake in more than $1 billion and turn a small profit.

7   Not without scratches. Last year a Chinese exporter sued Apex Digital, claiming it owed $18 million. In February a warehouse company tried to auction off a stash of Apex gear, alleging Apex was in arrears by $2 million. Hsu says in both cases Apex was wronged by partners. Hsu had a scrape with the law 11 years ago; he pleaded nolo contendere to not keeping proper payroll records, a misdemeanor.

8   And, Sony points out, Apex has had quality-control glitches. While analysts say that on average Apex Digital machines are about as reliable as any other, the company has had problems with some models. Its $340 high-end 7701 DVD player offered advanced features like progressive scan, which produces a better picture quality, and support for multiple audio and video formats. But the audio popped and hissed. And players couldn't recognize some discs. In February Apex halted production of the 7701 and arranged for customers to get refunds. Richard Feirstein, a lawyer in Albany, N.Y., returned four of the 7701 players before giving up and taking a refund. "My wife would divorce me if I tried again," he said. He bought a Sony player, which works fine.

9   With only eight technical support staffers, Apex can't keep up with the likes of Sony. But Ji and Hsu are trying. They paid $9 million to buy 60% of a Chinese DVD factory. They're also planning to hire engineers to design their own machines.

10   Meanwhile Apex Digital has struck a joint venture with a Chinese television manufacturer, Changhong Electric Ltd., and in January introduced 18 new TV models. Also planned for later this year: a digital camera that will play MP3 files.

11   Can a pair of hustling immigrants with little experience build an electronics giant? Demand, at least, is on their side. Sales of DVD players will reach $3.5 billion in the U.S. this year. And 75% of U.S. households still have not bought a DVD player.

12   Ji, 50, and Hsu, 41, insist they are merely doing what Sony, Hitachi and others disdain: making new technology affordable to the masses. They say Japanese companies have lost touch with U.S. consumers. "We are the only real American brand," Ji says. That should give the Japan-ese the willies. **F**

Discussion

1. How have David Ji and Ancle Hsu created a problem for Sony, the powerful Japanese corporation?

2. What has made it possible for Apex to market new high-tech gadgets earlier than other companies?

3. What does Sony think of Apex?

4. Describe the background of David Ji and Ancle Hsu.

5. How did Ji and Hsu become successful?

6. Explain the problems Apex has had.

7. How is Apex trying to keep up with companies like Sony?

8. How do Ji and Hsu differentiate their company from the Japanese technology companies?

9. If you decided to purchase a DVD player, would you buy a Sony or an Apex model? On what basis would you make this decision?

10. The title of this article, "Smart and Smarter," is modeled on the title of a 1994 Hollywood movie called *Dumb and Dumber*. This movie is a comedy about two friends who act in unintelligent ways. Explain how the title "Smart and Smarter" applies to this article.

11. Compare and contrast the three entrepreneurs described in the articles in this chapter: Monique Maddy in "Dream Deferred: The Story of a High-Tech Entrepreneur in a Low-Tech World" and David Ji and Ancle Hsu in "Smart and Smarter." In what ways are they similar, and in what ways are they different?

Teamwork

Working in a group, do an Internet research project to gather information on a well-known entrepreneur. Then write a short report about one of these businesspeople. Use this format for your report.

I. Abstract (50 words)

II. Introduction

III. Body

IV. Conclusion

For this project, you may choose an entrepreneur from your native country or investigate how one of the following people became successful: Michael Dell, Dell Computer Corporation (United States); Yue-Sai Kan, Yue-Sai Kan Cosmetics (China); Hiroshi

Mikitani, Rakuten cybermall (Japan); Anita Roddick, The Body Shop (Great Britain); Vera Wang, Vera Wang (United States) and Oprah Winfrey, Harpo Inc. (United States). You can find more information about these entrepreneurs on their Web sites.

- <http://www.dell.com>. Dell is the world's no. 1 computer systems company. Click on About Dell and then on Michael to read about Michael Dell, who founded the company in 1984.

- <http://www.yuesai.com>. Yue-Sai Kan has been called the most famous woman in China. She is a visionary entrepreneur with several companies. Click on About Yue-Sai Kan to read about her various projects.

- <http://www.rakuten.co.jp>. Hiroshi Mikitani founded the Rakuten cybermall in 1998, and its 8,000 retailers are extremely popular with Japanese Web users. Mikitani also owns Infoseek Japan and Bizseek, a used-goods trading Web site.

- <http://www.bodyshop.com>. The Body Shop is a global company that produces hair and body care products. It is an ethical business dedicated to the pursuit of social and environmental change. Click on Who We Are to read about Anita Roddick, who founded the company in 1976.

- <http://www.verawang.com>. Vera Wang, who founded her company in 1990, is a well-known fashion designer who specializes in luxurious wedding gowns. Click on About Vera Wang to learn how she rose to the top in a challenging profession.

- <http://www.oprah.com> Oprah Winfrey is a businesswoman, philanthropist, and talk show host. Click on About Oprah to read her biography.

Writing Assignments

1. Working in a team of three or four classmates, write a summary of "Dream Deferred: The Story of a High-Tech Entrepreneur in a Low-Tech World" by Monique Maddy, printed in this chapter.

2. Choose one of these business writing assignments.

   - Write a memorandum from Monique Maddy to the employees of Adesemi, informing them of the liquidation of the company and the reasons for this decision. The memorandum should be personal and informal in style and authoritative and straightforward in tone. (See Appendix B, Memorandum.)

   - Write a business letter from Monique Maddy to a potential investor. In the letter, describe Maddy's experience with Adesemi, the purpose of her new telecommunications business venture in Africa, the general business plan, and the reasons for the investor to invest in the company. The letter should be personal and formal in style and businesslike and persuasive in tone. (See Appendix B, Business Letter.)

3. Write a synthesis based on the articles printed in this chapter, "Dream Deferred: The Story of a High-Tech Entrepreneur in a Low-Tech World" and "Smart and Smarter." Also use an article by Nathan Vardi from *Forbes* magazine: "Bird in the Hand" (*Forbes,* 29 April 2002, 107–8). Vardi's article describes an entrepreneur who wants to provide news, information, and entertainment to Third-World countries through a global satellite radio service. Use the Internet business database ABI/Inform to locate the *Forbes* article or find it in the periodicals section of the library.

   Cite your sources in the in-text citation format (Vardi 107). List your sources at the end of the paper as Works Cited and alphabetize them according to the authors' last names. Develop your own thesis, or you may use the following thesis: Entrepreneurs who target markets in Third-World countries face more challenges than entrepreneurs working in developed countries.

4. Write a research paper on the topic of the entrepreneurial personality. You may use the articles printed or mentioned in this chapter, including the expansion readings as sources for your paper. Also find several recent sources. These books should be helpful.

   Ash, Mary Kay. *Mary Kay, You Can Have It All: Lifetime Wisdom from America's Foremost Woman Entrepreneur.* Rocklin, CA: Prima Publishers, 1996.

   Byron, Christopher M. *Martha Inc.: The Incredible Story of Martha Stewart Living Omnimedia.* New York: John Wiley, 2002.

   Heinecke, William. *The Entrepreneur: 21 Golden Rules for the Global Business Manager.* Singapore; New York: John Wiley, 2000.

   Walton, Sam. *Sam Walton: Made in America, My Story.* New York: Bantam Books, 1992.

Expansion Readings

Batten, Frank. "Out of the Blue and into the Black." *Harvard Business Review* 80, no. 4 (April 2002): 112–19.

Bricklin, Dan. "Natural-Born Entrepreneur." *Harvard Business Review* 79, no. 8 (September 2001): 53–59.

"Freddy Heineken." *The Economist,* 12 January 2002, 77.

"Copying Starbucks." *Harvard Business Review* 80, no. 1 (January 2002): 66.

Kawasaki, Guy. "The Top Ten Lies of Entrepreneurs." *Harvard Business Review* 79, no. 1 (January 2001): 22–23.

Kuemmerle, Walter. "A Test for the Fainthearted." *Harvard Business Review* 80, no. 5 (May 2002): 122–27.

Leonard, Dorothy, and Walter Swap. "Gurus in the Garage." *Harvard Business Review* 78, no. 1 (November–December 2000): 71–82.

Oral Presentation

Working with a partner, give a 20-minute oral presentation to the class on one of the articles listed under Expansion Readings or an article of your choice on entrepreneurship. Summarize the article by including the author's thesis, major points, and supporting data and evaluate its strengths and weaknesses. Be prepared to answer questions on your topic. If you have the technical capability, use the presentation graphics program PowerPoint for your presentation. Otherwise, make at least one overhead to use on the overhead projector. (See Appendix B, Oral Presentation.)

Travels on the Web

The Internet offers numerous opportunities to learn more about entrepreneurship.

1. Log on to the following Web site for *Entrepreneur Magazine* (Solutions for Growing Businesses): <http://www.entrepreneur.com>. Read the articles that appear on the home page of the Web site or select Starting Out under Small-Biz Essentials. Print out an article that is interesting and bring it to class.

2. Log on to the Web site for EntreWorld.org: A World of Resources for Entrepreneurs: <http://www.entreworld.org>. This site offers a variety of information on becoming an entrepreneur. For example, if you click on Starting Your Business, you can read about the beginning stage of entrepreneurship.

3. Log on to the following Web site for Scottish women entrepreneurs: <http://www.scottishbusinesswomen.com>. Write a summary of the information on this unique Web site. In your summary, include information on the mission statement.

4. Use the Internet business database LexisNexis Academic to locate current information on entrepreneurship and gender. Select Site Map, choose Business, and click on Business News. Do a Guided News Search using the terms *entrepreneur* and *gender*. After reading an article, print it out and bring it to class for discussion.

Appendixes

Appendix A

Definitions of Writing Terms and Examples of Writing Styles

Definitions of Writing Terms

Abstract: A very short summary of the main ideas and topics of a report, research paper, journal article, or technical document, which appears ahead of the document and is usually 150 words or less.

Analogy: Similarity in some respects between things otherwise unlike.

Example:
"Like an old married couple, the Americans and Europeans bicker about relatively minor issues, but make sure that their broader trade relationship does not break down" ("Trade Disputes: Dangerous Activities," *The Economist*, 11 May 2002, 64).

Analysis: Breaking up a whole into its parts and examining these parts to solve a problem or reach a conclusion.

Argument: An essay in which the writer presents a point of view and attempts to persuade others of the validity of his or her opinion.

Business Letter: Common form of external business correspondence, usually sent from a representative of an organization to people outside the organization.

Case Study: Method of instruction that is used in American business schools and involves the analysis of actual business situations to teach problem solving.

Critique: An essay based on critical reading of a text, in which the writer summarizes, reacts to, and evaluates an author's ideas.

Deductive Organization: Placement of the main idea of a text at the beginning; the writer gives the conclusion first and then presents supporting evidence.

Essay: An analytical or interpretative composition that deals with its subject in a limited way.

Figure of speech: An expression (metaphor or simile) using words in a nonliteral or unusual sense to add vividness to what is said and comparing dissimilar objects or ideas.

Examples:
Metaphor: "Companies that smash the glass ceiling also enjoy higher profits, a new study indicates" ("Women and Profits," *Harvard Business Review* 79, no. 10 [November 2001]: 30).

Simile: "Compaq is like a 6-foot-4 center in the National Basketball Association: the smallest big man in the league" (Randall E. Stross, "Can This Marriage Be Saved?" *U.S. News and World Report,* 17 December 2001, 41).

Format: The general arrangement or plan of a document; the physical presentation of a document on a page.

Idiom: An accepted phrase or expression that is contrary to the usual patterns of the language or that has a meaning different from the literal meaning of the words.

Example:
"Realizing your dream will always take longer and suck up more resources than you planned, and the process can drive well-meaning people around the bend" (Frank Batten, "Out of the Blue and into the Black," *Harvard Business Review* 80, no. 4 [April 2002]: 113).

Inductive Organization: Placement of the main idea of a text at the end; the writer gives supporting evidence and leads the reader to a conclusion.

In-Text Citation System: Citation system for documenting sources in a report, essay, research paper, journal article, or technical document; it places the author's last name and the page number within parentheses in the text (Martin 323). All sources are listed as Works Cited at the end of the document.

Irony: A method of humorous or sarcastic expression in which the intended meaning of the words used is the direct opposite of their usual sense.

Example:
"The board of directors is supposed to carefully calibrate compensation packages so that CEOs are paid just enough to be motivated to swing their weary legs out of bed each morning and clomp to work" (Randall E. Stross, "Masters of the Universe," *U.S. News and World Report,* 27 May 2002, 41).

Main Idea: The most important idea or unifying theme of a paragraph or longer text.

Memorandum: An informal written business communication, usually from one person or department to another within an organization.

Methods of Development: Organizational patterns used to structure the content; these include analysis, argument, cause-effect, chronology, classification, comparison-contrast, definition, description, enumeration, exemplification, problem-solution, process, and spatial order.

Parallelism: The use of the same or similar grammatical form to express the same or similar ideas.

Example:
"In the process of publicly voicing problems, owning them, and fixing them, we grew more powerful, nimble, and tough-minded. In the course of becoming comfortable with honesty, we learned to respond quickly to internal and external changes" (Ginger L. Graham, "If You Want Honesty, Break Some Rules," *Harvard Business Review* 80, no. 4 [April 2002]: 47).

Paraphrase: A rewording or restatement of an author's meaning.

Purpose Statement: A restatement of intention found in the abstract and introduction of a report; it announces the topic and tells readers why the report is being written.

Report: A written document that contains an objective presentation of the facts of an investigation; an organized presentation of data, serving a practical purpose by supplying needed information.

Research Paper: A lengthy paper based on research and using numerous sources to answer a specific question, support a thesis, or prove a hypothesis.

Style: The writer's manner of expression in language; the way of using words to express thoughts.

Summary: A brief restatement of the main ideas and major points of a longer written document, usually paraphrased.

Synthesis: An essay that is developed from two or more sources from which the writer selects information to support a thesis.

Thesis: The main idea of a text, expressed as a sentence; a statement assumed as a premise in a research paper, essay, argument, critique, or synthesis.

Tone: A manner of writing that shows the attitude of the writer toward the subject and audience and results from word choice, sentence structure, and phrasing.

Topic Sentence: A sentence that contains the main idea of a paragraph and often is the first or last sentence of a paragraph.

Examples of Writing Styles

Informal: Let's try to get together to talk about this right away, or else we won't be able to change the policy.

Formal: I suggest that we meet to discuss this issue at a mutually convenient time in the near future; otherwise, we will not be able to effect a change in the policy.

Impersonal: There have been reports that some managers are not complying with the smoking guidelines. This is having a negative impact on the company, and these guidelines must be followed by all employees.

Personal: I have heard that some managers are not complying with the smoking guidelines. This displeases me greatly, and I expect all employees to follow these guidelines.

Bureaucratic: Since first inventorying Agency activities subject to OMB Circular A-76, we have reviewed those activities for adequacy under revised guidelines from OMB. After recent discussions with the Productivity Clearinghouse, it has been determined that one Productivity Improvement Program (PIP) review category, "Accounts Management," is not an appropriate review activity for this Agency. That activity, therefore, is being deleted from the PIP review lists for this Agency.

Technical: CDC Systems, Inc., is a globally recognized custom designer, fabricator, manufacturer, and provider of turnkey antenna systems; earth stations; radio and optical telescopes for communications, telemetry, tracking control, and monitoring; and special-purpose antenna systems. Our complete antenna designs include Ku-band, C-band, E-band, and/or L-band performance capabilities. Included with our designs are antenna servo control and tracking-system products specializing in microprocessor-based controls and monopulse tracking.

Nontechnical: CDC Systems, Inc., is known worldwide for our custom design and production of antenna systems. We provide a large variety of communications equipment, including earth stations, radio and optical telescopes, and tracking systems.

Scientific: The Hemostasis and Thrombosis Group consists of five senior investigators and two junior investigators. The program trains predoctoral and postdoctoral fellows in biochemical, immunologic, physiologic, and pharmacologic approaches to problems in hemostasis thrombosis.

Business (Informal): ABC Corporation is pursuing a program to purchase minority interests in small-business companies that indicate potential growth opportunities in the future. We would like to discuss this aspect of our interest in small business at your convenience.

Business (Formal): This letter is to certify that a money-market account in the name of Sarah Hoffman was established today. Please be advised that this letter is issued at the aforementioned customer's request for whatever legal purpose it may serve her.

Legal: Before this Court is Defendant's motion for summary judgment pursuant to Fed. R. Civ. P. 50. The foundation for Defendant's request is Plaintiff's failure to establish any factual basis upon which liability may rest, thereby making appropriate disposition as a matter of law.

Conversational: "It's happened to you before. You call a meeting to try to convince your boss and peers that your company needs to make an important move—for instance, funding a risky but promising venture. Your argument is impassioned, your logic unassailable, your data bulletproof. Two weeks later, though, you learn that your brilliant proposal has been tabled. What went wrong?" (Gary A. Williams and Robert B. Miller, "Change the Way You Persuade," *Harvard Business Review* 80, no. 5 [May 2002]: 65–73).

Idiomatic: "Once you have earned credibility and are in a position to get what you want, you need to strike a series of devil's bargains. To horse-trade with the devil, you have to look him squarely in the eye and make the right demands from him. The deal I struck was to trade on my success as an actor in order to make films that otherwise wouldn't have been made because the studios thought they were not commercially viable" ("Turning an Industry Inside Out: A Conversation with Robert Redford," *Harvard Business Review* 80, no. 5 [May 2002]: 59).

Journalistic: "Carlos Ghosn, the CEO and president of Nissan Motor Co., is everywhere you look in Japan: lecturing audiences such as the Japan Association of

Corporate Executives, beaming from the pages of a comic book, *The True Story of Carlos Ghosn,* and signing copies of his book, *Renaissance*—which in Japan is outselling Jack Welch's autobiography. *Ghosn-Ryu,* or Ghosn-style, has entered the popular lexicon as shorthand for the take-no-prisoners restructuring this French trained executive imposed at Nissan" (Chester Dawson, "Ghosn's Way: Why Japan Inc. Is Following a Gaijin," *Business Week,* 20 May 2002, 58).

Academic: "There have been times in the history of science when the whole of orthodox science has been rightly thrown over because of a single awkward fact. It would be arrogant to assert that such overthrows will never happen again. But we naturally, and rightly, demand a higher standard of authentication before accepting a fact that would turn a major and successful scientific edifice upside down, than before accepting a fact which, even if surprising, is readily accommodated by existing science" (Richard Dawkins, *The Blind Watchmaker: Why the Evidence of Evolution Reveals a Universe without Design* [New York: W. W. Norton, 1995]: 293).

Colorful: "Consider the following four dead-end kids. One was spanked by his teachers for bad grades and a poor attitude. He dropped out of school at 16. Another failed remedial English and came perilously close to flunking out of college. The third feared he'd never make it through school—and might not have without a tutor. The last finally learned to read in third grade, devouring Marvel comics, whose pictures provided clues to help him untangle the words.

"These four losers are, respectively, Richard Branson, Charles Schwab, John Chambers, and David Boies. Billionaire Branson developed one of Britain's top brands with Virgin Records and Virgin Atlantic Airways. Schwab virtually created the discount brokerage business. Chambers is CEO of Cisco. Boies is a celebrated trial attorney, best known as the guy who beat Microsoft" (Betsy Morris, "Overcoming Dyslexia," *Fortune,* 13 May 2002, 53–59).

Pictorial: "In big businesses, when you need to cross a river, you simply design a bridge, build it, and march right across. But in a small venture, you must climb on the rocks. You don't know exactly where each step will take you, but you do know the general direction you're moving in. If you make a mistake, you get wet. If your calculations are wrong, you have to inch your way back to safety and find a different route. And, as you jump from rock to rock, you have to *like* the feeling" (Dan Bricklin, "Natural-Born Entrepreneur," *Harvard Business Review* 79, no. 8 [September 2001]: 53–59).

Literary: "It was later, much later, when the need to return was upon me and I yearned for the great, cool hall of our house in Tawasi, for the smell of the fields and the black, starry night of the countryside before the High Dam brought electricity to the villages—when I yearned for Cairo, for Abu el-'Ela bridge, for the feel of the dust gritty under my fingers as I trailed my hand along the iron railing, for the smell of salted fish that met you as you drew near to Fasakhani Abu el-'Ela, for the sight of fruit piled high in symmetrical pyramids outside a greengrocer's shop and the twist of the brown paper bag in which you carry the fruit home, when I yearned even for the khamaseen winds that make you cover your face against the dust and with bowed head hurry quickly home—it was only then that I understood how longing for a place can take you over so that you can do nothing except return." (Ahdaf Soueif, *The Map of Love* [New York: Anchor Books, 2000]: 119).

Poetic: "What she misses here is slow twilight, the sound of familiar trees. All through her youth in Toronto she learned to read the summer night. It was where she could be herself, lying in a bed, stepping onto a fire escape half asleep with a cat in her arms" (Michael Ondaatje, *The English Patient* [New York: Random House, 1993]: 49).

Appendix B

Strategies for Communication

A Note on Documentation Format

When writers incorporate another person's words, facts, or ideas into their own writing, they must cite the source of this information. The three most commonly used documentation formats in academic writing are the APA (American Psychological Association), the MLA (Modern Language Association), and the Turabian/*Chicago Manual of Style.* Many of the writing assignments in this text require the use of outside sources and the documentation of these sources. The documentation style that is suggested in the following guidelines is the MLA in-text citation format. This format gives the author's last name and the page number in parentheses in the text. It lists all sources as Works Cited at the end of the paper, arranged alphabetically by the author's last name or alphabetically by title if no author is identified. The recommended text is *The MLA Handbook for Writers of Research Papers,* 5th ed. (New York: MLA, 1999).

The following Web sites provide information about the three major documentation formats.

American Psychological Association: <http://www.apastyle.org> (contains guidelines and examples)

Modern Language Association: <http://www.mla.org> (contains links but not guidelines and examples)

Turabian/*Chicago Manual of Style:* <http://www.press.uchicago.edu> (contains links and FAQs but not guidelines and examples)

Summary

A summary is a brief restatement of a longer written document. Its purpose is to convey knowledge in a clear and concise form. The summarizer must extract only the most important information from the entire document. Writing effective summaries is challenging because it depends on the skills of reading comprehension, critical analysis, and paraphrasing.

In the business world, summary writing is a skill that is in great demand. Learning to present only the essential information takes time and effort, but it can be done by thinking logically and using a systematic approach. When summarizing a text, follow these four steps.

1. Read

2. Write

3. Edit

4. Rewrite

I. Read

   A. Read the text quickly, looking for major points.

   B. Reread the text carefully. Underline or highlight the author's main idea, major points, and key supporting data.

   C. Reread the underlined or highlighted statements, deleting any that are not relevant.

II. Write

   A. Using the underlined or highlighted statements, write a rough draft.

   B. In the first paragraph, give the author, title, source, date, and the main idea of the text.

   C. Paraphrase the author's words; do not copy directly from the text. However, you may include a few short quotations.

   D. Write in a clear, concise, and objective style.

   E. Do not add any extraneous information or give your opinion.

III. Edit

   A. Be certain that the content of the summary is accurate and coherent.

   B. Delete any unnecessary information from the summary.

   C. Add information if the meaning is not clear and complete.

   D. Rearrange the information if the organization is not logical.

   E. Follow quotations with in-text citation of the author's last name and the page number (Johnson 125).

IV. Rewrite

   A. Write the summary again, making the editorial changes.

   B. Proofread the summary for errors in grammar, punctuation, or spelling.

   C. Check the format for correct title, headings, spacing, and margins.

   D. Make all necessary corrections for the final copy of the summary.

   E. List your source as Works Cited at the end of the summary.

Example of a Summary (400 words)

"The Big Pitcher"

In "The Big Pitcher" (*The Economist,* January 20, 2001), the author argues that despite the increasing power of brewers around the world, the beer industry remains local and traditional rather than expanding into the international market. Not only is the major beer Budweiser mainly consumed in the United States, but Heineken and Carlsberg are primarily consumed in the European Union. Thus, beer brands remain weak in the international market. Even though mergers worth $13 billion took place between 1999 and 2001, "Beer is one of the least global consumer goods of all," writes the author (*The Economist* 63–64).

The beer industry has been having a hard time in global markets for several reasons. First, the beer business is divided within the international market, and even the 20 largest brand names added together have just 25% of the world market. For example, Budweiser, the largest global beer brand, had only 3.6% of the market shares in the beer industry in 1999 (*The Economist* 64). Furthermore, border taxes are costly, countries have a variety of legal restrictions that hinder global expansion, and a significant investment is required in order for a brewery and distribution system to be set up in a new location.

Beer is a slow-growing industry. The forecast for annual growth in world beer volumes between now and 2005 is "only 1.5 to 2%" (*The Economist* 64). Thus, there is pressure on brewers to merge and achieve larger market share. However, most brewers have focused on national mergers instead of international mergers. Although the major domestic brewers will soon have no choice but to expand beyond their borders, those that have tried to do so in the past have not been successful. These brewers were unsuccessful because they failed in their outreach to the new market, and they lost their focus on pleasing their traditional consumers.

The article suggests that marketing is a weak component in the beer industry and that most major brewers have not learned how to sell their product around the world. Nevertheless, beer consumers are changing and becoming more international, as tastes are becoming less divergent and more alike. Heineken's Mr. Vuursteen believes that "the future will be different" because young people, whether in Shanghai, Stockholm, or Munich, are basically the same (*The Economist* 64). Still, it may take the brewing industry some time to transform itself from a local operation to a global enterprise.

Works Cited

"The Big Pitcher." *The Economist,* 20 January 2001, 63–64.

Essay

An essay is an analytical or interpretative composition that deals with its subject in a limited way. It may be completely objective or contain the writer's opinion. Writing an essay can be done efficiently if the writer takes a systematic approach to the writing process by using the POWER method. The following are the five steps in the POWER method.

1. *Plan*

2. Outline

3. Write

4. Edit

5. Rewrite

   I. Plan

      A. Determine the purpose of the essay, the audience, and the type of information to be included.

      B. Collect and evaluate the information needed for the essay.

      C. Write a purpose statement for the essay.

      D. Choose a method of organization for the essay.

  II. Outline

      A. Write a one-sentence thesis or controlling idea for the essay.

      B. Write an outline of three or four major points, minor points, and supporting data.

      C. Arrange the major points and minor points in logical order.

      D. Write a topic sentence for each major point.

 III. Write

      A. Write the introduction to the essay, including the thesis (controlling idea).

      B. Write the body of the essay, following the outline and discussing each major point in a separate paragraph.

      C. Add supporting data (facts, examples, statistics, quotations) to the essay to support the major points.

      D. Cite your sources using in-text citation of the author's last name and the page number (Johnson 125).

      E. Write the conclusion to the essay by restating or paraphrasing the thesis and adding concluding data (summary, prediction, or solution).

IV. Edit

    A. Check for accurate and coherent content in the essay.

    B. Check for logical and clear organization in the essay.

    C. Be certain that the essay is written in a formal academic style.

    D. Delete any unnecessary information from and add missing information to the essay.

V. Rewrite

    A. Write the essay again, making the editorial changes.

    B. Proofread the essay for errors in grammar, punctuation, or spelling.

    C. Check the format for correct title, headings, spacing, and margins.

    D. Make all necessary corrections for the final copy of the essay.

Essay Outline Worksheet

General topic _____

Purpose statement _____

General method of organization (deductive or inductive) _____

  I. Paragraph 1: Introduction

    Controlling idea of the communication (thesis)

    _____

  II. Paragraph 2: Body

    A. Major point (aspect of controlling idea) _____

    B. Topic sentence _____

    C. Types of supporting data _____

  III. Paragraph 3: Body

    A. Major point (aspect of controlling idea) _____

    B. Topic sentence _____

    C. Types of supporting data _____

  IV. Paragraph 4: Body

    A. Major point (aspect of controlling idea) _____

    B. Topic sentence _____

    C. Types of supporting data _____

  V. Paragraph 5: Conclusion

    A. Major point (restatement of controlling idea) _____

    B. Topic sentence _____

    C. Types of concluding data _____

Examples of Essays

Yuhi Morita
March 2002

Major Differences between English and Japanese

When I first started to study English some years ago, I remember that many people used to ask me if it was hard to learn English. They must have thought that learning a completely new language would be as difficult as learning Japanese. Of course, it was not easy to learn English in the beginning, especially because English and Japanese have almost nothing in common. However, although my native language, Japanese, and English are different in alphabet, grammar, and levels of politeness, English is an easier language to learn than Japanese.

The primary factor that makes Japanese much more difficult than English is the Japanese alphabet. First of all, English uses the Roman alphabet, which consists of only 26 letters, while Japanese uses three different characters: Hiragana (squiggly letters), Katakana (boxy letters), and Kanji (Chinese characters). Hiragana is supposed to correspond to the alphabet in English. Katakana, on the other hand, is used only to spell out foreign words, such as *camera* or *guitar*. The most difficult characters, Kanji, are taken from Chinese, and each consists of several "strokes," which must be written in a specific order and convey a specific meaning. Kanji characters have various pronunciations, depending on their meanings in words and sentences. Kanji can also combine to form new words that will have unique meanings. For example, if one combines the Kanji for *hand* and *paper,* one gets the word for a *letter.* There are thousands of Kanji characters: an average Japanese adult has to memorize at least 2,000 characters of the 8,000 or so in regular use. Although Hiragana and Katakana are quite simple to learn, Kanji characters present a challenge even for Japanese native speakers. Thus, the alphabet makes English easier to master than Japanese.

The complicated grammar of Japanese is another factor that makes English less difficult than Japanese. First, the major grammatical difference between English and Japanese is the word order, and in particular, the placement of verbs in a sentence. For example, a verb in English comes toward the beginning of a sentence, usually after the subject, so it is easier to understand the context of the sentence. A verb in Japanese, however, comes at the end of a sentence, which means that the verb cannot help a reader to anticipate the meaning of the sentence. Once one becomes familiar with the structural patterns of Japanese, this word order will seem natural, and one can usually anticipate what the verb at the end of the sentence will be. However, it takes a long time to gain this familiarity. Second, Japanese speakers often do not include a subject in their sentences. In fact, Japanese does not have pronouns such as *I, me, them, him,* or *her,* so "He just kissed her" and "I just kissed her" sound exactly the same. Third, English has the present, past, and future tenses, whereas there is no future tense in Japanese. Therefore, context is important, and one must pay extra attention to it. These grammar rules make Japanese a complex language.

The levels of politeness in the Japanese language are the final reason that English is easier to learn than Japanese. Just as in spoken English, in written English there are basically two levels of politeness, formal and informal. In contrast, in Japanese there are at least four levels or forms of expression indicating politeness: futsugo, sonkeigo, kenjyougo, and teinego. Futsugo is the language spoken in everyday life, which is generally similar to informal English. The remainder of the three languages form a group of polite expressions, but each one has a particular usage. For example, sonkeigo, honorific language, is an expression implying a speaker's respect for the listener. Kenjyougo, modest language, is used when one steps down in order to show his or her respect for the listener. Teineigo, polite language, is an expression to show a speaker's respect for the listener directly. These rules are difficult to use perfectly even for Japanese, and one needs a lot of practice for this. Thus, English, which has simpler and fewer politeness levels, does not present learners with as many challenges as does Japanese.

It is a fact that one's native language is easily and naturally acquired in childhood. Generally, unless one has the basic knowledge of a language from an early age, it is hard to master a new language. There are many differences between English and Japanese, such as their alphabets, grammatical structures, and levels of politeness. Each of them has unique linguistic features. However, it is clear that Japanese is harder for most people to learn than English because of its alphabet, grammar, and levels of politeness.

Ayumu Kuroda
March 2001

Global Marketing of Japanese Box Lunches

According to Martin van Mesdag, the author of "Winging It in Foreign Markets" (*Harvard Business Review,* January–February 1987, 71–74), "food and drink products are the most difficult to take global." However, it is difficult, but it is not impossible. There are several examples of food and drink companies and products that have succeeded in global markets, such as McDonald's, Coca-Cola, Rocher chocolates, and others. Japan also has a product that can be sold globally. It is a packed box lunch. In fact, the packed box lunches sold at convenience stores in Japan are one of the most popular food products in Japan. I believe the box lunches will be successful in global markets for the following reasons: they are nutritious and delicious, and they are inexpensive.

First of all, since the packed box lunches are delicious and nutritious, almost everyone who tries them likes them. Of course, in Japan, the producers of these lunches adjust the taste in order to match local preferences. In some sections of the country, the lunches are less salty, for example. In Japan, a parent corporation of convenience stores employs dietitians, and they study the balanced nutrients that will be contained in the lunches. In addition, so as to make certain that the lunches remain popular with the majority of consumers, thorough taste tests are conducted repeatedly. Only those lunches that can pass through this process will be on the market. Therefore, people trust the taste and quality of the lunches and enjoy eating them.

The second reason for the likely global success of Japanese box lunches is the fact that the lunches are not only delicious but also inexpensive and ready-made. For this reason, the lunches appeal to those people who are so busy that they allocate little time for lunch, especially businesspeople. Furthermore, in view of the low cost, the box lunch is popular regardless of income bracket. The price is lower than the cost of a lunch at McDonald's. Thus, its sales cut across all levels of society. Executives as well as factory laborers prefer to eat box lunches.

In order to market these lunches internationally, companies should do market research, analysis, and reformulation. First, it is necessary to make the taste appealing to a large general market rather than the specific Japanese market. In this way, the lunches will appeal to the taste preferences of as many consumers as possible. Next, we should consider in which areas to sell the lunches. Downtown areas, university neighborhoods, and suburban shopping malls would be the best targets, since they are frequented by busy professionals, students, and family shoppers. For this marketing project to succeed, I recommend careful and detailed research and preparation rather than the inadequate and uncertain shot-in-the-dark method described by van Mesdag.

In conclusion, considering the reasons discussed above, I am convinced that the packed box lunches will be as successful in the global market as they are in Japan. They will meet the need of the ever-increasing workforce around the world by providing healthful, delicious, and convenient lunches at a reasonable price.

Entering the global food and drink market, while difficult because of people's traditional preferences, is an exciting challenge. Although the risk is quite large, it is worth taking in order to attain the profits that will accompany the sale of Japanese packed box lunches in the international arena.

Works Cited

van Mesdag, Martin. "Winging It in Foreign Markets." *Harvard Business Review* 65 (January–February 1987): 71–74.

Synthesis

A synthesis is an essay that is developed from two or more sources from which the writer selects information to support a thesis. A synthesis may be organized according to various organizational patterns: argument, comparison-contrast, cause-effect, definition, description, example, or process. Writing a synthesis requires that the writer find relationships among the several reading selections being analyzed. The following sequence is recommended for the process of writing a synthesis.

1. Read

2. Underline

3. Outline

4. Write

5. Edit

6. Rewrite

  I. Read

    A. Read the selections carefully.

    B. Think about the authors' themes and main ideas.

    C. Develop a tentative thesis (controlling idea) that can be supported by all the readings.

  II. Underline

    A. Read the selections again, underlining the sentences that relate to your thesis.

    B. Underline any other major points or key terms that support your thesis.

  III. Outline

    A. Write a one-sentence thesis that is the foundation for the synthesis.

    B. Write an outline of three or four major points, minor points, and supporting data.

    C. Arrange the major points and minor points in logical order.

    D. Write a topic sentence for each major point.

IV. Write

    A. Write an introduction for the synthesis, including your sources (authors, titles, and dates) and thesis.

    B. Write the body of the synthesis, following the outline and discussing each major point in a separate paragraph.

    C. Use brief quotations or paraphrased passages from the readings to support your thesis and cite your sources using in-text citation of the author's last name and the page number (Johnson 125).

    D. Write the conclusion to the synthesis by paraphrasing your thesis and adding concluding data (summary, prediction, or solution).

V. Edit

    A. Check for accurate and coherent content in the synthesis.

    B. Check for logical and clear organization in the synthesis.

    C. Be certain that the synthesis is written in a formal academic style.

    D. Be certain that the body paragraphs support your thesis.

VI. Rewrite

    A. Write the synthesis again, making the editorial changes.

    B. Proofread the synthesis for errors in grammar, punctuation, or spelling.

    C. Check the format for correct title, headings, spacing, and margins.

    D. Make all necessary corrections for the final copy of the synthesis.

    E. List your sources as Works Cited at the end of the synthesis. Alphabetize them by the authors' last names.

Example of a Synthesis

Outline and Synthesis
Maxim Sigarev
March 2002

I. Introduction

  A. Authors, titles, sources, dates

  B. Globalization has many advantages, but it also has harmful effects, which can be seen in the terrorist attacks of 9-11-01 and the collapse of Argentina.

II. Openness allows citizens in such countries to live more freely and prosperously.

  A. Openness leads to increased investment and trade.

  B. This results in the transfer of technology, improved resource allocation, increased competition, lower prices, and greater access to foreign capital.

III. Too much openness can have its own disadvantages.

  A. International conflicts accompany openness (terrorist attacks).

  B. If growth in global trade is disrupted or slows, the most exposed countries pay the price (Argentina).

IV. The terrorist attacks resulted in an economic downturn, which affected the global economy.

  A. A "security tax" was imposed, so cross-border transfers will now take longer.

  B. The attacks revealed the risk of global connectivity.

V. Conclusion

  A. Life has changed since September 11, 2001.

  B. Globalization was a contributing cause of 9-11 and of Argentina's collapse, which means that globalization has harmful consequences.

Globalization

The articles "Sizing Up Global Integration" by Moisés Naím and Paul A. Laudicina (*Christian Science Monitor*, 28 February 2001) and "Special Report: Globalisation: Is It at Risk?" (*The Economist*, 2 February 2002) focus on how globalization has affected the modern world. Naím and Laudicina discuss the first annual report on the Globalization Index, which measures global integration by considering technology, personal contact, finance, and goods/services in 50 countries. According to Naím and Laudicina, "ongoing debates over the relative merits of global integration have very real implications, both for countries and for the people who live in them" (Naím and Laudicina 11). One year later, the *Economist* discussed the economic impact of the September 11, 2001, terrorist attacks and questioned the endurance of globalization, which may be at risk. Moreover, the authors of both articles acknowledge the advantages of globalization but admit that it can be harmful.

According to the article "Sizing Up Global Integration," globalization and openness allow citizens in such countries to live more freely and more prosperously. The author says: "Openness allows access to goods, services, and capital not readily available at home" (Naím and Laudicina 11). Nations more open to trade are the ones best positioned to grow and develop in the long term and therefore represent more attractive investment opportunities. In general, openness equates to the transfer of technology, improved resource allocation, increased competition, lower prices, and greater access to foreign capital. This openness accounts for the fact that Singapore was the most globally integrated country in 2000. Singapore "boasts high levels of trade, heavy capital flows, and an annual stream of international travelers nearly three times higher than the country's population of a little more than 4 million" (Naím and Laudicina 11).

On the other hand, too much openness can have its own disadvantages. It is possible that international conflicts will accompany openness because governments can't control "the rise of transnational crime" (Naím and Laudicina 11). This can be seen in the September 11, 2001, terrorist attacks. The *Economist* author writes: "The horror at the World Trade Centre exposed the dark side of global interconnections: the ease with which the West's enemies and their resources can move around the world" ("Special Report: Globalisation" 65). Furthermore, if growth in global trade is disrupted or slows, the most exposed countries pay the price. This happened in Argentina, which "opened its capital markets to international money and sold everything, from banks to ports, to foreign investors" ("Special Report: Globalisation" 65). The consequences of this openness were severe. Last year in December "Argentina defaulted on $155 billion of debt and collapsed ignominiously into political and economic chaos" ("Special Report: Globalisation" 65).

As a result of the terrorist attacks of September 11, 2001, the world suffered an economic downturn, which affected the global economy in a variety of ways. The *Economist* provides some reactions to this. For example, after the tragedy at the World Trade Center and the Pentagon, John Gray, a British political scientist, wrote: "The era of globalisation is over. The entire view of the world that supported the markets' faith in globalisation has melted down" ("Special Report: Globalisation" 65). The devastating events of September 11 have resulted in a new "security tax," which will make it more difficult to achieve global integration. The security of national borders will now have to be tightened, hardly an inexpensive endeavor, so cross-border transfers will take longer. According to the *Economist*, the terrorist attacks revealed the risk of global connectivity and also raised the fear as to what might come next ("Special Report: Globalisation" 65).

Globalization is a complex world system that does not benefit all countries equally: "Global integration is a selective phenomenon. Many countries benefit; many do not" ("Special Report: Globalisation" 66). The terrorist attacks, which were related to globalization, have affected not only the United States but also the whole world. In fact, this tragedy has certainly affected the forces of globalization, which once seemed unstoppable, and several economic changes have taken place since September 11, 2001. A country that defaulted on its debt in the period of just one month (Argentina) and a new tax on the price of cross-border connectivity are major examples of these changes. The high costs of globalization confirm that this phenomenon does not necessarily bring harmony and happiness, but it also has dramatic and negative consequences.

Works Cited

Naím, Moisés, and Paul A. Laudicina. "Sizing Up Global Integration." *Christian Science Monitor,* 28 February 2001, 11.

"Special Report: Globalisation: Is It at Risk?" *The Economist,* 2 February 2002, 65–68.

Critical Review

A critical review is a type of essay in which the writer gives his or her response to the argument that an author has presented in an article or a book. Other names for a critical review are *reaction paper* and *critique*. In a critical review, the writer should express an overall opinion in the introduction and summarize the author's argument. Then he or she should evaluate the author's argument according to several criteria, such as logic, accuracy, completeness, and clarity. The following format is suggested for writing a critical review.

   I. Introduction

      A. Background information about the author and topic

      B. Thesis (the writer's evaluation of the author's argument)

  II. Summary of article or book

      A. Major points

      B. Supporting points

 III. Critique

      A. Analysis of the author's argument

      B. Agreement or disagreement with the author's argument

 IV. Conclusion

      A. Summary

      B. Restatement of thesis

The following sequence is suggested for the process of writing a critical review.

1. Read
2. Underline
3. Outline
4. Write
5. Edit
6. Rewrite

I. Read

   A. Read the book or article carefully.

   B. Think about the author's argument and main ideas.

   C. Develop a tentative thesis (controlling idea) that contains your evaluation of the author's argument.

II. Underline

   A. Read the book or article again, underlining the sentences that relate to your thesis.

   B. Underline any other major points or key terms that support your thesis.

III. Outline

   A. Write a one-sentence thesis that is the foundation for the critical review.

   B. Write an outline of three or four major points, minor points, and supporting data.

   C. Arrange the major points and minor points in logical order, beginning with the summary.

   D. Write a topic sentence for each major point.

IV. Write

   A. Write an introduction for the critical review, including the title and author of the book or article and your thesis.

   B. Write the body of the critical review, following the outline and discussing each major point in a separate paragraph.

   C. Use brief quotations or paraphrased passages from the book or article to support your thesis, and cite your sources using in-text citation of the author's last name and page number (Johnson 125).

   D. Write the conclusion to the critical review by paraphrasing your thesis and adding concluding data (summary, prediction, or solution).

V. Edit

   A. Check for accurate and coherent content in the critical review.

   B. Check for logical and clear organization in the critical review.

   C. Be certain that the critical review is written in a formal academic style.

   D. Be certain that the body paragraphs support your thesis (your evaluation of the author's argument).

VI. Rewrite

    A. Write the critical review again, making the editorial changes.

    B. Proofread the critical review for errors in grammar, punctuation, or spelling.

    C. Check the format for correct title, headings, spacing, and margins.

    D. Make all necessary corrections for the final copy of the critical review.

    E. List your sources as Works Cited at the end of the critical review. Alphabetize them by the authors' last names.

Examples of Theses for Critical Reviews

- Although Karen Field makes a compelling argument for home schooling, she does not provide justification for her belief that home-schooled children score higher on standardized tests than students who attend traditional schools.

- Robert Martelli presents a variety of psychological theories to support his proposal that marijuana should be legalized; however, his argument is weak in logic and lacks objectivity.

- While the author has assembled a strongly argued case for abolishing capital punishment, his argument that capital punishment is not a deterrent to crime is unsupported by recent data.

Examples of Critical Reviews

Misako Schreim
February 2002

"How I Caused That Story"

In the article "How I Caused That Story," which appeared in *Time* (February 4, 2002), Doris Kearns Goodwin explains how she unintentionally plagiarized in one of her books fourteen years ago. Because of the significant number of reference materials needed for her complicated historical research, she says that the possibility of error was great. Moreover, there is no guarantee that she will not make an error again, even though she is now using a computer to avoid mistakes. Her explanation makes her errors seem understandable. However, if a professional historian is allowed to make these citation mistakes, historical information will not be accurate for future reference. Moreover, as a professional historian, she must take responsibility for using citations correctly and in accordance with U.S. copyright laws. Therefore, her explanation about her plagiarism sounds somewhat unprofessional and is not convincing.

According to Goodwin, after she published *The Fitzgeralds and the Kennedys,* she was accused of plagiarism, which she claimed happened by mistake. Goodwin explains that the 900-page book, which she wrote over a ten-year period, had 3,500 footnotes based on 300 reference books. She had taken an enormous number of notes by hand, and she checked the accuracy of her sources carefully, but somehow she confused her paraphrased sentences with direct quotes taken from another author: "If I had had the books in front of me, rather than my notes, I would have caught mistakes in the first place and placed any borrowed phrases in direct quotes" (Goodwin 69). Goodwin believes that the only way to prevent plagiarism is to organize research materials by using computer technology. However, it is still possible to make an error, especially when a historian's research is complicated and lengthy (Goodwin 69).

I understand that a historian's work is complex, involving significant numbers of sources, in this case, 300 reference books and 3,500 footnotes. Nevertheless, when it comes to history, incomplete documentation is not acceptable. It is critical that historical writing contain accurate quotations and footnotes that will give additional meaning to the work under discussion. If a citation in historical writing is omitted, future historians will be confused, and the situation might cause questions about the historian's work. As a result, the historical record might be misinterpreted because of incorrect information. In other words, any piece of information about history should be cited correctly because correct evidence is essential.

Regarding rules related to her work as a professional writer, Goodwin should be aware of the importance of U.S. copyright laws, which prohibit a person from using someone else's writing as if it were his or hers. This is an ethical and legal issue regarding acknowledgement of and respect for other people's original work. In addition, Goodwin is paid for her work as a professional writer, so she should be held responsible for her work just like all paid employees have to take responsibility for fulfilling the requirements of their jobs.

In conclusion, I don't agree with Goodwin's opinion that under certain circumstances, there is an excuse for plagiarism to occur. Even if Goodwin's plagiarism was unintentional, it is not justifiable. It is important for historians to make an effort to fully cite their sources and to use quotation marks for direct quotations. Plagiarism is not acceptable under any circumstances.

Works Cited

Goodwin, Doris Kearns. "How I Caused That Story." *Time,* 4 February 2002, 69.

Dominique Fotso
February 2002

"How I Caused That Story"

In "How I Caused That Story" (*Time,* February 4, 2002), Doris Kearns Goodwin, a Pulitzer-prizewinning historian, tries to clarify how author Lynne McTaggart's writing appeared in her book *The Fitzgeralds and the Kennedys* without being correctly attributed. She describes the research process of a historian and concludes that mistakes are likely to happen in this kind of complicated work. I agree with her persuasive piece of writing, which my own experience tends to verify.

In her article, Goodwin relates how the incident happened. Fourteen years ago, after McTaggart complained that Goodwin used her language without quotation marks, Goodwin corrected the omissions, but in February 2002, the *Weekly Standard* reported the incident. As a consequence, she published this article describing the process of writing a historical book in order to convince readers that an error can easily occur. While writing *The Fitzgeralds and the Kennedys,* Goodwin read many materials, took notes, and classified them by source and author. She checked her footnotes against her sources to catch any mistakes. However, in this complex process, Goodwin did not get rid of every inaccuracy. She admits her fault but tries to make it appear less serious than one might think it is and says that now she uses computer technology to lessen the chance of errors.

I find Goodwin's explanation for her plagiarism reasonable because of my own experience. College students are assigned many essays with citations and references that require a great deal of work to be effective and without error. In fact, who has never made a mistake in doing this task? At the college level, it is hardly possible to do comprehensive research without making a single mistake. Thus, I believe that Goodwin's research, which was more complex than college writing, required more effort and had a greater chance of errors. In addition, the author may have had good methodology in the research process, but she didn't have modern computer technology to prevent mistakes from slipping into her work.

Furthermore, Goodwin has the impressive ability to persuade readers with her writing style. First of all, she admits her responsibility in this issue: "I failed to provide quotation marks for phrases that I had taken verbatim . . ." (Goodwin 69). More to the point, she uses many skillful methods to convey the immensity of a historian's research. She gives enormous numbers related to the project: "900-page book," "3,500 footnotes," "300 books," "thousands of family letters" (Goodwin 69). Also she uses several action verbs to illustrate the difficult work she has to do: take, read, categorize, revisit, arrange, recheck (Goodwin 2002). The author shows us her talent in writing, and it contributes to the persuasive tone.

Goodwin clearly defends her position and explains how her plagiarism occurred. Admitting her responsibility and outlining the research process of a historian, she successfully clarifies the issue and justifies her actions. In the end, she describes herself as a "fallible person" (Goodwin 69). I believe this is a reasonable depiction of any human being.

Works Cited

Goodwin, Doris Kearns. "How I Caused That Story." *Time,* 4 February 2002, 69.

Memorandum

TO: CDC Information Systems Division

FROM: Charles Fredericks, Manager

SUBJECT: Work Schedule

DATE: October 23, 2002

Lately, I have noticed that some employees have not been conforming to their assigned work schedules. Although this is not yet a widespread practice, I have decided to take a proactive approach to prevent this from becoming a major problem. Thus, I am sending this memorandum to all Information Systems Division employees to ask that you follow your work schedule. This is a serious matter to the company, not only because of the cost it represents to CDC, but also because of the impact it has on employee morale.

The most common violation has been late arrival to work. It has come to my attention that several employees are consistently late. Also, certain employees leave early without asking permission to do so. The company will no longer accept this kind of unprofessional behavior. This misconduct has resulted in deadlines not being met and projects not being completed. Therefore, I remind all the division's employees that everyone is responsible for complying with the company rules on work schedules.

Following these rules is mandatory, and lack of compliance will lead to disciplinary actions. Anyone who arrives late or leaves the office early without permission will receive a letter of warning. If this happens again within the month, he or she will be suspended for three days without pay. If there is a third violation within 30 days, the employee will be subject to dismissal.

I hope that after this reminder, no further measures will be necessary. Following your assigned work schedule will be to everyone's advantage. Thank you for your cooperation on this important issue.

cc: Elizabeth Perez

Business Letter

2700 Fleetwood Road
Apartment 330
McLean, VA 22101
November 12, 2002

Mr. Alexander Booth, Director
Human Resources Department
Globaltech, Inc.
2207 Wisconsin Avenue, NW
Washington, DC 20007

Dear Mr. Booth:

This is in response to the advertisement (*Washington Post,* 11-10-02) for an administrative assistant at Globaltech, Inc. I believe my education and professional experience qualify me for this position. Currently, I am studying for an MBA at American University. Because I am a part-time graduate student, I am interested in finding a challenging job that complements my overall career objective to work in international business.

In June 1996, I graduated with honors from Michigan State University with a major in business management and a minor in finance. Prior to entering graduate school, I was employed for two years in Casablanca, Morocco, as an office administrator. During this overseas opportunity, I maintained financial records for a rural project involving over $1.5 million, while supervising a large office staff. My administrative responsibilities ranged from tracking the mileage and repairs of a fleet of four-wheel-drive vehicles to planning procurement and banking trips to Rabat, Morocco.

My administrative abilities are excellent and include proficiency in office organization, scheduling, ordering supplies, and handling telephone, e-mail, and fax communications. My English language skills are above average, and I am also fluent in French and Arabic. My computer skills include mastery of WordPerfect, Microsoft Word, Microsoft Excel, and PowerPoint.

I am enclosing my résumé and would be happy to provide you with references from my previous positions. I hope to have the opportunity to meet with you to discuss this position in detail. If you wish to contact me, please telephone me at 703-555-1234, send a fax to 703-555-4321, or e-mail me at angela@erols.com. I look forward to hearing from you.

Sincerely,

Angela Callahan

Angela Callahan

Enclosure: résumé

Résumé

A résumé tells potential employers about a job applicant in one or two pages. Thus, it should be a readable document that highlights education, experience, and accomplishments. It is a good idea to write an appropriate objective that tailors your résumé to the job for which you are applying. A résumé includes the following information.

- Name, address, phone and fax numbers, and e-mail address (centered at the top of the page)
- Employment objective
- Education
  - Schools, dates, and locations
  - Awards and honors
- Employment experience
  - Positions, dates, locations, and responsibilities
  - Awards and honors
- Skills, activities, and affiliations
- References (optional)

Examples of Employment Objectives

- To find a challenging position in an international trade organization where my analytical skills can be utilized.
- To contribute my expertise and knowledge of information technology to a multinational corporation.
- To work in the public policy area of a nongovernmental organization that specializes in Latin America.
- To attain a communications position in the public or private sector utilizing my skills and knowledge.
- To join an innovative company in a sales or training capacity where my background and experience in education can be used.
- To have a challenging position in a progressive company that will encourage the use of my foreign language proficiency, communication skills, and program development background.
- To obtain a position in a global enterprise that will use my education and work experience in international business, telecommunications, and market analysis.

. . . .

Martha Madison Richmond
403 Macomb Street, NW, Washington, D.C. 20016
202-555-5555   martha@talk.com

OBJECTIVE: To contribute my knowledge of public policy law to the development of regulatory policies in a governmental organization.

EDUCATION
University of Virginia, School of Law, Charlottesville, Virginia
JD, May 2002
Honor: Winner of Moot Court Competition, May 2002
Justice Anthony Kennedy presiding

University of Virginia, Charlottesville, Virginia
Bachelor of Arts in Government, May 1998
Semester in Florence, Italy, spring 1997

EXPERIENCE
Professional Services Council, Washington, DC
Public Policy Intern, 1998–1999
- Researched and wrote issue papers to be used in a briefing book for the press and PSC members
- Covered congressional hearings on defense procurement, the effects of federal policy on small businesses, and tax reform
- Researched and wrote reports and news updates on legislative issues for PSC newsletter
- Attended meetings and worked with CEOs
- Assembled news articles on PSC issues

Barrington & Sheffield Law Offices, Washington, DC
Intern, summers 1995, 1996, 1997
- Performed accounting, administrative, research, and supervisory duties
- Implemented a computerized billing system
- Trained and managed summer interns and supervised a project in the accounting department

Virginia Congressional Primary Campaign, McLean, VA
Campaign Volunteer, 1994
- Organized mailings and scheduled events

Paine-Webber Investment Campaign, Washington, DC
Investment Research Assistant, 1993–1994
- Recruited new clients

NBC-TV, *The Sandy Bell Show,* Washington, DC
Production Intern, summer 1993
- Researched show topics and wrote summaries of shows for syndication purposes

SKILLS
- **Computer:** Proficient in WordPerfect, Microsoft Word, Microsoft Excel, PowerPoint, Microsoft Office, Quattro Pro, LexisNexis
- **Language:** Fluent in Italian and French

ACTIVITIES
- Academics Committee for Student Council, University of Virginia, 1995–1996
- Thomas Jefferson National Affairs Study Group, University of Virginia, 1996–1997
- Big Brother–Big Sister Association, University of Virginia, 1997–1998
- University of Virginia Orchestra, 1994–1998

Guidelines for Written Assignments

Format

1. Use 12-point Times Roman font.

2. Use 1.5 spacing or double spacing.

3. Number the pages.

4. Indent the first word of a paragraph five spaces.

5. Use one-inch margins.

6. Be consistent in format and graphics.

7. Do not leave a title or subtitle at the bottom of a page. Move it to the next page.

Process

1. Consider the type of assignment and the audience and purpose of the paper.

2. Write a purpose statement and a thesis statement for the paper.

3. Make an outline before beginning to write the paper.

4. Edit the paper after you have finished writing it.

5. Rewrite the paper at least once, incorporating revisions.

6. Use spell check and grammar check on the paper.

7. Proofread the paper before making the final copy.

Example of a Purpose Statement

- The purpose of this essay is to compare the information technology infrastructure in Brazil with the information technology infrastructure in the United States.

Example of a Thesis Statement

- Although Brazil is technologically advanced, the information technology infrastructure in that country is not as strong as the infrastructure in the United States.

Oral Presentation

To be successful in giving an oral presentation, speakers should use a simple, direct, and relaxed style. They must know their subject very well and present the information in logical order. They should speak naturally to the audience, rather than reading from their index cards or, if they are using the presentation graphics program PowerPoint, from the screen. Planning, preparation, and practice are the keys to effective oral presentations.

The following are seven suggestions for giving a successful oral presentation.

1. Know the subject well by planning, preparing, and practicing in advance.

2. Organize the material logically so that one idea leads to the next.

3. State the purpose and thesis in the beginning of the presentation.

4. Speak in a loud, clear voice, and do not speak too quickly.

5. Maintain eye contact with every member of the audience.

6. Stand up straight, and use natural gestures.

7. Use concrete language and words that create mental images.

The following are seven suggestions for organizing an oral presentation.

1. Organize the material into a thesis, major points, and supporting details or examples.

2. Divide the presentation into four parts: introduction, summary, evaluation, and conclusion.

3. In the introduction of the presentation, state your purpose and thesis, along with background information.

4. Organize the major points of the presentation logically, and explain them clearly.

5. Restate the thesis in the conclusion of the presentation.

6. Use visual aids (pictures, charts, or graphs) to support your major points.

7. Put the information for the presentation in outline form on three-by-five-inch index cards that you can refer to whenever necessary. Do not read the entire oral presentation from the index cards or, if you are using PowerPoint, from the screen.

Example of a Purpose Statement

- The purpose of this presentation is to describe "A Long Trip to School," published in *Business Week* (August 27, 2001) and written by Moon Ihlwan in Seoul.

Example of a Thesis Statement

- Thousands of Korean students are enrolled in secondary schools and universities in English-speaking countries, where they master English, a prized asset in Korea, and receive a better education than they would in Korea.

Outline for an Oral Presentation (Summary and Evaluation of an Article)

I. Introduction

    A. Purpose statement

    B. Thesis statement

II. Summary of article

    A. Major points

    B. Supporting points

III. Evaluation of article

    A. Strengths

    B. Weaknesses

IV. Conclusion

    A. Restatement of thesis

    B. Value of article

Example of an Outline for an Oral Presentation

I. Introduction

   A. Purpose statement
      The purpose of this presentation is to describe "A Long Trip to School," published in *Business Week* (August 27, 2001) and written by Moon Ihlwan in Seoul.

   B. Thesis statement
      Thousands of Korean students are enrolled in secondary schools and universities in English-speaking countries, where they master English, a prized asset in Korea, and receive a better education than they would in Korea.

II. Summary of article

   A. Major points

- A growing number of Korean children are studying abroad because the Korean education system is weak in developing children's creativity and individuality and in teaching English.

- Korean families are willing to sacrifice because they want their children to develop the creativity that is needed to build a knowledge-based economy.

- With an increasing number of Korean children studying abroad, the Korean government is trying to reform its education system so that Korean students will attend schools in Korea.

   B. Supporting points

- Parents in Korea send their children abroad because Korean schools have large classes, emphasize rote learning, and use a rigid curriculum developed by bureaucrats.

- The Korean government earmarked $12.8 billion from 2001 to 2004 to hire 23,600 teachers, to reduce class size, and to train instructors to teach more creatively.

- The government wants to let top foreign graduate schools open branches in Korea.

- The government has developed more than 500 education Web sites.

III. Evaluation of article

   A. Strengths
      The article explains why thousands of Korean parents agree to send their children to study abroad despite the high cost and the separation of family members that result. It shows how important education is to Koreans and,

in particular, that knowledge of English is valuable. The article is clearly written, easy to read, and filled with current facts and statistics.

B. Weaknesses
The article would have been more interesting if it had contained interviews with Korean students attending schools in the United States, Canada, New Zealand, or Australia.

IV. Conclusion

A. Restatement of thesis
A growing number of Korean children are studying abroad because the Korean education system is weak in developing children's creativity and in teaching English. Even though study abroad requires a sacrifice from families, they see its long-term benefits for their country.

B. Value of article
This article was useful to read because it focused on the importance of knowing English in Korea today and explained the causal relationship between well-educated citizens and a country's economic success in the global economy.

Appendix C

"Globalization's Last Hurrah?" *Foreign Policy,* January–February 2002, 38–50

*The shock of terrorist attacks and a worldwide economic slowdown have prompted many observers to declare globalization's end. But any recent reversals in global integration must be measured against the remarkable advances of 2000. The second annual A.T. Kearney/*FOREIGN POLICY *Magazine Globalization Index, which ranks the 20 most global nations, also sheds light on a crucial question: Has globalization hit a bump in the road, or is it on the verge of a fundamental shift?*

"The era of globalization is over," declared John Gray, a professor of European thought at the London School of Economics and Political Science, less than two weeks after the terrorist attacks upon the United States. Gray had been a staunch critic of globalization, so it might be tempting to dismiss his musings as ideological triumphalism. But longtime proponents of globalization also had their faith shaken by the events of the past year. Even before terrorism, anthrax, and war dominated the headlines, other forces threatened to transform the process of global integration into one of disintegration. Beginning in spring 2000, the tech bubble burst, prompting a free fall in stock markets worldwide. The United States, Japan, and Europe faced simultaneous economic slumps for the first time since the oil shocks of the 1970s, with the United States experiencing its longest decline in industrial production since World War II. Argentina

teetered on the brink of default, portending a Latin American replay of the financial crises that swept Asian markets and Russia in 1998. Turkey faced its worst economic crisis in decades, and the value of the lira plunged by nearly 50 percent. At the outset of 2001, the Bush administration's unilateralist rejection of treaties on arms control and climate change renewed tensions with Russia and China while engendering bitter disputes between the United States and Europe.

Just as success in the stock market is ultimately measured by long-term gains instead of year-to-year returns, so too might it be premature to proclaim that 2001 sounded the death knell of globalization. After all, those countries that find themselves enmeshed in a global slowdown are measuring their losses against an unprecedented surge of economic growth and global integration in the preceding years. And at the moment, the world that has grown more integrated also seems to be more volatile. As Nobel laureate and former World Bank Chief Economist Joseph Stiglitz recently observed, "The borderless world through which goods and services flow is also a borderless world through which other things can flow that are less positive." The very forces that drove global inte-

Ireland surged ahead as the most global nation, thanks in part to the foreign investment attracted by its favorable tax climate and proximity to the euro zone but also because of its high ranking on personal contact. The United States remains at number 12, while Singapore, last year's leader, is now third.

Economic integration: trade, foreign direct investment and portfolio capital flows, and income payments and receipts (including compensation of nonresident employees and income earned and paid on assets held abroad)

Personal contact: international travel and tourism, international telephone traffic, and cross-border transfers

Technology: number of Internet users, Internet hosts, and secure servers

Political engagement: number of memberships in international organizations, U.N. Security Council missions in which each country participates, and foreign embassies that each country hosts

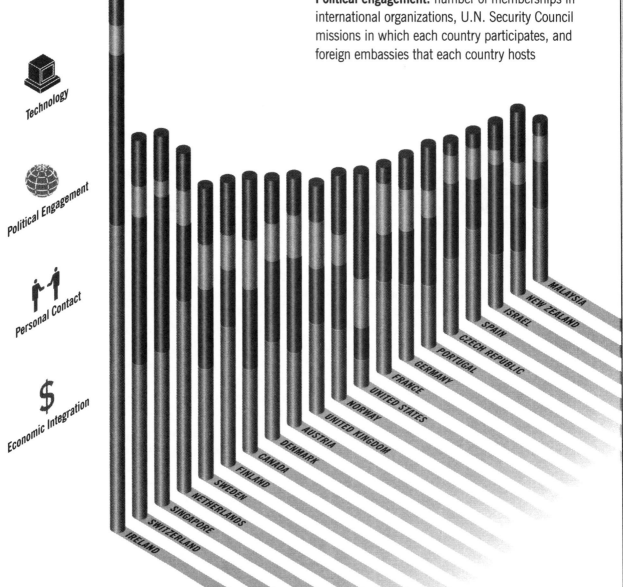

CHARTS BY AGNEW MOYER SMITH

gration over the past decade—the free flow of capital, immigration, airline travel, the Internet, and the global media—can be used by terrorist networks as well as businesses.

In our own attempt to make sense of this borderless world, we present the second edition of the annual A.T. Kearney/FOREIGN POLICY Magazine Globalization Index. We created this index to quantify what has arguably become the new century's most abused buzzword. Advocates and detractors alike bend the definition of "globalization" to fit their arguments. In truth, globalization entails a dense web of cross-border relationships that range from the very evident (the spread of disease) to the very subtle (the spread of ideas).

One aspect frequently missed in the debates about globalization is its measurement: How exten-sive is globalization? Which countries are the most globalized? The least? And why? Those rare instances in which anyone attempts to gauge globalization typically rely on data concerning international trade and investment flows, to the exclusion of other aspects of global integration. To fill this gap, FOREIGN POLICY teamed up with management consulting firm A.T. Kearney to create an index that employs indicators spanning information technology, finance, trade, politics, travel, and personal communication to evaluate levels of global integration in dozens of advanced economies and key emerging markets worldwide.

Last year's Globalization Index yielded many surprising revelations about the shape of global integration through 1998. We found that the world's most global countries boast greater income equality

How the Index Is Calculated

The Globalization Index brings globalization into sharper focus by assessing changes in its most important components, whether engagement in international relations and policymaking, trade and financial flows, or the movement of people, ideas, and information across borders. The index tracks these changes across 62 advanced economies and key emerging markets (up from 50 last year) to draw a picture of globalization across all the world's regions.

The index quantifies economic integration by combining data on trade, foreign direct investment (FDI) and portfolio capital flows, and income payments and receipts, which includes compensation of nonresident employees and income earned and paid on assets held abroad. (Convergence between domestic and international price levels, an indicator included in last year's index, was removed in this year's revision in favor of more direct measures that focus on causes of globalization rather than effects.) It charts personal contact via levels of international travel and tourism, international telephone traffic, and

Technology: number of Internet users, Internet hosts, and secure servers

Political Engagement: number of memberships in international organizations, U.N. Security Council missions in which each country participates, and foreign embassies that each country hosts

Personal Contact: international travel and tourism, international telephone traffic, and cross-border transfers

Economic Integration: trade, foreign direct investment and portfolio capital flows, and income payments and receipts

cross-border transfers, including remittances. The index also gauges technological connect-edness by counting Internet users and the Internet hosts and secure servers through which they communicate and conduct business transactions. And beginning this year, it also assesses political engagement by taking stock of the number of international organizations and U.N. Security Council missions in which each country participates, as well as the number of foreign embassies that each country hosts.

For most variables, each year's inward and outward flows are added, and the sum is divided by the country's nominal economic output or, where appropriate, its population. Political engagement figures are treated differently, with participation in U.N. Security Council missions divided by the total number of missions active in each year and embassies and international organizations than their less global counterparts—a counterpoint to the common argument that developing countries are poor and unequal because of globalization, suggesting instead that history, economic policies, welfare programs, and education policies may play an important role in shaping income distribution. Moreover, we learned that the most global economies tend to be small nations for which openness allows access to goods, services, and capital not readily available at home. Last year, tiny Singapore ranked as the world's most global nation, with the Netherlands, Sweden, and Switzerland not far behind. By contrast, the United States came in 12th place.

Also, with few exceptions, countries that scored high on the Globalization Index enjoyed greater political freedom, as measured by the annual Freedom House survey of civil liberties and political rights. And a comparison of our index rankings with Transparency International's survey of perceived corruption suggested that public officials in the most global countries are less corrupt than their counterparts in closed economies. Moreover, various indicators of Internet use and access indicated that significant gaps exist within the global digital divide, with the United States, Canada, and Scandinavian countries like Finland and Sweden far outpacing other advanced countries in the diffusion of new information technologies.

The second iteration of the Globalization Index examines global integration through the end of 2000, with several important changes that provide a greater degree of focus than ever before possible. First, we have expanded our coverage by adding a dozen new countries to the 50 covered previously.

remaining as absolute numbers. This process produces panels of data that enable comparisons between countries of all sizes.

The resulting data panels for a given variable are then compared and "normalized" through a process that values the single lowest data point at zero and the highest at one, while assigning relative values between zero and one to the remaining data points in the panel. Suppose the variable is trade. The maximum value of inward and outward trade flows is 348 percent of gross domestic product (GDP) recorded for Singapore in 1995, while the minimum is 15.7 percent of GDP for Brazil in 1996. These data points are valued at one and zero, respectively, with all others falling in between.

Country scores are summed across the panels, with double weighting on FDI and portfolio capital flows due to their particular importance in the ebb and flow of globalization. Internet indicators and political indicators are collapsed into a single variable each. The Internet variable is then double weighted in the final calculation, as are the international telephone traffic scores, reflecting their status as important means by which ideas and information are spread across national borders. Globalization Index scores for every country and year are derived by summing the scores across panels.

Small trading nations tend to take top places in the index, leading some observers last year to speculate that size plays an undue role in determining levels of globalization. A closer look, however, suggests otherwise. Statistically speaking, there is very little direct correlation between the size of a country's economy and its globalization rank. Big economies rank from 12th (United States) to 53rd (China), while smaller economies rank from 1st (Ireland) to 45th (Egypt) and 57th (Venezuela). But size is not irrelevant, either; it is only in combination with the level of economic development, as measured by per capita income, that the relationship becomes clear. Simply put, small countries tend to have an advantage over larger countries at similar levels of per capita income.

These key indicators only scratch the surface of globalization's complexity. Many other aspects of global integration—including culture—defy measurement. Cultural exchange has undoubtedly grown in tandem with the movement of people and ideas across borders and with the growing use of communications technology, but little accurate data are available. For instance, statistics on trade flows in music or books might show a country's comparative advantages in manufacturing these products, such as CDs and technical manuals, but would not reveal whether the goods reflect the ideas and culture of the exporting nation. Consequently, cultural trends are not included in this index.

The index now accounts for nearly 85 percent of the world's population and more than 90 percent of its economic output, with enhanced coverage of Africa, Central and Eastern Europe, and South Asia. Second, the revised index incorporates new political variables that help assess the level of a country's engagement in matters concerning diplomacy and international security by measuring membership in international organizations, commitments to international peace-keeping missions, and diplomatic representations hosted from abroad. Third, the index makes use of the latest available forecasts to make better sense of the world we are about to enter, as well as the one we are leaving behind.

These changes not only broaden our understanding of last year's findings, they also reveal important new details of the changing geography of the digital divide, the status of emerging markets, the impact of globalization on government spending, and even whether globalization relates to perceptions of personal happiness. The consequences of September 11, 2001, and the events that have followed remain uncertain, but the data presented in this index will make it easier to assess whether global integration has hit a temporary roadblock or whether it is about to make a fundamental shift in direction.

GLOBALIZATION'S BEST YEAR?

Spurred by robust economic growth, global integration deepened substantially in 2000, a year that saw record gains in most indicators of international exchange. The value of world merchandise exports, for instance, surged by more than 12 percent in 2000, while trade in services jumped by 6.1 percent—both more than triple the previous year's growth rate. Similarly, foreign direct investment (FDI) marked a spectacular increase in 2000, growing from $1.08 trillion in 1999 to $1.27 trillion in 2000, compared with only $203 billion in 1990. Much of this investment was driven by corporations buying or merging with companies in other countries, contributing to increasingly global multinational firms. In but one example of the results, top French firms earned more than two times more revenue from their foreign affiliates than from their domestic sales in 2000, double the level early in the 1990s. And foreign sales, on average, nearly equaled domestic sales for leading firms in the United Kingdom, Germany, and Italy.

The strong global economy and a host of events tied to the millennium also prompted the most extensive growth in global tourism in at least a decade. Worldwide, travelers made an additional 50 million trips across national borders in 2000 to reach 698.8 million international arrivals, up from 457.2 million a decade before. Asia and the Pacific saw the most substantial growth, but virtually all regions experienced considerable new flows of visitors from abroad. Other aspects of personal connectedness also grew. Cross-border telephone traffic, for example, saw a steady growth of roughly 10 bil-

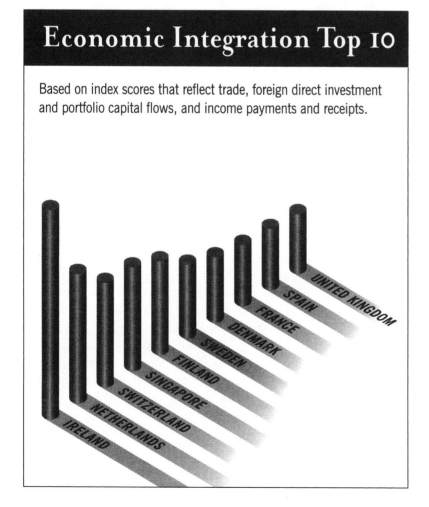

Economic Integration Top 10

Based on index scores that reflect trade, foreign direct investment and portfolio capital flows, and income payments and receipts.

IRELAND
NETHERLANDS
SWITZERLAND
SINGAPORE
FINLAND
SWEDEN
DENMARK
FRANCE
SPAIN
UNITED KINGDOM

lion minutes in 2000, driven primarily by rapidly declining costs.

At the same time, the number of Internet hosts (computers that allow users to communicate with one another along the Internet) continued to climb, growing by 44 percent in 2000. Yet this expansion was substantially slower than in earlier years and about one-third less than the explosive growth in 1999, a boom year for Internet-related businesses. In part, this slowdown reflects the downturn in the dot-com economy, but it may also have to do with saturation in some key markets, with growth in Internet users also cooling in 2000 to its lowest rate since the Internet's emergence as a mass communications medium in the mid-1990s. Even so, 80 million new users logged on to the Internet for the first time in 2000. And as a sign of changes to come, 2000 may well have been the first year in which English was no longer the majority language on the Web. Estimates show that 192 million English speakers had regular access to the Internet, compared with 211 million non-English speakers. Although English remained the single most dominant language, Japanese, Chinese, and German were gaining ground, with the population of Spanish speakers set to experience substantial growth in coming years.

Moreover, political engagement has shown signs of slow but steady growth. Between 1995 and 2000, the advanced economies and key emerging markets tracked in the Globalization Index established 344 new embassies around the world. Only a handful of countries—including Bangladesh, Senegal, Turkey, and Venezuela—experienced a decline in the number of diplomatic representations they hosted from abroad. At the same time, 342 new memberships in international organizations were extended to the nations in our index, including new seats for Peru, Russia, and Vietnam in the Asia-Pacific Economic Cooperation forum. And while the number of active peacekeeping and nation-building missions approved

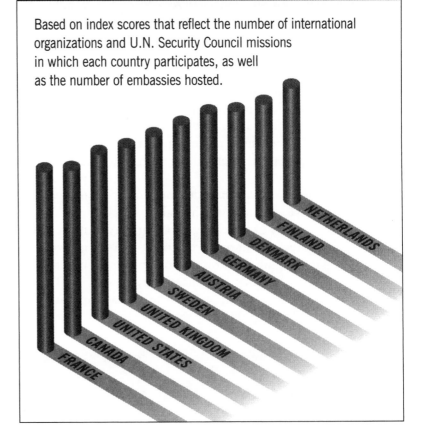

Political Engagement Top 10

Based on index scores that reflect the number of international organizations and U.N. Security Council missions in which each country participates, as well as the number of embassies hosted.

FRANCE
CANADA
UNITED STATES
UNITED KINGDOM
SWEDEN
AUSTRIA
GERMANY
DENMARK
FINLAND
NETHERLANDS

by the U.N. Security Council declined slightly (from 20 in 1995 to 18 in 2000), the number of participating countries increased. By 2000, some 66 nations were contributing military and civilian police personnel, money, medicine, or other equipment. Of these, a diverse group of 11 countries—Austria, Bangladesh, Canada, Denmark, Finland, France, Ireland, Italy, Poland, Russia, and Sweden—made direct contributions to more than half the active missions that year, ranging from the U.N. Organization Mission in the Democratic Republic of the Congo to the U.N. Transitional Authority in East Timor.

In short, levels of global integration reached new highs in 2000, capping a decade of dramatic expansion in global economic flows and political engagement as well as the increased mobility of people, information, and ideas. While such free movement is likely to remain a defining characteristic of our suddenly smaller world, its persistence in the coming years cannot be taken for granted. Indeed, many of the countries that score high on the index are the ones most likely to bear the brunt of globalization's unwinding.

WINNERS AND LOSERS

The Celtic Tiger Roars | As was true in last year's index, small trading nations tend to show higher levels of integration with other countries than their larger neighbors, although the relationship between size and globalization remains complex. Last year, the A.T. Kearney/FOREIGN POLICY Magazine Globalization Index revealed that Singapore was the "most global" nation. Topping this year's list is Ireland, a country whose levels of economic integration have boomed since 1998, the end of our previous survey, in which Ireland ranked sixth.

Ireland's strong pro-business policies and English-speaking population have long drawn interest from overseas business, helping to transform the island into a highly attractive location for foreign investors. Yet in the past two years, the Celtic Tiger has really begun to roar. In a bid to attract more international capital and technology investments, the country has cut corporate tax rates (already among Europe's lowest) and adopted a National Development Plan designed to improve infrastructure and government efficiency. Privatization of state assets in telecommunications and banking have created positive signals for investment, while Ireland's decision to join the euro currency zone has dramatically reduced barriers against financial flows to and from other euro zone countries.

Ireland was also among the world's largest beneficiaries of the global boom in high tech and information technologies. Its success in attracting IT investments in earlier years gave it a "first mover" advantage when these industries began to experience truly global growth. By 2000, technology giants such as Microsoft, Intel, Gateway, and Global Crossing were calling the "Silicon Isle" their European home. These high-tech investments help explain Ireland's steadily growing FDI inflows, which rose from an average of close to $3 billion per year throughout the mid-1990s to $20.5 billion in 2000, or nearly $5,500 per resident (three times more than the $1,653 per resident in Finland).

Even more dramatic has been the increase in portfolio capital flows, marking Ireland's rise as an important center for international financial transactions. These inflows and outflows totaled a scant 1.6 percent of the national economy in 1996, on par with countries like Chile, the Czech Republic, and Israel. By 2000, however, portfolio flows had grown to the world's largest when measured as a share of gross domestic product, owing largely to the growth of Dublin's International Financial Services Center, a leading location for international banking, investment funds, corporate treasury, and insurance activities.

Ireland also scores high in other indicators. Its growing tourist industry and advanced telecommunications infrastructure, for example, place the country atop the ranking for personal connections across international borders,

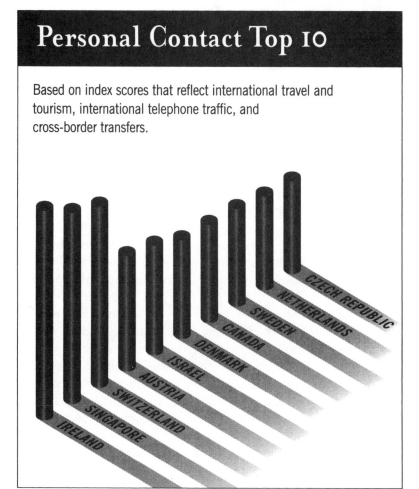

Personal Contact Top 10

Based on index scores that reflect international travel and tourism, international telephone traffic, and cross-border transfers.

IRELAND
SINGAPORE
SWITZERLAND
AUSTRIA
ISRAEL
DENMARK
CANADA
SWEDEN
NETHERLANDS
CZECH REPUBLIC

and its rapidly growing online population places it among Europe's Internet leaders.

Singapore slipped to third place in this year's Globalization Index, largely as a result of its performance in certain economic indicators. While the island economy remained the world's top trading nation, it struggled to take full advantage of the rising tide of global portfolio capital flows. A reorganization of its primary stock exchange helped to pull in some additional capital and position the country as a future financial center, but the country evidently proved less attractive than others with larger or more dynamic economic hinterlands, including the combined euro zone. Thus, while portfolio inflows to Ireland grew by some $26 billion between 1998 and 2000, Singapore saw only $1.3 billion in additional inflows.

Yet Singapore continued to score well in a variety of other categories, most notably in terms of personal connectedness. Although already leading the world in international telephone traffic per capita, for example, residents increased average call times in 2000 by another 2.5 percent, bringing the total to nearly 400 minutes per person in outgoing international calls alone (with another 317 minutes per person in incoming calls).

Up From Down Under | The United States and Canada remain the leaders in Internet penetration. Nearly 35 percent of the U.S. population and 41 percent of the Canadian population were online by January 2001, putting the two countries well within the world's top 10, if slightly behind the competition in Scandinavia. The United States excels in levels of IT infrastructure development, with one Internet host for every three residents—more than triple the number in Sweden, Norway, and Finland and more than 10 times the number in the United Kingdom. The United States also maintains some 77,000 of the world's 118,000 secure servers (computers capable of supporting encryption and other advanced functions necessary for e-commerce trans-

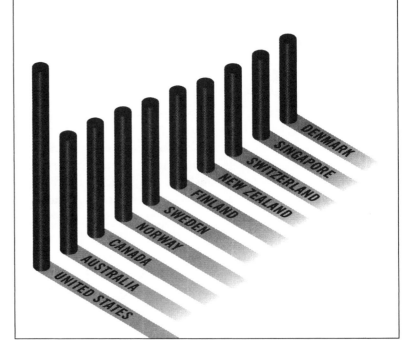

Technology Top 10

Based on index scores that reflect number of Internet users, hosts, and secure servers.

UNITED STATES
AUSTRALIA
CANADA
NORWAY
SWEDEN
FINLAND
NEW ZEALAND
SWITZERLAND
SINGAPORE
DENMARK

actions). And the vast majority of worldwide Internet content is physically housed in the United States, which helps to explain why 95 percent of the bandwidth that ties together world regions flows to and from the country.

Last year's Globalization Index revealed that, in terms of Internet use and development, Scandinavian countries had far outpaced their continental neighbors in the closing years of the 1990s. By 2000, however, Oceania (comprising Australia and New Zealand) began to emerge as a new regional center, with higher average levels of connectedness than even the Scandinavian countries [see chart on page 257]. In Australia, the online population topped 35 percent in 2000, surpassing the United States, while New Zealand ranked fourth in the number of Internet hosts per resident. Both countries also ranked within the world's top five in providing secure servers per capita. As in Scandinavia, this dramatic growth may have as much to do with a combination of economic prosperity and a sense of geographic isolation—along with the convenience of Internet com-

Globalization and Happiness

Does globalization make people happy? We don't know. But countries that have a large portion of their population who describe themselves as "happy" or "very happy" and indicate a high degree of satisfaction with life also tend to be the most globally integrated countries. This measure of "subjective well-being" is part of the *World Values Survey*, conducted by researchers in more than 65 societies.

Income alone cannot account for the relationship between globalization and happiness. Ireland is happier than Germany, although not as well-to-do by half. And the Taiwanese are about as happy as the Japanese, although the Japanese are three times more wealthy.

Source: *World Values Survey* (Ann Arbor: Institute for Social Research, 1996)

IRELAND
SWITZERLAND
NETHERLANDS
SWEDEN
FINLAND
CANADA
DENMARK
AUSTRIA
UNITED KINGDOM
UNITED STATES
NORWAY
GERMANY *
FRANCE
PORTUGAL
CZECH REPUBLIC
SPAIN
NEW ZEALAND
AUSTRALIA
HUNGARY
SLOVAKIA
ITALY
POLAND
CROATIA
SLOVENIA
TAIWAN
SOUTH KOREA
CHILE
NIGERIA
JAPAN
ROMANIA
RUSSIA
UKRAINE
ARGENTINA
BANGLADESH
INDIA
MEXICO
PHILIPPINES
CHINA
SOUTH AFRICA
TURKEY
PAKISTAN
BRAZIL
COLOMBIA
PERU
BULGARIA
GHANA

Globalization

Happiness

★ *World Values Survey* data derived from former West Germany only.

munication across the vast distances of sparsely populated countries—as it does with supportive policy environments.

Taxes Stay Intact | One of the most heated debates about globalization today is whether competition between countries forces them to cut taxation—as well as social spending—in order to attract foreign investors and other international business interests. Some observers have argued that, in this way, globalization generates a race to the bottom in which local populations lose out as their governments curtail spending on the jobs, education, and social safety nets that higher taxation levels might support.

To test this hypothesis, we looked closely at World Bank statistics on each country's level of taxation as well as government expenditures on the full range of public goods and then compared each against Globalization Index scores. Our findings show that taxation levels and spending levels go hand-in-hand but that neither correlates well with levels of globalization. In fact, some of the highest levels of taxation are in countries that are also highly globalized, and levels of spending vary across the board [see chart on page 256]. Israel and the Czech Republic, for example, rank among the most global of emerging markets, yet collect taxes totaling more than 40 percent of national economic output. Those levels are far above tax collection rates in such countries as Colombia, Indonesia, and Pakistan, which rank much lower on the Globalization Index. By the same token, Sweden and Finland, which rank among the world's most global countries, boast levels of social spending that are among the most generous in the world—all supported by relatively high tax rates. And with Scandinavian countries attracting record levels of FDI in recent years, there is little evidence that high tax rates are driving away investors, who appear more concerned about economic prospects, available infrastructure, education levels, and other fundamentals.

Don't Worry, Be Happy | Since 1995, an international network of social scientists has collaborated on a global investigation of sociocultural and political change known as the *World Values Survey*. These researchers conduct national surveys in more than 65 societies, accounting for almost 80 percent of the world population. Each survey features hundreds of questions, ranging from assessments of personal satisfaction and financial security to views on whether local governments are capable of coping with environmental decay or runaway crime.

What happened when we examined the *World Values Survey*'s measure of "subjective well-being"—the share of people in each country who describe themselves as "very happy" or "happy"

Many of the countries that score high on the index are the ones most likely to bear the brunt of globalization's unwinding.

and the share indicating high satisfaction with life as a whole—with each country's Globalization Index score? The results [see chart on facing page] did not necessarily prove that globalization brings happiness, but they clearly showed that people in highly globalized countries (including Ireland, Denmark, and the United Kingdom) tend to have higher levels of perceived well-being than do people in societies that are not as well connected to the outside world.

Although most of the highly globalized countries tend also to be wealthy, the correlations among globalization, wealth, and happiness are fuzzy at best. Researchers from the *World Values Survey*, for example, have found that per capita income correlates well with happiness levels up to a certain level of economic development, beyond which happiness becomes a much more subjective phenomenon.

The Divides Deepen | Although 2000 saw an unprecedented surge in global integration, a closer look at the data reveals a more mixed picture for the developing world. For instance, although emerging markets have seen Internet access grow at remarkable rates (on average twice the rate in the developed world in recent years), those same markets are still dwarfed by the industrialized countries. The Organization for Economic Co-operation and Development (OECD) estimates that 95.6 percent of the world's Internet hosts in 2000 were located in its member countries. Hong Kong, Singapore, and Taiwan accounted for more than half of the remainder, leaving little for the rest of the world. By the end of 2001, OECD countries are likely to have had more than 100 Internet hosts for every 1,000 inhabitants, while the rest of the world may be lucky to average 1 for every 1,000.

This digital abyss only made it more difficult for many emerging markets to expand their integration with the rest of the world in 2000 (although emerging markets might make up ground in 2001). While no region experienced net "de-globalization," several individual countries—including Botswana, Egypt, Peru, and Saudi Arabia—saw their levels of integration decline relative to the rest of the world, suggesting an inability to keep pace with the

scale—a snapshot of global integration in the period before September 11, 2001. We are not yet certain to what extent the globalization skyline has been damaged by recent events, but we can make some educated guesses.

Even before the terrorist attacks, a number of globalization's key components showed signs of setting a slower pace. International Monetary Fund projections showed global economic growth slowing from 4.7 percent in 2000 to a mere 2.4 percent in 2001, just below levels considered to be recessionary. Similarly, global trade growth in 2001 was expected to remain nearly flat, while predictions showed FDI flows dropping more than 40 percent from the record highs in 2000.

Some of the highest levels of taxation are in countries that are also highly globalized, and levels of spending vary across the board.

---

increased movement of goods, capital, people, and ideas (as well as technological developments) at a global level. Even as emerging markets attracted $265 billion of new FDI, for example, their share of total flows declined for the fourth year in a row—from 43 percent in 1997, followed in each year by 30 percent, 23 percent, and 21 percent. Meanwhile, African countries attracted several million new tourists but saw their combined share of the booming global tourism market hover at 4 percent of the global total.

Moreover, evidence suggests that some regions are becoming relatively less integrated within the world economy. The African countries, for example, saw their average level of economic integration fall, then rise, then fall again over the past six years, a reflection of variable economic performance and the rise and fall of prices for oil and commodity exports, their main connection to global economic markets.

COLLATERAL DAMAGE

By now, we've all seen the before-and-after photos of the New York City skyline, perhaps forever altered by terrorism. In a similar vein, this year's A.T. Kearney/FOREIGN POLICY Magazine Globalization Index presents a "before" photo on a worldwide

In the aftermath of the attacks, however, even these dire predictions appear optimistic, as heightened security concerns compel nations to tighten their borders. Rising public anxiety and new travel restrictions, for example, appear likely to curtail travel between countries, perhaps leading to a decline in global tourism for the first time in the last 50 years. And with global investors skittish about all but the safest opportunities, developed markets may see slow growth in equities, and emerging markets may see portfolio investment from abroad draining away more rapidly than at any time since the mid-1980s.

These trends are likely to affect disproportionately those countries that are closely integrated into the world economy. The global downturn in the IT sector and tourism has hit Ireland particularly hard, and some forecasts see its growth slowing to 3 percent in 2002, compared with 11 percent in 2000. Singapore, with its small domestic economy and heavy reliance on trade, has already begun to feel the pain of globalization's downturn, with exports and imports alike plummeting more rapidly than at any time since the country's independence in 1965. Other countries in which trade accounts for the lion's share of integration with global markets—including Malaysia, Slovakia, Panama, Thailand, and the Philippines—may also see globalization levels affected over the coming year. Others that are heavily exposed to international portfolio capital and FDI flows—including Ireland, the Netherlands, Finland, Spain, and even the United States—could likewise struggle to maintain their overall globalization scores.

Yet even as the global economy retrenches, other aspects of globalization are likely to sustain their forward momentum. These include personal contact across borders, which has become an indelible part of an increasingly globalized world. Telephone calls and Internet messages may well come to substitute for "being there" at a time when travel has grown more difficult. With the International Telecommunications Union estimating that call rates are falling 20 percent per year, on average, there is no reason that international telephone traffic—which has maintained a steady growth of roughly 10 billion minutes per year since 1997—would be reversed because of the events of September 11. In fact, international calls to the United States now average less than $0.50

Sitting Out the Race to the Bottom

Some analysts worry that open societies feel added pressure to keep taxes low to encourage investment and that such countries therefore have less to spend on their social safety nets. But data from the Globalization Index do not support this "race to the bottom" theory: many highly global countries have retained high levels of taxation and public spending.

Height of bars represents degree of globalizaton

Less Expenditures

Greater Tax Revenue

Less Tax Revenue

Greater Expenditures

Venezuela, India, Colombia, Pakistan, Thailand, Peru, Philippines, Indonesia, Sri Lanka, United States, Iran, Russia, Chile, Australia, Turkey, Slovakia, Poland, South Africa, Tunisia, New Zealand, Denmark, United Kingdom, Czech Republic, Sweden, Italy, Slovenia, Austria, Hungary, Israel, Croatia

Source: Taxation and expenditure data from *World Development Indicators* (Washington: World Bank, 2001)

Digital Divide

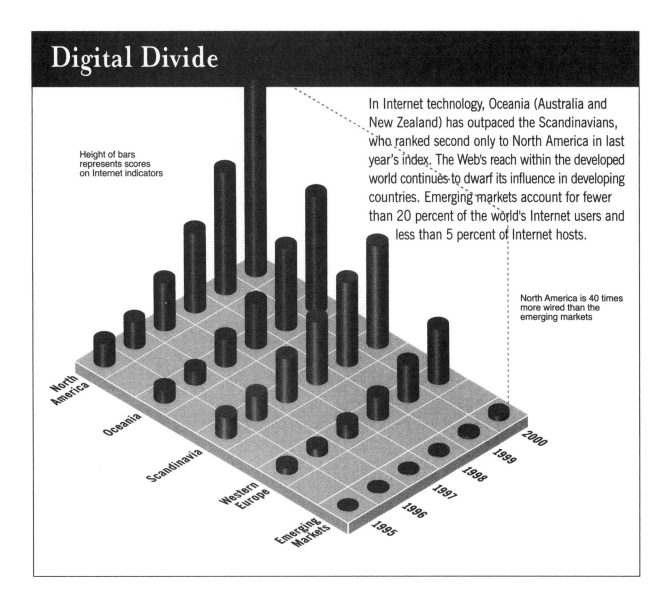

Height of bars represents scores on Internet indicators

In Internet technology, Oceania (Australia and New Zealand) has outpaced the Scandinavians, who ranked second only to North America in last year's index. The Web's reach within the developed world continues to dwarf its influence in developing countries. Emerging markets account for fewer than 20 percent of the world's Internet users and less than 5 percent of Internet hosts.

North America is 40 times more wired than the emerging markets

North America
Oceania
Scandinavia
Western Europe
Emerging Markets

1995 1996 1997 1998 1999 2000

per minute, no more than domestic long distance rates in many countries. The Internet, too, will continue its impressive expansion, particularly in developing countries like China and India, where penetration remains low. And the new global emphasis on fighting terrorism on military, diplomatic, and economic fronts could serve to increase levels of international political engagement over the coming years.

Nor can forward momentum in the global economy be ruled out. Even as nations are struggling to pull themselves out of recession, they are continuing to strengthen the mechanisms for global integration. Two years after WTO negotiations broke down amidst tear gas and rioting in Seattle, the delegates in Qatar agreed to launch a new round of talks to cut trade barriers on a wide

range of industrial and agricultural goods. After 15 years of tortuous negotiations, China has finally acceded to the World Trade Organization, and Russia—enjoying a second honeymoon in East-West relations following the September 11 attacks—is optimistic about joining the global trading body by the end of 2002.

Next year's Globalization Index will begin to assess whether these predictions will come to pass. But even our most pessimistic scenarios do not portend the end of global integration. They merely highlight the extent to which global integration has made us more vulnerable, even as it has made us more prosperous. Perhaps the most profound ideological casualty of the September 11 attacks was the belief that a more globalized world would necessarily be a safer one. **FP**

Index